D0870134

G.A. HENTY

December 8, 1832   ---
            November 16, 1902

THE YOUNG CARTHAGINIAN

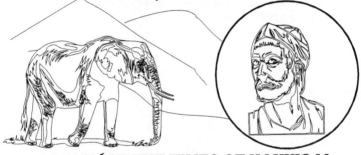

A STORY OF THE TIMES OF HANNIBAL

BY

G.A. HENTY

ILLUSTRATED BY C.J. STANILAND, R.I.

Preston
Speed
ublications

Pennsylvania

A note about our name: Preston/Speed Publications
In an age where it has become fashionable to denigrate fathers, we
have decided to honor ours. Our name is in loving memory of Preston
Louis Schmitt and Speed - Lester Herbert Maynard ("Speed" was a
nickname that was earned for prowess in baseball).

This book is printed on acid-free paper, and its binding
materials have been chosen for strength and durability.

Published June 8, 1886 by
BLACKIE & SON, LONDON

Blackie & Son Title Page Date: 1887

ISBN 1-887159-12-6
Printed in the U.S.A.

PRESTON/SPEED PUBLICATIONS
RR #4, BOX 705
MILL HALL, PENNSYLVANIA 17751
(717) 726-7844
1997

INTRODUCTION:

G. A. Henty's life was filled with exciting adventure. Completing Westminster School, he attended Cambridge University. Along with a rigorous course of study, Henty participated in boxing, wrestling and rowing. The strenuous study and healthy, competitive participation in sports prepared Henty to be with the British army in Crimea, as a war correspondent witnessing Garibaldi fight in Italy, visiting Abyssinia, being present in Paris during the Franco-Prussian war, in Spain with the Carlists, at the opening of the Suez Canal, touring India with the Prince of Wales (later Edward VII) and a trip to the California gold fields. These are only a few of his exciting adventures.

G. A. Henty lived during the reign of Queen Victoria (1837-1901) and began his story telling career with his own children. After dinner, he would spend an hour or two in telling them a story that would continue the next day. Some stories took weeks! A friend was present one day and watched the spell-bound reaction of his children suggesting that he write down his stories so others could enjoy them. He did. Henty wrote approximately 144 books plus stories for magazines and was dubbed as "The Prince of Story-Tellers" and "The Boy's Own Historian." One of Mr. Henty's secretaries reported that he would quickly pace back and forth in his study dictating stories as fast as the secretary could record them.

Henty's stories revolve around a fictional boy hero during fascinating periods of history. His heroes are diligent, courageous, intelligent and dedicated to their country and cause in the face, at times, of great peril. His histories, particularly battle accounts, have been recognized by historian scholars for their accuracy. There is nothing dry in Mr. Henty's stories and thus he removes the drudgery and laborious task often associated with the study of history.

Henty's heroes fight wars, sail the seas, discover land, conquer evil empires, prospect for gold, and a host of other exciting adventures. They meet famous personages like Josephus, Titus, Hannibal, Robert the Bruce, Sir William Wallace, General Marlborough, General Gordon, General Kitchner, Robert E. Lee, Frederick the Great, the Duke of Wellington, Huguenot leader Coligny, Cortez, King Alfred, Napoleon, and Sir Francis Drake just to mention a *few*. The heroes go through the fall of Jerusalem, the Roman invasion of Britain, the Crusades, the Viking invasion of Europe, the Reformation in various countries, the Reign of Terror, etc. In short, Henty's heroes live through tumultuous historic eras meeting the leaders of that time. Understanding the culture of the time period becomes second nature as well as comparing/contrasting the society of various European and heathen cultures.

Preston/Speed Publications is delighted to offer again the works of G. A. Henty. Action-packed exciting adventure awaits adults and a whole new generation. The books have been reproduced with modern type-setting. However, the original grammar, spellings and punctuation remains the same as the original versions.

Malchus brought before the Roman general

PREFACE.

MY DEAR LADS,

When I was a boy at school, if I remember rightly, our sympathies were generally with the Carthaginians as against the Romans. Why they were so, except that one generally sympathizes with the unfortunate, I do not quite know; certainly we had but a hazy idea as to the merits of the struggle and knew but little of its events, for the Latin and Greek authors, which serve as the ordinary text-books in schools, do not treat of the Punic wars. That it was a struggle for empire at first, and latterly one for existence on the part of Carthage, that Hannibal was a great and skilful general, that he defeated the Romans at Trebia, Lake Trasimenus, and Cannæ, and all but took Rome, and that the Romans behaved with bad faith and great cruelty at the capture of Carthage, represents, I think, pretty nearly the sum total of our knowledge.

I am sure I should have liked to know a great deal more about this struggle for the empire of the world, and as I think that most of you would also like to do so, I have chosen this subject for my story. Fortunately there is no lack of authentic material from which to glean the incidents of the struggle. Polybius visited all the passes of the Alps some forty years after the event, and conversed with tribesmen who had witnessed the passage of Hannibal, and there can be no doubt that his descriptions are far more accurate than those of Livy, who wrote somewhat later and had no personal knowledge of the affair. Numbers of books have been written as to the identity of the passes traversed by Hannibal. The whole of these have been discussed and summarized by Mr. W. J. Law, and as it appears to me that his arguments are quite conclusive I have adopted the line which he lays down as that followed by Hannibal.

In regard to the general history of the expedition, and of the manners, customs, religion, and politics of Carthage, I have followed M. Hennebert in his most exhaustive and important work on the subject. I think that when you have read to the end you will perceive that although our sympathies may remain with Hannibal and the Carthaginians, it was nevertheless for the good of the world that Rome was the conqueror in the great struggle for empire. At the time the war began Carthage was already corrupt to the core, and although she might have enslaved many nations she would never have civilized them. Rome gave free institutions to the people she conquered, she subdued but she never enslaved them, but rather strove to plant her civilization among them and to raise them to her own level. Carthage, on the contrary, was from the first a cruel mistress to the people she conquered. Consequently while all the peoples of Italy rallied round Rome in the days of her distress, the tribes subject to Carthage rose in insurrection against her as soon as the presence of a Roman army gave them a hope of escape from their bondage.

Had Carthage conquered Rome in the struggle she could never have extended her power over the known world as Rome afterwards did, but would have fallen to pieces again from the weakness of her institutions and the corruption of her people. Thus then, although we may feel sympathy for the failure and fate of the noble and chivalrous Hannibal himself, we cannot regret that Rome came out conqueror in the strife, and was left free to carry out her great work of civilization.

Yours sincerely,

G. A. Henty

CONTENTS

ILLUSTRATIONS

THE YOUNG CARTHAGINIAN

CHAPTER I: THE CAMP IN THE DESERT

IT is afternoon, but the sun's rays still pour down with great power upon rock and sand. How great the heat has been at midday may be seen by the quivering of the air as it rises from the ground and blurs all distant objects. It is seen, too, in the attitudes and appearance of a large body of soldiers encamped in a grove. Their arms are thrown aside, the greater portion of their clothing has been dispensed with. Some lie stretched on the ground in slumber, their faces protected from any chance rays which may find their way through the foliage above by little shelters composed of their clothing hung on two bows or javelins. Some, lately awakened, are sitting up or leaning against the trunks of the trees, but scarce one has energy to move.

The day has indeed been a hot one even for the southern edge of the Libyan desert. The cream-coloured oxen stand with their heads down, lazily whisking away with their tails the flies that torment them. The horses standing near suffer more; the lather stands on their sides, their flanks heave, and from time to time they stretch out their extended nostrils in the direction from which, when the sun sinks a little lower, the breeze will begin to blow.

The occupants of the grove are men of varied races, and, although there is no attempt at military order, it is clear at once that they are divided into three parties. One is composed of men more swarthy than the others. They are lithe and active in figure, inured to hardship, accustomed to the burning sun. Light shields hang against the trees with bows and gaily-painted quivers full of arrows, and near each man are three or four light short

1

javelins. They wear round caps of metal, with a band of the skin of the lion or other wild animal, in which are stuck feathers dyed with some bright colour. They are naked to the waist, save for a light breastplate of brass. A cloth of bright colours is wound round their waist and drops to the knees, and they wear belts of leather embossed with brass plates; on their feet are sandals. They are the light armed Numidian horse.

Near them are a party of men lighter in hue, taller and stouter in stature. Their garb is more irregular, their arms are bare, but they wear a sort of shirt, open at the neck and reaching to the knees, and confined at the waist by a leather strap, from which hangs a pouch of the same material. Their shirts, which are of roughly made flannel, are dyed a colour which was originally a deep purple, but which has faded, under the heat of the sun, to lilac. They are a company of Iberian slingers, enlisted among the tribes conquered in Spain by the Carthaginians. By them lie the heavy swords which they use in close quarters.

The third body of men are more heavily armed. On the ground near the sleepers lie helmets and massive shields. They have tightly fitting jerkins of well-tanned leather, their arms are spears and battle-axes. They are the heavy infantry of Carthage. Very various is their nationality; fair-skinned Greeks lie side by side with swarthy negroes from Nubia. Sardinia, the islands of the Ægean, Crete and Egypt, Libya and Phoenicia are all represented there.

They are recruited alike from the lower orders of the great city and from the tribes and people who own her sway.

Near the large grove in which the troops are encamped is a smaller one. A space in the centre has been cleared of trees, and in this a large tent has been erected. Around this numerous slaves are moving to and fro.

A Roman cook, captured in a sea fight in which his master, a wealthy tribune, was killed, is watching three Greeks, who are under his superintendence, preparing a repast. Some Libyan grooms are rubbing down the coats of four horses of the purest breed of the desert, while two Nubians are feeding, with large flat cakes, three elephants, who, chained by the leg to trees, stand rocking themselves from side to side.

The exterior of the tent is made of coarse white canvas; this is thickly lined by fold after fold of a thin material, dyed a dark blue, to keep out the heat of the sun, while the interior is hung with silk, purple and white. The curtains at each end are looped back with gold cord to allow a free passage of the air.

A carpet from the looms of Syria covers the ground, and on it are spread four couches, on which, in a position half-sitting half-reclining, repose the principal personages of the party. The elder of these is a man some fifty years of age, of commanding figure, and features which express energy and resolution. His body is bare to the waist, save for a light short-sleeved tunic of the finest muslin embroidered round the neck and sleeves with gold.

A gold belt encircles his waist, below it hangs a garment resembling the modern kilt, but reaching half-way between the knee and the ankle. It is dyed a rich purple, and three bands of gold embroidery run round the lower edge. On his feet he wears sandals with broad leather lacings covered with gold. His toga, also of purple heavily embroidered with gold, lies on the couch beside him; from one of the poles of the tent hang his arms, a short heavy sword, with a handle of solid gold in a scabbard incrusted with the same metal, and a baldrick, covered with plates of gold beautifully worked and lined with the softest leather, by which it is suspended over his shoulder.

Two of his companions are young men of three or four and twenty, both fair like himself, with features of almost Greek regularity of outline. Their dress is similar to his in fashion, but the colours are gayer. The fourth member of the party is a lad of some fifteen years old. His figure, which is naked to the waist, is of a pure Grecian model, the muscles, showing up clearly beneath the skin, testify to hard exercise and a life of activity.

Powerful as Carthage was, the events of the last few years had shown that a life-and-death struggle with her great rival in Italy was approaching. For many years she had been a conquering nation. Her aristocracy were soldiers as well as traders, ready at once to embark on the most distant and adventurous voyages, to lead the troops of Carthage on toilsome expeditions against insurgent tribes of Numidia and Libya, or to launch their triremes to engage the fleets of Rome.

The severe checks which they had lately suffered at the hands of the newly-formed Roman navy, and the certainty that ere long a tremendous struggle between the two powers must take place, had redoubled the military ardour of the nobles. Their training to arms began from their very childhood, and the sons of the noblest houses were taught, at the earliest age, the use of arms and the endurance of fatigue and hardship.

Malchus, the son of Hamilcar, the leader of the expedition in the desert, had been, from his early childhood, trained by his father in the use of arms. When he was ten years old Hamilcar had taken him with him on a campaign in Spain; there, by a rigourous training, he had learned to endure cold and hardships.

In the depth of winter his father had made him pass the nights uncovered and almost without clothing in the cold. He had bathed in the icy water of the torrents from the snow-clad hills, and had been forced to keep up with the rapid march of the light-armed troops in pursuit of the Iberians. He was taught to endure long abstinence from food and to bear pain without flinching, to be cheerful under the greatest hardships, to wear a smiling face when even veteran soldiers were worn out and disheartened.

"It is incumbent upon us, the rulers and aristocracy of this great city, my son, to show ourselves superior to the common herd. They must recognize that we are not only richer and of better blood, but that we are stronger, wiser, and more courageous than they. So, only, can we expect them to obey us, and to make the sacrifices which war entails upon them. It is not enough that we are of pure Phoenician blood, that we come of the most enterprising race the world has ever seen, while they are but a mixed breed of many people who have either submitted to our rule or have been enslaved by us.

"This was well enough in the early days of the colony when it was Phoenician arms alone that won our battles and subdued our rivals. In our days we are few and the populace are many.

4

THE CAMP IN THE DESERT

Our armies are composed not of Phoenicians, but of the races conquered by us. Libya and Numidia, Sicily, Sardinia, and Spain, all in turn conquered by us, now furnish us with troops.

"Carthage is a mighty city, but it is no longer a city of Phoenicians. We form but a small proportion of the population. It is true that all power rests in our hands, that from our ranks the senate is chosen, the army officered, and the laws administered, but the expenses of the state are vast. The conquered people fret under the heavy tributes which they have to pay, and the vile populace murmur at the taxes.

"In Italy, Rome looms greater and more powerful year by year. Her people are hardy and trained to arms, and some day the struggle between us and her will have to be fought out to the death. Therefore, my son, it behoves us to use every effort to make ourselves worthy of our position. Set before yourself the example of your cousin Hannibal, who, young as he is, is already viewed as the greatest man in Carthage. Grudge no hardship or suffering to harden your frame and strengthen your arms.

"Some day you too may lead armies in the field, and, believe me, they will follow you all the better and more cheerfully if they know that in strength and endurance, as well as in position, their commander is the foremost man in his army."

Malchus had been an apt pupil, and had done justice to the pains which his father had bestowed upon him and to the training he had undergone. He could wield the arms of a man, could swim the coldest river, endure hardship and want of food, traverse long distances at the top of his speed, could throw a javelin with unerring aim, and send an arrow to the mark as truly as the best of the Libyan archers.

"The sun is going down fast, father," the lad said, "the shadows are lengthening and the heat is declining."

"We have only your word for the decline of the heat, Malchus," one of the younger men laughed; "I feel hotter than ever. This is the fifteenth time that you have been to the door of the tent during the last half-hour. Your restlessness is enough to give one the fever."

"I believe that you are just as eager as I am, Adherbal," the boy replied laughing. "It's your first lion hunt as well as mine,

5

and I am sure you are longing to see whether the assault of the king of beasts is more trying to the nerves than that of the Iberian tribesmen."

"I am looking forward to it, Malchus, certainly," the young man replied; "but as I know the lions will not quit their coverts until after nightfall, and as no efforts on my part will hasten the approach of that hour, I am well content to lie quiet and to keep myself as cool as may be."

"Your cousin is right," the general said, "and impatience is a fault, Malchus. We must make allowances for your impatience on the present occasion, for the lion is a foe not to be despised, and he is truly as formidable an antagonist when brought to bay as the Iberians on the banks of the Ebro—far more so than the revolted tribesmen we have been hunting for the past three weeks."

"Giscon says nothing," Adherbal remarked; "he has a soul above even the hunting of lions. I warrant that during the five hours we have been reclining here his thoughts have never once turned towards the hunt we are going to have to-night."

"That is true enough," Giscon said, speaking for the first time. "I own that my thoughts have been of Carthage, and of the troubles that threaten her owing to the corruption and misgovernment which are sapping her strength."

"It were best not to think too much on the subject, Giscon," the general said; "still better not to speak of it. You know that I lament, as you do, the misgovernment of Carthage, and mourn for the disasters which have been brought upon her by it. But the subject is a dangerous one; the council have spies everywhere, and to be denounced as one hostile to the established state of things is to be lost."

"I know the danger," the young man said passionately. "I know that hitherto all who have ventured to raise their voices against the authority of these tyrants have died by torture—that murmuring has been stamped out in blood. Yet were the danger ten times as great," and the speaker had risen now from his couch and was walking up and down the tent, "I could not keep silent. What have our tyrants brought us to? Their extravagance, their corruption, have wasted the public funds and have paralyzed our arms. Sicily and Sardinia have been lost; our allies in Africa have been goaded by their exactions again and again into rebellion, and Carthage has more than once lately been obliged to fight hard for her very existence. The lower classes in the city are utterly disaffected; their earnings are wrung from them by the tax-gatherers. Justice is denied them by the judges, who are the mere creatures of the committee of five. The suffetes are mere puppets in their hands. Our vessels lie unmanned in our harbours, because the funds which should pay the sailors are appropriated by our tyrants to their own purposes. How can a Carthaginian who loves his country remain silent?"

"All you say is true, Giscon," the general said gravely, "though I should be pressed to death were it whispered in Carthage that I said so; but at present we can do nothing. Had the great Hamilcar Barca lived I believe that he would have set himself to work to clear out this Augean stable, a task greater than that accomplished by our great hero, the demigod Hercules; but no less a hand can accomplish it. You know how every attempt at revolt has failed; how terrible a vengeance fell on Matho and the mercenaries; how the down-trodden tribes have again and again, when victory seemed in their hands, been crushed into the dust.

"No, Giscon, we must suffer the terrible ills which you speak of until some hero arises—some hero whose victories will bind not only the army to him, but will cause all the common people of Carthage—all her allies and tributaries—to look upon him as their leader and deliverer.

"I have hopes, great hopes, that such a hero may be found in my nephew, Hannibal, who seems to possess all the genius, the wisdom, and the talent of his father. Should the dream which he cherished, and of which I was but now speaking to you, that of leading a Carthaginian army across the Ebro, over the Apennines, through the plains of lower Gaul, and over the Alps into Italy, there to give battle to the cohorts of Rome on their own ground,—should this dream be verified I say, should success attend him, and Rome be humbled to the dust, then Hannibal would be in a position to become the dictator of Carthage, to overthrow the corrupt council, to destroy this tyranny—

misnamed a republic–and to establish a monarchy, of which he should be the first sovereign, and under which Carthage, again the queen of the world, should be worthy of herself and her people. And now let us speak of it no more. The very walls have ears, and I doubt not but even among my attendants there are men who are spies in the pay of the council. I see and lament as much as any man the ruin of my country; but, until I see a fair hope of deliverance, I am content to do the best I can against her enemies, to fight her battles as a simple soldier."

There was silence in the tent. Malchus had thrown himself down on his couch, and for a time forgot even the approaching lion hunt in the conversation to which he had listened.

The government of Carthage was indeed detestable, and was the chief cause both of the misfortunes which had befallen her in the past, and of the disasters which were in the future to be hers. The scheme of government was not in itself bad, and in earlier and simpler times had acted well. Originally it had consisted of three estates, which answered to the king, lords, and commons. At the head of affairs were two suffetes chosen for life. Below them was the senate, a very numerous body, comprising all the aristocracy of Carthage. Below this was the democracy, the great mass of the people, whose vote was necessary to ratify any law passed by the senate.

In time, however, all authority passed from the suffetes, the general body of the senate and the democracy, into the hands of a committee of the senate, one hundred in number, who were called the council, the real power being invested in the hands of an inner council, consisting of from twenty to thirty of the members. The deliberations of this body were secret, their power absolute. They were masters of the life and property of every man in Carthage, as afterwards were the council of ten in the republic of Venice. For a man to be denounced by his secret enemy to them as being hostile to their authority was to ensure his destruction and the confiscation of his property.

The council of a hundred was divided into twenty sub-committees, each containing five members. Each of these committees was charged with the control of a department—the army, the navy, the finances, the roads and communications, agriculture, religion, and the relations with the various subject tribes, the more important departments being entirely in the hands of the members of the inner council of thirty.

The judges were a hundred in number. These were appointed by the council, and were ever ready to carry out their behest, consequently justice in Carthage was a mockery. Interest and intrigue were paramount in the law courts, as in every department of state. Every prominent citizen, every successful general, every man who seemed likely, by his ability or his wealth, to become a popular personage with the masses, fell under the ban of the council, and sooner or later was certain to be disgraced. The resources of the state were devoted not to the needs of the country but to aggrandizement and enriching of the members of the committee.

Heavy as were the imposts which were laid upon the tributary peoples of Africa for the purposes of the state, enormous burdens were added by the tax-gatherers to satisfy the cupidity of their patrons in the council. Under such circumstances it was to be wondered at that Carthage, decaying, corrupt, ill-governed, had suffered terrible reverses at the hands of her young and energetic rival Rome, who was herself some day, when she attained the apex of her power, to suffer from abuses no less flagrant and general than those which had sapped the strength of Carthage.

With the impetuosity of youth Malchus naturally inclined rather to the aspirations of his kinsman Giscon than to the more sober counsels of his father. He had burned with shame and anger as he heard the tale of the disasters which had befallen his country, because she had made money her god, had suffered her army and her navy to be regarded as secondary objects, and had permitted the command of the sea to be wrested from her by her wiser and more far-seeing rival.

As evening closed in the stir in the neighbouring camp aroused Malchus from his thoughts, and the anticipation of the lion hunt, in which he was about to take part, again became foremost.

THE YOUNG CARTHAGINIAN

The camp was situated twenty days' march from Carthage at the foot of some hills in which lions and other beasts of prey were known to abound, and there was no doubt that they would be found that evening.

The expedition had been despatched under the command of Hamilcar to chastise a small tribe which had attacked and plundered some of the Carthaginian caravans on their way to Ethiopia, then a rich and prosperous country, wherein were many flourishing colonies, which had been sent out by Carthage.

The object of the expedition had been but partly successful. The lightly clad tribesmen had taken refuge far among the hills, and, although by dint of long and fatiguing marches several parties had been surprised and slain, the main body had evaded all the efforts of the Carthaginian general.

The expedition had arrived at its present camping place on the previous evening. During the night the deep roaring of lions had been heard continuously among the hills, and so bold and numerous were they that they had come down in such proximity to the camp that the troops had been obliged to rise and light great fires to scare them from making an attack upon the horses.

The general had therefore consented, upon the entreaties of his nephew Adherbal, and his son, to organize a hunt upon the following night. As soon as the sun set the troops, who had already received their orders, fell into their ranks. The full moon rose as soon as the sun dipped below the horizon, and her light was ample for the object they had in view.

The Numidian horse were to take their station on the plain; the infantry in two columns, a mile apart, were to enter the mountains, and having marched some distance, leaving detachments behind them, they were to move along the crest of the hills until they met; then, forming a great semicircle, they were to light torches, which they had prepared during the day, and to advance towards the plain shouting and clashing their arms, so as to drive all the wild animals inclosed in the arc down into the plain.

THE CAMP IN THE DESERT

The general with the two young officers and his son, and a party of fifty spearmen, were to be divided between the two groves in which the camps were pitched, which were opposite the centre of the space facing the line inclosed by the beaters. Behind the groves the Numidian horse were stationed, to give chase to such animals as might try to make their escape across the open plain. The general inspected the two bodies of infantry before they started, and repeated his instructions to the officers who commanded them, and enjoined them to march as noiselessly as possible until the semicircle was completed and the beat began in earnest.

The troops were to be divided into groups of eight, in order to be able to repel the attacks of any beasts which might try to break through the line. When the two columns had marched away right and left towards the hills, the attendants of the elephants and baggage animals were ordered to remove them into the centre of the groves. The footmen who remained were divided into two parties of equal strength. The general with Malchus remained in the grove in which his tent was fixed with one of these parties, while Adherbal and Giscon with the others took up their station in the larger grove.

"Do you think the lions are sure to make for these groves?" Malchus asked his father as, with a bundle of javelins lying by his side, his bow in his hand, and a quiver of arrows hung from his belt in readiness, he took his place at the edge of the trees.

"There can be no certainty of it, Malchus; but it seems likely that the lions, when driven out of their refuges among the hills, will make for these groves, which will seem to offer them a shelter from their pursuers. The fires here will have informed them of our presence last night; but as all is still and dark now they may suppose that the groves are deserted. In any case our horses are in readiness among the trees close at hand, and if the lions take to the plains we must mount and join the Numidians in the chase."

"I would rather meet them here on foot, father."

"Yes, there is more excitement, because there is more danger in it, Malchus; but I can tell you the attack of a wounded lion is no

THE YOUNG CARTHAGINIAN

CHAPTER II: A NIGHT ATTACK

THE time seemed to Malchus to pass slowly indeed as he sat waiting the commencement of the hunt. Deep roars, sounding like distant thunder were heard from time to time among the hills. Once or twice Malchus fancied that he could hear other sounds such as would be made by a heavy stone dislodged from its site leaping down the mountain side; but he was not sure that this was not fancy, or that the sound might not be caused by the roaring of lions far away among the hills.

His father had said that three hours would probably elapse before the circuit would be completed. The distance was not great; but the troops would have to make their way with the greatest care along the rocky hills through brushwood and forest, and their advance would be all the more slow that they had to take such pains to move noiselessly.

It was indeed more than three hours after the column had left the camp when the sound of a distant horn was heard far up the hillside. Almost instantaneously lights burst out in a great semicircle along the hillside, and a faint confused sound, as of the shouting of a large body of men, was heard on the still night air.

"That is very well done," the general said in a tone of satisfaction. "I had hardly expected it to be so well managed; for the operation on such broken and difficult ground was not easy to carry out, even with the moon to help them."

"But see, father!" Malchus said, "there are many patches of darkness in the line, and the lions might surely escape through these."

13

"It would not be possible, Malchus, to place the parties at equal distances over such broken ground. Nor are the lions likely to discover the gaps in the line; they will be far too much terrified by the uproar and sudden blaze of light to approach the troops. Hark, how they are roaring! Truly it is a majestic and terrible sound, and I do not wonder that the wild natives of these mountains regard the animals with something of the respect which we pay to the gods. And now do you keep a sharp eye along the foot of the hills. There is no saying how soon the beasts may break cover."

Slowly the semicircle of light was seen to contract as the soldiers who formed it moved forward towards the foot of the hill; but although Malchus kept his eyes strained upon the fringe of trees at its foot, he could see no signs of movement.

The roaring still continued at intervals, and it was evident that the beasts inclosed in the arc had descended to the lower slopes of the hill.

"They may be upon us sooner than you expect, Malchus. Their colour well-nigh matches with that of the sand, and you may not see them until they are close upon us."

Presently a Nubian soldier standing behind Malchus touched him on the shoulder and said in a whisper:

"There they are!" pointing at the same time across the plain.

Malchus could for a time see nothing; then he made out some indistinct forms.

"There are six of them," the general said, "and they are making for this grove. Get your bows ready."

Malchus could now clearly see the lions approaching. They were advancing slowly, turning occasionally to look back as if reluctant to quit the shelter of the hills; and Malchus could hardly resist a start of uneasiness as one of them suddenly gave vent to a deep, threatening roar, so menacing and terrible that the very leaves of the trees seemed to quiver in the light of the moon under its vibrations. The lions seemed of huge dimensions, especially the leader of the troop, who stalked with a steady and majestic step at their head. When within fifty yards of the grove the lions suddenly paused; their leader apparently scented danger. Again the deep terrible roar rose in the air, answered

14

by an angry snarling noise on the part of the females.

"Aim at the leader," the general whispered, "and have your brands in readiness."

Immediately behind the party a fire was burning; it had been suffered to die down until it was a mere pile of glowing embers, and in this the ends of a dozen stakes of dried wood were laid. The glow of the fire was carefully hidden by a circle of sticks on which thick cloths had been hung. The fire had been prepared in readiness in case the lions should appear in numbers too formidable to be coped with. The leading lion was within twenty-five paces of the spot where the party was standing when Hamilcar gave the word, and a volley of arrows shot forth from their hiding-place.

The lion gave a roar of rage and pain, then, crouching for a moment, with a few tremendous bounds he reached the edge of the wood. He could see his enemies now, and with a fierce spring threw himself upon them. But as soon as they had discharged their arrows the soldiers had caught up their weapons and formed in a close body, and the lion was received upon the points of a dozen spears.

There was a crashing of wood and a snarling growl as one of the soldiers was struck dead with a blow of the mighty paw of the lion, who, ere he could recover himself, received half a dozen javelins thrust deep into his flanks, and fell dead. The rest of the troop had followed him as he sprang forward, but some of the soldiers, who had been told off for the purpose, seized the lighted brands and threw them over the head of the leader among his followers. As the glowing brands, after describing fiery circles in the air, fell and scattered at their feet, the lions paused, and turning abruptly off dashed away with long bounds across the front of the grove.

"Now, Malchus, to horse!" Hamilcar exclaimed. And the general and his son, leaping upon their steeds, dashed out from the grove in pursuit of the troop of lions. These, passing between the two clumps of trees, were making for the plain beyond, when from behind the other grove a dark band of horsemen rode out.

"Let them pass," Hamilcar shouted; "do not head them back."

The cavalry reined up until the troop of lions had passed. Hamilcar rode up to the officer in command.

"Bring twenty of your men," he said; "let the rest remain here. There will doubtless be more of them yet."

Then with the twenty horsemen he rode on in pursuit of the lions.

The chase was an exciting one. For a time the lions, with their long bounds, kept ahead of the horsemen; but the latter, splendidly mounted on their well-bred steeds, soon began to gain. When they were within a hundred yards of them one of the lions suddenly faced round. The Numidians, well accustomed to the sport, needed no orders from their chief. They scattered at once and broke off on each flank so as to encircle the lion, who had taken his post on a hummock of sand and lay couched on his haunches, with his tail lashing his sides angrily, like a great cat about to make his spring.

The horsemen circled round him, dashing up to within five-and-twenty yards, discharging their arrows, and then wheeling away. Each time the lion was struck he uttered a sharp, angry growl, and made a spring in the direction of the horsemen, and then fell back to his post.

One of the soldiers, thinking that the lion was now nearly crippled, ventured to ride somewhat closer; he discharged his arrow, but before he could wheel his horse the lion with two tremendous springs was upon him.

A single blow of his paw brought the horse to the ground. Then the lion seized the soldier by the shoulder, shook him as a cat would a mouse, and throwing him on the sand lay with his paw across him. At this moment Malchus galloped past at full speed, his bow drawn to the arrow head and fixed. The arrow struck the lion just behind its shoulder. The fierce beast, which was in the act of rising, sank down quietly again; its majestic head drooped between its forepaws on to the body of the Nubian, and there it lay as if overtaken with a sudden sleep. Two more arrows were fired into it, but there was no movement.

"The brave beast is dead," Malchus said. "Here is the arrow with which I slew it."

Malchus at the lion hunt

"It was well done, Malchus, and the hide is yours. Let us set off after the others."

But the stand which the lion had made had been sufficiently long to enable the rest of the troop to escape. Leaving two or three of their comrades to remove the body of the soldier, the horsemen scattered in various directions; but although they rode far over the plain, they could see no signs of the troop they had pursued.

After a time they gave up the pursuit and rode back towards the camp. When they reached it they found that another troop of lions, eight in number, had approached the other grove, where two had been killed by the party commanded by Adherbal and Giscon, and the rest of the cavalry were still in pursuit of the others. They presently returned, bringing in four more skins; so that eight lions in all had fallen in the night's work.

"Well, Malchus, what do you think of lion hunting?" Adherbal asked as they gathered again in the general's tent.

"They are terrible beasts," Malchus said. "I had not thought that any beast could make so tremendous a roar. Of course I have heard those in captivity in Carthage, but it did not seem nearly so terrible as it sounded here in the stillness of the desert."

"I own that it made my blood run cold," Adherbal said; "and their charge is tremendous—they broke through the hedge of spears as if they had been reeds. Three of our men were killed."

"Yes," Malchus agreed; "it seemed almost like a dream for a minute when the great beast was among us. I felt very glad when he rolled over on to his side."

"It is a dangerous way of hunting," Hamilcar said. "The chase on horseback in the plains has its dangers, as we saw when that Numidian was killed; but with proper care and skill it is a grand sport. But this work on foot is too dangerous, and has cost the republic the loss of five soldiers. Had I had nets with me I would have adopted the usual plan of stretching one across the trees ten paces in front of us. This breaks the lion's spring, he becomes entangled in its meshes, and can be destroyed with but

18

little danger. But no skill or address avails against the charge of a wounded lion. But you are wounded, Giscon."

"It is a mere nothing," Giscon said.

"Nay," Hamilcar replied, "it is an ugly scratch, Giscon; he has laid open your arm from the shoulder to the elbow as if it were by the cut of a knife."

"It served me right for being too rash," Giscon said. "I thought he was nearly dead, and approached with my sword to give him a finishing thrust. When he struck viciously at me I sprang back, but one of his claws caught my shoulder. A few inches nearer and he would have stripped the flesh from my arm, and perhaps broken the limb and shoulder-bone."

While he was speaking a slave was washing the wound, which he then carefully bandaged up. A few minutes later the whole party lay down to sleep. Malchus found it difficult to close his eyes. His pulse was still throbbing with excitement, and his mind was busy with the brief but stirring scene of the conflict.

Two or three hours passed, and he felt drowsiness creeping over him, when he heard a sudden challenge, followed instantly by a loud and piercing yell from hundreds of throats. He sprang in an instant to his feet, as did the other occupants of the tent.

"To arms!" Hamilcar cried; "the enemy are upon us."

Malchus caught up his shield and sword, threw his helmet on his head, and rushed out of the tent with his father.

A tremendous din had succeeded the silence which had just before reigned in the desert, and the yells of the barbarians rose high in the air, answered by shouts and loud words of command from the soldiers in the other grove. The elephants in their excitement were trumpeting loudly; the horses stamped the ground; the draught cattle, terrified by the din, strove to break away.

Large numbers of dark figures occupied the space some two hundred yards wide between the groves. The general's guards, twenty in number, had already sprung to their feet and stood to arms; the slaves and attendants, panic-stricken at the sudden attack, were giving vent to screams and cries and were running about in confusion.

Hamilcar sternly ordered silence.

"Let each man," he said, "take a weapon of some kind and stand steady. We are cut off from the main body and shall have to fight for our lives. Do you," he said to the soldiers, "lay aside your spears and shoot quickly among them. Fire fast. The great object is to conceal from them the smallness of our number."

Moving round the little grove Hamilcar posted the slaves at short distances apart, to give warning should the enemy be attempting an attack upon the other sides, and then returned to the side facing the other grove, where the soldiers were keeping up a steady fire at the enemy.

The latter were at present concentrating their attention upon their attack upon the main body. Their scouts on the hills during the previous day had no doubt ascertained that the Carthaginian force was encamped here, and the occupants of the smaller grove would fall easy victims after they had dealt with the main body. The fight was raging furiously here. The natives had crept up close before they were discovered by the sentries, and with a fierce rush they had fallen upon the troops before they had time to seize their arms and gather in order.

The fight raged hand to hand, bows twanged and arrows flew, the light javelins were hurled at close quarters with deadly effect, the shrill cries of the Numidians mingled with the deeper shouts of the Iberians and the yells of the natives. Hamilcar stood for a minute irresolute.

"They are neglecting us," he said to Adherbal, "until they have finished with the main body; we must go to their assistance. At present our men are fighting without order or regularity; unless their leaders are with them they are lost, our presence will encourage and reanimate them. Bring up the elephants quickly."

The three elephants were at once brought forward, their drivers mounted on their necks. Four soldiers with their bows and arrows took their places on the back of each, the general with the rest of the fighting men followed closely behind.

At the orders of their drivers the well-trained animals broke into a trot, and the party advanced from the shadow of the grove. The natives scattered between it and the wood fired a volley of arrows and then broke as the elephants charged down upon them.

20

A NIGHT ATTACK

Trained to warfare the elephants dashed among them, catching some up in their trunks and dashing them lifeless to the ground, knocking down and trampling upon others, scattering terror wherever they went, while the archers on their backs kept up a deadly fire. As soon as the way was open Hamilcar led the little party on foot at full speed towards the wood.

As he entered it he ordered his trumpeter to blow his horn. The well-known signal revived the hopes and courage of the sorely pressed troops, who, surprised and discouraged, had been losing ground, great numbers falling before the arrows and javelins of their swarming and active foes. The natives, surprised at the trumpet sound in the rear, paused a moment, and before they could turn round to face their unexpected adversaries, Hamilcar with his little band burst his way through them and joined his soldiers, who, gathered now in a close body in the centre of the grove, received their leader with a shout of welcome.

Hamilcar's measures were promptly taken. He saw that if stationary his band must melt away under the shower of missiles which was being poured upon them. He gave the command and the troops rapidly formed into three groups, the men of each corps gathering together. Adherbal, who was in command of the Numidians, placed himself at their head, Giscon led the Iberians, and Hamilcar headed the heavily armed troops, Malchus taking his place at his side. Hamilcar had already given his orders to the young officers. No response was to be made to the fire of the arrows and javelins, but with spear, sword, and battle-axe the troops were to fall upon the natives.

"Charge!" he shouted in a voice that was heard above the yells of the barbarians. "Clear the wood of these lurking enemies, they dare not face you. Sweep them before your path."

With an answering shout the three bodies of men sprang forward, each in a different direction. In vain the natives poured in volleys of arrows and javelins; many fell, more were wounded, but all who could keep their feet rushed forward with fury upon their assailants.

The charge was irresistible. The natives, fighting each for himself, were unable for a moment to withstand the torrent, and, vastly superior in numbers as they were, were driven headlong before it. When they reached the edge of the wood each of the bodies broke into two. The Numidians had directed their course towards their horses, which a party of their own men were still defending desperately against the attacks of a large body of natives. Through these they cut their way, and springing upon their steeds dashed out into the plain, and sweeping round the grove fell upon the natives there, and cut down the parties of men who emerged in confusion from its shelter, unable to withstand the assaults of Hamilcar and his infantry within.

The heavy infantry and the Iberians, when they gained the edge of the wood, had swept to the right and left, cleared the edge of the grove of their enemies until they met, then joining they again plunged into the centre. Thus they traversed the wood in every direction until they had completely cleared it of foes.

When the work was done the breathless and exhausted troops gathered outside, in the light of the moon. More than half their number had fallen; scarce one but was bleeding from wounds of arrow or javelin. The plain beyond was thickly dotted to the foot of the hills with the bodies of the natives who had been cut up by the Numidian horse or trampled by the elephants, while the grove within was thickly strewn with their bodies.

As there was no fear of a renewal of the attack, Hamilcar, ordered the men to fall out of ranks, and the hours until daybreak were passed in extracting arrows and binding up wounds, and in assisting their comrades who were found to be still living in the grove. Any natives still breathing were instantly slain.

Hamilcar found that a party of the enemy had made their way into his own camp. His tent had been hastily plundered, but most of the effects were found in the morning scattered over the ground between the groves and the hills, having been thrown away in their flight by the natives when the horsemen burst out of the wood in pursuit. Of the slaves and attendants several had been killed, but the greater portion had, when Hamilcar left the grove with the troops, climbed up into trees, and remained there concealed until the rout of the assailants.

It was found in the morning that over one hundred and fifty of the three hundred Carthaginian troops had fallen, and that four hundred of the natives had been slain either in the grove or in the pursuit by cavalry.

The following day two envoys arrived from the hostile tribe offering the submission of their chief.

As pursuit in the hills would be useless Hamilcar offered them comparatively easy terms. A heavy fine in horses and cattle was to be paid to the republic, and ten of the principal members of the tribe were to be delivered up as hostages for their future good behaviour. The next day the hostages were brought into the camp with a portion of the ransom; and Hamilcar, having thus accomplished the mission he had been charged to perform, marched away with his troops to Carthage.

As they approached the coast the whole character of the scenery changed. The desert had been left behind them, and they entered a fertile tract of country which had been literally turned into a garden by the skill and industry of the Carthaginian cultivators, at that time celebrated throughout the world for their knowledge of the science of agriculture. The rougher and more sterile ground was covered with groves of olive trees, while rich vineyards and orchards of fig and other fruit trees occupied the better soil. Wherever it was possible little canals leading water from reservoirs and dammed-up streams crossed the plains, and every foot of the irrigated ground was covered with a luxuriant crop.

The villages were scattered thickly, and when the troops arrived within a day's march of Carthage they came upon the country villas and mansions of the wealthy inhabitants. These in the richness of their architecture, the perfection and order of their gardens, and the beauty and taste of the orchards and grounds which surrounded them, testified alike to the wealth and taste of their occupants.

Fountains threw their water into the air, numerous waterfalls splashed with a cool, soothing sound over artificial rocks. Statues wrought by Greek sculptors stood on the terraces, shady walks offered a cool retreat during the heat of the day, the vine, the pomegranate, and the fig afforded refreshment to the palate as well as pleasure to the eye. Palm trees with their graceful foliage waved gently in the passing breezes. All the countries with which the Carthaginians traded had supplied their contingent of vegetation to add to the beauty and production of these gardens, which were the admiration and envy of the civilized world.

Crossing the brow of a low range of hills the detachment came in sight of Carthage. The general and his three companions, who were riding in the rear of the column, drew in their horses and sat for awhile surveying the scene. It was one which, familiar as it might be, it was impossible to survey without the deepest feeling of admiration.

In the centre stood the great rock of Byrsa, a flat topped eminence with almost perpendicular sides rising about two hundred feet above the surrounding plain. This plateau formed the seat of the ancient Carthage, the Phoenician colony which Dido had founded. It was now the acropolis of Carthage. Here stood the temples of the chief deities of the town; here were immense magazines and storehouses capable of containing provisions for a prolonged siege for the fifty thousand men whom the place could contain. The craggy sides of the rock were visible but in few places. Massive fortifications rising from its foot to its summit defended every point where the rock was not absolutely perpendicular. These walls were of enormous thickness, and in casemates or recesses in their thickness were the stables for the elephants, horses, and cattle of the garrison.

Round the upper edge of the rock extended another massive wall, above which in picturesque outline rose the temple and other public edifices. At the foot of this natural citadel stretched the lower town, with its crowded population, its dense mass of houses, its temples and forum. The style of architecture was peculiar to the city. The Carthaginians abhorred straight lines, and all their buildings presented curves. The rooms were for the most part circular, semicircular, or oval, and all exterior as well as interior angles were rounded off. The material used in their construction was an artificial stone composed of pieces of rock cemented together with fine sand and lime, and as hard as natural conglomerate. The houses were surmounted by domes or cupolas. Their towers were always round, and throughout the city scarce an angle offended the eye of the populace.

Extending into the bay lay the isthmus, known as the Tana, some three miles in length, communicating with the mainland by a tongue of land a hundred yards wide.

This was the maritime quarter of Carthage; here were the extensive docks in which the vessels which bore the commerce of the city to and from the uttermost parts of the known world loaded and unloaded. Here were the state dockyards where the great ships of war, which had so long made Carthage the mistress of the sea, were constructed and fitted out. The whole line of the coast was deeply indented with bays, where rode at anchor the ships of the mercantile navy. Broad inland lakes dotted the plain; while to the north of Byrsa, stretching down to the sea and extending as far as Cape Quamart, lay Megara, the aristocratic suburb of Carthage.

Here, standing in gardens and parks, were the mansions of the wealthy merchants and traders, the suburb presenting to the eye a mass of green foliage dotted thickly with white houses. Megara was divided from the lower town by a strong and lofty wall, but lay within the outer wall which inclosed Byrsa and the whole of Carthage and stretched from sea to sea.

The circumference of the inclosed space was fully twenty miles; the population contained within it amounted to over eight hundred thousand. On the north side near the sea, within the line of the outer fortifications, rose a low hill, and here on the face which sloped gently down to the sea was the great necropolis— the cemetery of Carthage, shaded by broad spreading trees, dotted with the gorgeous mausoleums of the wealthy and the innumerable tombs of the poorer families, and undermined by thousands of great sepulchral chambers, which still remain to testify to the vastness of the necropolis of Carthage, and to the pains which her people bestowed upon the burying-places of their dead.

Beyond all, from the point at which the travellers viewed it, stretched the deep blue background of the Mediterranean, its line broken only in the foreground the lofty citadel of Byrsa, and far out at sea by the faint outline of the Isle of Zinbre.

For some minutes the party sat immovable on their horses, then Hamilcar broke the silence:

"'Tis a glorious view," he said; "the world does not contain a site better fitted for the seat of a mighty city. Nature seems to have marked it out. With the great rock fortress, the splendid bays and harbours, the facilities for commerce, the fertile country stretching away on either hand; give her but a government strong, capable, and honest, a people patriotic, brave, and devoted, and Carthage would long remain the mistress of the world."

"Surely she may yet remain so," Adherbal exclaimed.

"I fear not," Hamilcar said gravely shaking his head. "It seems to be the fate of all nations, that as they grow in wealth so they lose their manly virtues. With wealth comes corruption, indolence, a reluctance to make sacrifices, and a weakening of the feeling of patriotism. Power falls into the hands of the ignorant many. Instead of the destinies of the country being swayed by the wisest and best, a fickle multitude, swayed by interested demagogues, assumes the direction of affairs, and the result is inevitable—wasted powers, gross mismanagement, final ruin."

So saying Hamilcar set his horse in motion and, followed silently by his companions, rode with a gloomy countenance after his little columns towards the capital.

THE YOUNG CARTHAGINIAN

CHAPTER III: CARTHAGE

CARTHAGE was at that time divided between two factions, the one led by the relatives and friends of the great Hamilcar Barca and known as the Barcine party. The other was led by Hanno, surnamed the Rich. This man had been the rival of Hamilcar, and the victories and successes of the latter had been neutralized by the losses and defeats entailed upon the republic by the incapacity of the former. Hanno, however, had the support of the greater part of the senate, of the judges, and of the lower class, which he attached to himself by a lavish distribution of his vast wealth, or by the common tie of wholesale corruption.

The Barcine party were very inferior in numbers, but they comprised among them the energy, the military genius, and the patriotism of the community. They advocated sweeping reforms, the purification of the public service, the suppression of the corruption which was rampant in every department, the fair administration of justice, the suppression of the tyranny of the committee, the vigourous prosecution of the struggle with Rome. They would have attached to Carthage the but half-subdued nations round her who now groaned under her yoke, ground down to the dust by the enormous tribute necessitated by the extravagance of the administration of the state, the corruption and wholesale peculation of its officials.

Hamilcar Barca had been the founder of the party; in his absence at the seat of war it had been led at Carthage by his son-in-law Hasdrubal, whose fiery energy and stirring eloquence had rendered him a popular idol in Carthage. But even the genius of Hamilcar and the eloquence of Hasdrubal would not have sufficed to enable the Barcine party to make head against the enormous power of the council and the judges, backed by the wealth of Hanno and his associates, had it not been for the military successes which flattered the patriotic feelings of the populace.

The loss of Sardinia, Corsica, and Sicily had been atoned for by the conquest of the greater portion of Spain by Hamilcar, and that general might eventually have carried out his plans for the purification of the government of Carthage had he not fallen in a battle with the Iberians. This loss was a terrible blow to the Barcine faction, but the deep feeling of regret among the population at the death of their great general enabled them to carry the election of Hasdrubal to be one of the suffetes in his place, and to obtain for him the command of the army in Spain.

There was the less difficulty in the latter appointment, since Hanno's party were well content that the popular leader should be far removed from the capital. Hasdrubal proved himself a worthy successor of his father-in-law. He carried out the policy inaugurated by the latter, won many brilliant victories over the Iberians, fortified and firmly established Carthagena as a port and city which seemed destined to rival the greatness of its mother-city, and Carthage saw with delight a great western settlement growing in power which promised to counterbalance the influence of the ever-spreading territory of her great rival in Italy.

After seeing his detachment safely lodged in the barracks Hamilcar and his companions rode along the streets to the Barcine Syssite, or club, one of the grandest buildings in Carthage. Throwing the reins of their horses to some slaves who stood in readiness at the foot of the steps, they entered the building. As they rode through the streets they had noticed that the population appeared singularly quiet and dejected, and the agitation which reigned in the club showed them that something unusual had happened. Groups of men were standing talking excitedly in the great hall. Others with dejected men were pacing the marble pavement. As Hamilcar entered, several persons hurried up to him.

"Welcome back again!" they exclaimed; "your presence is most opportune at this sad moment."

"What has happened?" Hamilcar asked; "I have but this moment arrived, and rode straight here to hear the news of what has taken place in my absence."

"What ! have you not heard?" they exclaimed; "for the last four days nothing else has been talked of, nothing else thought of—Hasdrubal has been assassinated!"

Hamilcar recoiled a step as if struck.

"Ye gods!" he exclaimed, "can this be so? Hasdrubal the handsome, as he was well called, the true patriot, the great general, the eloquent orator, the soul of generosity and patriotism, our leader and hope, dead! Surely it cannot be."

"It is too true, Hamilcar. Hasdrubal is dead—slain by the knife of an Iberian, who, it seems, has for months been in his service, awaiting the chance for revenge for some injuries which his family or people have suffered from our arms.

"It is a terrible blow. This morning a swift-sailing ship has arrived with the news that the army of Spain have with one voice acclaimed the young Hannibal as their general, and that they demand the ratification of their choice by the senate and people. Need I tell you how important it is that this ratification should be gained? Hanno and his satellites are furious, they are scattering money broadcast, and moving heaven and earth to prevent the choice falling upon Hannibal, and to secure the appointment for Hanno himself or one of his clique. They say that to appoint a youth like this to such a position would be a thing unheard of, that it would bring countless dangers upon the head of the republic. We know, of course, that what they fear is not the youth and inexperience, but the talent and genius of Hannibal.

"Young though he is, his wonderful abilities are recognized by us all. His father, Hamilcar, had the very highest hopes of him, Hasdrubal has written again and again saying that in his young kinsman he recognized his superior, and that in loftiness of aim, in unselfish patriotism, in clearness of judgment, in the marvellous ascendency he has gained over the troops, in his talent in administration, and in the greatness of his military conceptions, he saw in him a genius of the highest order. If it be in man to overthrow the rising greatness of Rome, to reform our disordered administration, to raise Carthage again to the climax of her glory and power, that man is Hannibal.

"Thus, then, on him our hopes rest. If we can secure for him the command of the army in Spain, he may do all and more than all that Hamilcar and Hasdrubal have done for us. If we fail, we are lost; Hanno will be supreme, the official party will triumph, man by man we shall be denounced and, destroyed by the judges, and, worse than all, our hopes of saving Carthage from the corruption and tyranny which have so long been pressing her into the dust are at an end. It is a good omen of success that you have returned from your expedition at such a critical moment. All has gone well with you, I hope. You know the fate that awaits an unsuccessful general here."

"Ay, I know," Hamilcar said bitterly; "to be judged by a secret tribunal of civilians, ignorant of even the rudimentary laws of war, and bent not upon arriving at the truth, but of gratifying their patrons and accomplices; the end, disgrace and execution.

"No, my success has been complete, although not brilliant. I have obtained the complete submission of the Atarantes, and have brought with me ten of their principal chiefs as hostages; but my success narrowly escaped being not only a failure but a disaster. I had in vain striven to come to blows with them, when suddenly they fell upon me at night, and in the desperate combat which followed, well-nigh half my force fell; but in the end we inflicted a terrible chastisement upon them and completely humbled their pride."

"So long as you succeeded in humbling them and bringing home hostages for their good behaviour, all is well; the lives of a few score of soldiers, more or less, matters little to Carthage. We have but to send out an order to the tribes and we can replace them a hundred-fold in a week; 'tis only a failure which would be fatal. Carthage has suffered such terrible disasters at the hands of her tributaries that she trembles at the slightest rising, for its success might be the signal for another general insurrection. If you have humbled the Atarantes, all is well.

"I know the council have been anxiously expecting news of

your expedition. Our opinion here has been from the first that, from the small force they placed at your command, they purposely sent you to disaster, risking the chance of extended trouble in order to obtain a ground of complaint by which they could inflame the minds of the populace against our party. But now, I recommend you to take some refreshment at once after your journey. The inner council of the club will meet in an hour, and their deliberations are likely to be long as well as important, for the whole future of our party, and of Carthage itself, depends upon the issue."

"Malchus," Hamilcar said, "do you mount your horse and ride out at once and tell your mother that all has gone well with us, but that I am detained here on important business, and may not return until nightfall."

"May I come back here, father, after I see my mother? I would fain be of some use, if I may. I am known to many of the sailors down at the port; I might go about among them trying to stir them up in favour of Hannibal."

"You may come back if you like, Malchus; your sailors may aid us with their voices, or, should it come to anything like a popular disturbance, by their arms. But, as you know, in the voting the common people count for nothing, it is the citizens only who elect, the traders, shopkeepers, and employers of labour. Common people count for no more than the slaves, save when it comes to a popular tumult, and they frighten the shopkeeping class into voting in accordance with their views. However, we will leave no stone unturned that may conduce to our success. Do not hurry away from home, my boy, for your mother would think it unkind after three months' absence. Our council is likely to last for some hours; when it is at an end I will look for you here and tell you what has been determined upon."

Malchus mounted his horse and rode out through the narrow streets of the lower city, through the gateway leading into the suburb, then he loosed the rein and the horse started at a gallop along the broad road, lined with stately mansions, and in a quarter of an hour stopped in front of the villa of Hamilcar.

Throwing his bridle to a slave he ran up the broad steps of the portico and entered the hall. His mother, a stately woman, clad in a long flowing garment of rich material embroidered in gold, arms and neck bare, her hair bound up in a knot at the back of her head, which was encircled by a golden fillet, with pendants of the same metal encrusted with gems falling on her forehead, rose eagerly to meet him, and his two sisters, girls older than himself, clad in white robes, confined at the waist with golden belts, leaped to their feet with a cry of gladness.

"Welcome back, my own son," his mother said; "all is well, I hope, with your father. It is so, I am sure, for I should read evil news in your face."

"He is well, mother, well and victorious, though we had a rare fight for it, I can tell you. But he is kept at the Barcine Syssite on matters connected with this terrible business of the death of Hasdrubal. He bade me give you his love, and say he would be back here as soon as he could get away."

"It is terrible news indeed, Malchus. The loss is a grievous blow to Carthage, but especially to us who are his near kinsfolk; but for the moment let us set it aside and talk of your doings. How the sun has bronzed your face, child! You seem to have grown taller and stouter since you have been away."

"Yes," one of the sisters laughed, "the child is growing up, mother; you will have to choose another name for him."

"I think it is about time," Malchus said, joining in the laugh, "considering that I have killed a lion and have taken part in a desperate hand-to-hand fight with the wild Atarantes. I think even my mother must own that I am attaining the dignity of youth."

"I wonder your father let you take part in such strife," the mother said anxiously; "he promised me that he would, as far as possible, keep you out of danger."

"Why, mother," Malchus said indignantly, "you don't suppose that my father was going to coddle me as he might do one of the girls here. You know he has promised that I shall soon enter the Carthaginian guard, and fight in the next campaign. I think it has been very hard on me not to have had a chance of distinguishing myself as my cousin Hannibal did when he was no older than I am."

"Poor boy," his sister laughed, "he has indeed been

unfortunate. Who can say but that if he had only had opportunities he would have been a general by this time, and that Rome would have been trembling at the clash of his armour."

Malchus joined heartily in the laugh about himself.

"I shall never grow to be a general," he said, "unless you get me some food; it is past mid-day, and I have not broken my fast this morning. I warn you that I shall not tell you a word of our adventures until I have eaten, therefore the sooner you order a meal to be served the better."

The meal was speedily served, and then for an hour Malchus sat with his mother and sisters, giving them a history of the expedition. There was a little playful grumbling on the part of his sisters when he told them that he was going to return to the Syssite to hear what had been determined by the conclave.

"Surely you can wait until our father returns here, Malchus," Thyra, the elder, said.

"Yes; but I may be useful," Malchus replied. "There will be lots to be done, and we shall all do our utmost."

"Listen to him, mother," Anna, the younger sister, said, clapping her hands; "this comes of slaying lions and combating with the Atarantes; do not let us hinder him; beg the slaves to bring round a horse instantly. Carthage totters, let Malchus fly to its support. What part are you thinking of taking, my brother, do you mean to harangue the people, or to urge the galley slaves to revolt, or to lead the troops against the council?"

The two girls burst into a peal of merry laughter, in which Malchus, although colouring a little, joined heartily.

"You are too bad, Anna; what I want is, of course, to hear what has been done, and to join in the excitement, and really I am not such a boy as you girls think me, just because you happen to be two or three years older than I am. You persist in regarding me as a child; father doesn't do so, and I can tell you I may be more good than you think."

"Well, go along, Malchus, do not let us keep you, and don't get into mischief; and remember, my boy," his mother added, "that Carthage is a place where it is well that no one should make more enemies than he can help. A secret foe in the council or among the judges is enough to ruin the strongest. You know how many have been crucified or pressed to death without a shadow of pretext, save that they had foes. I would not see you other than your father's son; you will belong, of course, to the Barcine party, but there is no occasion to draw enmity and hate upon yourself before you are in a position to do real service to the cause. And now ride off with you; I know all our words are falling on deaf ears, and that willful lads will go their own way."

A few minutes later and Malchus was on his way back to the club. On his arrival there he found that the sitting of the inner council was not yet finished. The building was thronged with the adherents of the party waiting to ascertain what course was determined upon. He presently came across Adherbal and Giscon. The former, as usual, was gay, light-hearted, and disposed to view matters in a humorous light; Giscon was stern and moody.

"So, here you are again, Malchus," Adherbal said. "I thought you would soon be back. I am glad you have come, for Giscon here grows monotonous as a companion. Nature in making him forgot to give him that spice of humour which is to existence what seasoning is to meat. I am ready to fight if it comes to fighting, to orate if talking is necessary, and to do anything else which may be within the limits of my powers, but I can't for the life of me take matters as if the existence of the state depended on me alone. I have already heard that all is well with you at home. I shall ride out there and see your mother when this business is over. What they can find to talk about so long I can't make out.

"The question is a simple one, surely. Will it be better for Carthage at large, and our party in particular, for Hannibal to stay at the head of the army in Spain, or to come home and bring the influence of his popularity and reputation to bear upon the populace? There is the question put in a nutshell, and if they can't decide upon it let them toss up. There is virtue, I am ready to maintain, in an appeal to dame Fortune.

"Look round now, Malchus, is it not amusing to study men's

characters. Look at little Philene going about among the groups, standing on tiptoe to whisper into the ear first of one and then of another. He prides himself on his knowledge of affairs, and in his heart believes that he is shamefully wronged inasmuch as he is not already on the secret committee.

"Look at Bomilca leaning against that pillar and lazily pulling his mustache, an easy-going giant, who looks upon the whole thing as a nuisance, but who, if he received orders from the conclave, would put himself at the head of the Libyans, and would march to storm Hanno's house, and to slaughter his Nubian guard without a question.

"Look at Magon's face of importance as he walks about without speaking to anyone. He is trying to convey to all the impression that he knows perfectly well what is going on inside, and could if he chose tell you what the decision will be. There is Carthalon, who is thinking at present, I warrant, more of the match which he has made of his Arab steed against that of his comrade Phano, than of the matter in hand. But see, there is a stir, the curtains are drawing aside at last, the meeting is over."

As he spoke the heavy curtains which shut off an inner room from the hall were drawn aside, and the council of the Syssite came out. Each was speedily surrounded by a group of the members of his own family, or those who specially looked up to him as a leader. Malchus and the two young officers were among those who gathered round Hamilcar.

"It has been decided," the general said, "that Hannibal shall be retained in his command. Therefore, now let all set to work each in his own sphere. The populace must be stirred up. We have a small majority in the council, but the middle class, the men who will vote, are with Hanno. Some have been bought with his gold, some of the weak fools dream that Carthage can be great simply as a trading power without army or navy, and think only of the present advantage they would gain by remission of taxation. It is these we have to fear, and we must operate upon them by means of the populace.

"If the people gather in the streets and shout for Hannibal, these cowards will hesitate. They are accessible only in their money-bags, and rather than risk a riot they would vote for the destruction of Moloch's temple. Giscon and Adherbal, do you go to the barracks, get as many of your comrades together as are of our way of thinking, talk to the soldiers of the glories of Hamilcar Barca, of the rich booty they won under him, of the glory of their arms when he led them, tell them that in Hannibal they have their old commander revived, and that Hanno and his companions seek only to have him removed, because they fear that the luster of his deeds will overshadow them.

"Urge that he is the elect of the army of Spain, that the voice of the soldiers has acclaimed him, and that the troops here should join their voices to those of their comrades in Spain. They too may ere long have to take share in the war, and would it not be far better for them to be led by a soldier like Hannibal than by Hanno, whose incapacity has been proved a score of times, and who is solely chosen because he is rich, and because he has pandered to the fat traders and lazy shopkeepers?

"Do you, Stryphex, go to the weavers' quarter; you have influence there. Work upon the men, point out to them how, since Hamilcar and Hasdrubal have conquered Spain, and the gold and silver from the mines have poured into Carthage, their trade has flourished. Before that gold was scarce known in the city, none could purchase their choice productions, their wages would scarce keep the wolf from the door. Show them that under Hanno disaster will be sure to befall our arms, that the Iberians will reconquer their soil, that the mines will be lost, and we shall have to return to the leather money of twenty years back."

So one by one Hamilcar despatched the groups round him on various missions, until Malchus alone remained.

"You, Malchus, can, as you suggested, go down to the port; ask the sailors and fishermen what will become of their trade were the Roman galleys cruising in our bay. Point out that our conquests in Spain have already caused the greatest alarm in Rome, and that under Hannibal our arms will so flourish that Rome will be glad to come to terms with us, and to leave us free to trade with the world.

"Point out how great is the trade and commerce which Carthagena has already produced. Ask them if they are willing that all this shall be hazarded, in order that Hanno may gratify his personal ambition, and his creatures may wring the last penny from the over-taxed people of Carthage. Don't try too much, my boy. Get together a knot of men whom you know; prime them with argument, and send them among their fellows. Tell them to work day and night, and that you will see that their time is well paid. Find out if there are any men who have special influence with their fellows, and secure them on our side. Promise them what they will; the Syssite will spend money like water to carry its object. Be discreet, Malchus; when you have lit the fire, and see that it is well on its way, withdraw quietly."

Malchus hurried off, and in half an hour was down by the port. Through the densely packed district which lay behind the lofty warehouses crammed with goods brought by sea from all parts of the world, he made his way until he reached the abode of a fisherman, in whose boat he often put to sea.

The old man, with three or four grown-up sons, was reclining on a pile of rushes.

"Welcome back, my lord Malchus," he said; "glad am I to see you safely returned. We have often talked of you, me and my sons, and wondered when you would again go out for a night's fishing with us. You have come back at the right time. The tunny are just entering the bay, and in another week we shall have rare sport."

"I shall be glad, indeed, of another sail with you," Malchus said; "but at present I have other matters in hand. Hanno and his friends have determined to oppose the appointment of Hannibal to the army in Spain." The fisherman gave a grunt, which signified that the matter was one of which he knew nothing, and which affected him not in the slightest.

"Don't you see the importance of this?" Malchus said. "If Hannibal doesn't get the command our troops will be beaten, and we shall lose all our trade with Spain." The fisherman still appeared apathetic.

"My sons have all taken to fishing," he said indifferently, "and it matters nothing to them whether we lose the trade of Spain or not."

"But it would make a difference," Malchus said, if no more gold and silver came from Spain, because then, you know, people wouldn't be able to pay a good price for fish, and there would be bad times for you fishermen. But that is not the worst of it. The Romans are so alarmed by our progress in Spain that they are glad to keep friends with us, but if we were driven out from there they would soon be at war again. You and your sons would be pressed for the ships of war, and like enough you might see the Roman fleets hovering on our coasts and picking up our fishing-boats."

"By Astarte," the fisherman exclaimed, "but that would be serious, indeed; and you say all this will happen unless Hannibal remains as general in Spain?"

"That is so," Malchus nodded.

"Then I tell you what, my boys," the fisherman said, rising and rubbing his hands, "we must put our oars into this business. You hear what my lord Malchus tells us. Get up, there is work to be done. Now, sir, what is the best way to stop this affair you tell us of ? If it's got to be done we will do it, and I think I can answer for three or four thousand fishing hands here who ain't going to stand by any more than I am and see the bread taken out of their mouths. They know old Calcon, and will listen to what he says. I will set about it at once."

"That is just what I want," Malchus said. "I want you and your sons to go about among the fishermen and tell them what is proposed to be done, and how ruinous it will be for them. You know how fond of fishermen I am, and how sorry I should be to see them injured. You stir them up for the next three or four days, and get them to boiling point. I will let you know when the time comes. There are other trades who will be injured by this business, and when the time comes you fishermen with your oars in your hands must join the others and go through the streets shouting "Hannibal for general! Down with Hanno and the tax-gatherers!"

"Down with the tax-gatherers is a good cry," the old fisherman said. "They take one fish of every four I bring in, and always choose the finest. Don't you be afraid, sir; we will be there, oars and all, when you give the word."

"And now I want you to tell me the names of a few men who have influence among the sailors of the mercantile ships, and among those who load and discharge the cargoes; their interest is threatened as well as yours. I am commissioned to pay handsomely all who do their best for the cause, and I promise you that you and your sons shall earn as much in four days' work as in a month's toiling on the sea. The Barcine Club is known to be the true friend of Carthage, the opponent of those who grind down the people, and it will spare no money to see that this matter is well carried out."

The fisherman at once went round with Malchus to the abodes of several men regarded as authorities by the sailors and stevedores. With these, partly by argument, but much more by the promises of handsome pay for their exertions, Malchus established an understanding, and paved the way for a popular agitation among the working-classes of the water-side in favour of Hannibal.

THE YOUNG CARTHAGINIAN

CHAPTER IV: A POPULAR RISING

DAY after day Malchus went down to the port. His father was well pleased with his report of what he had done, and provided him with ample funds for paying earnest-money to his various agents, as a proof that their exertions would be well rewarded. He soon had the satisfaction of seeing that the agitation was growing.

Work was neglected, the sailors and labourers collected on the quays and talked among themselves, or listened to orators of their own class, who told them of the dangers which threatened their trade from the hatred of Hanno and his friends the tax-collectors for Hannibal, whose father and brother-in-law had done such great things for Carthage by conquering Spain and adding to her commerce by the establishment of Carthagena and other ports. Were they going to stand tamely by and see trade ruined, and their families starving, that the tyrants who wrung from them the taxes should fatten at ease?

Such was the tenor of the orations delivered by scores of men to their comrades on the quays. A calm observer might have noticed a certain sameness about the speeches, and might have come to the conclusion that the orators had received their instructions from the same person, but this passed unnoticed by the sailors and workmen, who were soon roused into fury by the exhortations of the speakers. They knew nothing either of Hannibal or of Hanno, but they did know that they were ground down to the earth with taxation, and that the conquest of Spain and the trade that had arisen had been of enormous benefit to them. It was, then, enough to tell them that this trade was

40

threatened, and that it was threatened in the interest of the tyrants of Carthage, for them to enter heart and soul into the cause.

During these four days the Barcine Club was like the headquarters of an army. Night and day the doors stood open, messengers came and went continually, consultations of the leading men of the city were held almost without a break. Every man belonging to it had his appointed task. The landed proprietors stirred up the cultivators of the soil, the manufacturers were charged with the enlightenment of their hands as to the dangers of the situation, the soldiers were busy among the troops; but theirs was a comparatively easy task, for these naturally sympathized with their comrades in Spain, and the name of the great Hamilcar was an object of veneration among them.

Hanno's faction was not idle. The Syssite which was composed of his adherents was as large as its rival. Its orators harangued the people in the streets on the dangers caused to the republic by the ambition of the family of Barca, of the expense entailed by the military and naval establishments required to keep up the forces necessary to carry out their aggressive policy, of the folly of confiding the principal army of the state to the command of a mere youth. They dilated on the wealth and generosity of Hanno, of his lavish distribution of gifts among the poor, of his sympathy with the trading community. Each day the excitement rose, business was neglected, the whole population was in a fever of excitement.

On the evening of the fourth day the agents of the Barcine Club discovered that Hanno's party were preparing for a public demonstration on the following evening. They had a certainty of a majority in the public vote, which, although nominally that of the people, was, as has been said, confined solely to what would now be called the middle class.

Hitherto the Barcine party had avoided fixing any period for their own demonstration, preferring to wait until they knew the intention of their opponents. The council now settled that it should take place on the following day at eleven o'clock, just when the working-classes would have finished their morning meal.

The secret council, however, determined that no words should be whispered outside their own body until two hours before the time, in order that it should not be known to Hanno and his friends until too late to gather their adherents to oppose it. Private messengers were, however, sent out late to all the members to assemble early at the club.

At nine o'clock next morning the Syssite was crowded, the doors were closed, and the determination of the council was announced to the members, each of whom was ordered to hurry off to set the train in motion for a popular outbreak for eleven o'clock. It was not until an hour later that the news that the Barcine party intended to forestall them reached Hanno's headquarters. Then the most vigourous efforts were made to get together their forces, but it was too late. At eleven o'clock crowds of men from all the working portions of the town were seen making their way towards the forum, shouting as they went, "Hannibal for general!" "Down with Hanno and the tax-gatherers!"

Conspicuous among them were the sailors and fishermen from the port, armed with oars, and the gang of stevedores with heavy clubs. Hanno and a large number of his party hurried down to the spot and tried to pacify the crowd, but the yells of execration were so loud and continuous that they were forced to leave the forum. The leaders of the Barcine party now appeared on the scene, and their most popular orator ascended the rostrum. When the news spread among the crowd that he was a friend of Hannibal and an opponent of Hanno, the tumult was stayed in order that all might hear his words.

"My friends," he said, "I am glad to see that Carthage is still true to herself, and that you resent the attempt made by a faction to remove the general of the army's choice, the son of the great Hamilcar Barca. To him and to Hasdrubal, his son-in-law, you owe the conquest of Spain, you owe the wealth which has of late years poured into Carthage, you owe the trade which is already doing so much to mitigate your condition. What have Hanno and his friends done that you should listen to him? It is their incapacity which has lost Carthage so many of its possessions. It is their greed and corruption which place such burdens on your backs. They claim that they are generous. It is easy to be generous with the money of which they have plundered you; but let them know your will, and they must bend before it. Tell them that you will have Hannibal and none other as the general of your armies, and Spain is secure, and year by year your commerce with that country will increase and flourish."

A roar of assent arose from the crowd. At the same instant a tumult was heard at the lower entrance to the forum, and the head of a dense body of men was seen issuing from the street, with shouts of "Hanno forever!" They were headed by the butchers and tanners, an important and powerful body, for Carthage did a vast trade in leather.

For a time they bore all before them, but the resistance increased every foot they advanced. The shouts on both sides became louder and more angry. Blows were soon exchanged, and ere long a pitched battle was raging. The fishermen and sailors threw themselves into the thick of it, and for ten minutes a desperate fight raged in the forum. Soon the battle extended, as bodies of men belonging to either faction encountered each other as they hurried towards the forum.

Street frays were by no means unusual in Carthage, but this was a veritable battle. Hanno had at its commencement, accompanied by a strong body of his friends, ridden to Byrsa, and had called upon the soldiers to come out and quell the tumult. They, however, listened in sullen silence, their sympathies were entirely with the supporters of Hannibal, and they had already received orders from their officers on no account to move, whosoever might command them to do so, until Hamilcar placed himself at their head.

The general delayed doing this until the last moment. Hannibal's friends had hoped to carry their object without the intervention of the troops, as it was desirable in every way that the election should appear to be a popular one, and that Hannibal should seem to have the suffrages of the people as well as of the army. That the large majority of the people were with them they knew, but the money which Hanno's friends had lavishly spent among the butchers, skinners, tanners, and smiths had raised up a more formidable opposition than they had counted upon.

Seeing that their side was gaining but little advantage, that already much blood had been shed, and that the tumult threatened to involve all Carthage, Hamilcar and a number of officers rode to the barracks. The troops at once got under arms, and, headed by the elephants, moved out from Byrsa. Being desirous to avoid bloodshed, Hamilcar bade his men leave their weapons behind them, and armed them with headless spear shafts, of which, with all other things needed for war, there was a large store in the citadel. As the column sallied out it broke up into sections. The principal body marched toward the forum, while others, each led by officers, took their way down the principal streets.

The appearance of the elephants and troops, and the loud shouts of the latter for Hannibal, quickly put an end to the tumult. Hanno's hired mob, seeing that they could do nothing against such adversaries, at once broke up and fled to their own quarters of the city, and Hanno and his adherents sought their own houses. The quiet citizens, seeing that the fight was over, issued from their houses, and the forum was soon again crowded.

The proceedings were now unanimous, and the shouts raised that the senate should assemble and confirm the vote of the army were loud and strenuous. Parties of men went out in all directions to the houses of the senators to tell them the people demanded their presence at the forum. Seeing the uselessness of further opposition, and fearing the consequences if they resisted, Hanno and his friends no longer offered any opposition.

The senate assembled, and, by a unanimous vote the election of Hannibal as one of the suffetes in place of Hasdrubal, and as commander-in-chief of the army in Spain, was carried, and was ratified by that of the popular assembly, the traders and manufacturers of Hanno's party not venturing to oppose the will of the mass of mechanics and sea-faring population.

"It has been a victory," Hamilcar said, when, accompanied by a number of his friends, he returned to his home that evening, "but Hanno will not forget or forgive the events of this day. As long as all goes well in Spain we may hope for the support of the people, but should any disaster befall our arms it will go hard with all who have taken a prominent part in this day's proceedings.

Hanno's friends have so much at stake that they will not give up the struggle. They have at their back all the moneys which they wring from the people and the tributaries of Carthage, and they will work night and day to strengthen their party and to buy over the lower classes. We are the stronger at present; but to carry the popular vote on a question which would put a stop to the frightful corruption of our administration, to suppress the tyranny of the council, to sweep away the abuses which prevail in every class in the state—for that we must wait till Hannibal returns victorious. Let him but humble the pride of Rome, and Carthage will be at his feet."

The party were in high spirits at the result of the day's proceedings. Not only had they succeeded in their principal object of electing Hannibal, but they had escaped from a great personal danger; for, assuredly, had Hanno and his party triumphed, a stern vengeance would have been taken upon all the leading members of the Barcine faction.

After the banquet, while Hamilcar and his companions reclined on their couches at tables, a Greek slave, a captive in war, sang songs of his native land to the accompaniment of the lyre. A party of dancing girls from Ethiopia performed their rhythmical movements to the sound of the tinkling of a little guitar with three strings, the beating of a small drum, the clashing of cymbals, and the jingling of the ornaments and little metal bells on their arms and ankles. Perfumes were burned in censers, and from time to time soft strains of music, played by a party of slaves among the trees without, floated in through the casements.

Malchus was in wild spirits, for his father had told him that it was settled that he was to have the command of a body of troops which were very shortly to proceed to Spain to reinforce the army under Hannibal, and that he should allow Malchus to enter the band of Carthaginian horse which was to form part of the body under his command.

The regular Carthaginian horse and foot formed but a very small portion of the armies of the republic. They were a corps *d'élite*, composed entirely of young men of the aristocratic families of Carthage, on whom it was considered as almost a matter of obligation to enter this force. They had the post of honour in battle, and it was upon them the Carthaginian generals relied principally to break the ranks of the enemy in close battle. All who aspired to distinguish themselves in the eyes of their fellow-citizens, to rise to power and position in the state, to officer the vast bodies of men raised from the tributary nations, and to command the armies of the country, entered one or other of these bodies. The cavalry was the arm chosen by the richer classes. It was seldom that it numbered more than a thousand strong. The splendour of their armour and appointments, the beauty of their horses, the richness of the garments of the cavaliers, and the trappings of their steeds, caused this body to be the admiration and envy of Carthage. Every man in it was a member of one of the upper ranks of the aristocracy; all were nearly related to members of the senate, and it was considered the highest honour that a young Carthaginian could receive to be admitted into it.

Each man wore on his wrist a gold band for each campaign which he had undertaken. There was no attempt at uniformity as to their appointments. Their helmets and shields were of gold or silver, surmounted with plumes or feathers, or with tufts of white horse-hair. Their breastplates were adorned with arabesques or repoussé work of the highest art. Their belts were covered with gold and studded with gems. Their short-kilted skirts were of rich Tyrian purple embroidered with gold.

The infantry were composed of men of good but less exalted families. They wore a red tunic without a belt. They carried a great circular buckler of more than a yard in diameter, formed of the tough hide of the river-horse, brought down from the upper Nile, with a central boss of metal with a point projecting nearly a foot in front of the shield, enabling it to be used as an offensive weapon in a close fight. They carried short heavy swords similar to those of the Romans, and went barefooted. Their total strength seldom exceeded two thousand.

These two bodies constituted the Carthaginian legion, and formed but a small proportion indeed of her armies, the rest of her forces being entirely drawn from the tributary states. The fact that Carthage, with her seven hundred thousand inhabitants, furnished so small a contingent of the fighting force of the republic, was in itself a proof of the weakness of the state. A country which relies entirely for its defence upon mercenaries is rapidly approaching decay.

She may for a time repress one tributary with the soldiers of the others; but when disaster befalls her she is without cohesion and falls to pieces at once. As the Roman orator well said of Carthage: "She was a figure of brass with feet of clay"—a noble and imposing object to the eye, but whom a vigourous push would level in the dust. Rome, on the contrary, young and vigourous, was a people of warriors. Every one of her citizens who was capable of bearing arms was a soldier. The manly virtues were held in the highest esteem, and the sordid love of wealth had not as yet enfeebled her strength or sapped her powers. Her citizens were men, indeed, ready to make any sacrifice for their country; and such being the case, her final victory over Carthage was a matter of certainty.

The news which afforded Malchus such delight was not viewed with the same unmixed satisfaction by the members of his family. Thyra had for the last year been betrothed to Adherbal, and he, too, was to accompany Hamilcar to Spain, and none could say how long it might be before they would return.

While the others were sitting round the festive board, Adherbal and Thyra strolled away among the groves in the garden.

"I do not think you care for me, Adherbal," she said reproachfully as he was speaking of the probabilities of the campaign. "You know well that this war may continue in Spain for years, and you seem perfectly indifferent to the fact that we must be separated for that time."

"I should not be indifferent to it, Thyra, if I thought for a moment that this was to be the case. I may remain, it is true, for years in Spain; but I have not the most remote idea of remaining there alone. At the end of the first campaign, when our army goes into winter quarters, I shall return here and fetch you."

"That's all very well," the girl said, pouting; "but how do you know that I shall be willing to give up all the delights of

Carthage to go among the savage Iberians, where they say the ground is all white in winter and even the rivers stop in their courses?"

Adherbal laughed lightly.

"Then it is not for you to talk about indifference, Thyra; but it won't be so bad as you fear. At Carthagena you will have all the luxuries of Carthage. I do not say that your villa shall be equal to this; but as you will have me it should be a thousand times dearer to you."

"Your conceit is superb, Adherbal," Thyra laughed. "You get worse and worse. Had I ever dreamed of it I should never have consented so submissively when my father ordered me to regard you as my future husband."

"You ought to think yourself a fortunate girl, Thyra," Adherbal said, smiling; "for your father might have taken it into his head to have done as Hamilcar Barca did, and married his daughters to Massilian and Numidian princes, to become queens of bands of nomad savages."

"Well, they were queens, that was something, even if only of nomads."

"I don't think that it would have suited you, Thyra—a seat on horseback for a throne, and a rough tent for a palace, would not be in your way at all. I think a snug villa on the slopes of the bay of Carthagena, will suit you better, not to mention the fact that I shall make an infinitely more pleasant and agreeable master than a Numidian chief would do."

"You are intolerable, Adherbal, with your conceit and your mastership. However, I suppose when the time comes I shall have to obey my father. What a pity it is we girls cannot choose our husbands for ourselves! Perhaps the time may come when we shall do so."

"Well, in your case, Thyra," Adherbal said, "it would make no difference, because you know you would have chosen me anyhow; but most girls would make a nice business of it. How are they to know what men really are? They might be gamesters, drunkards, brutal and cruel by nature, idle and spendthrift. What can maidens know of a man's disposition? Of course they only see him at his best. Wise parents can make careful inquiries, and have means of knowing what a man's disposition and habits really are."

"You don't think, Adherbal," Thyra said earnestly, "that girls are such fools that they cannot read faces; that we cannot tell the difference between a good man and a bad one."

"Yes, a girl may know something about every man save the one she loves, Thyra. She may see other's faults clearly enough; but she is blind to those of the man she loves. Do you not know that the Greeks depict Cupid with a bandage over his eyes?"

"I am not blind to your faults," Thyra said indignantly. "I know that you are a great deal more lazy than becomes you; that you are not sufficiently earnest in the affairs of life; that you will never rise to be a great general like my cousin Hannibal."

"That is all quite true," Adherbal laughed; "and yet you see you love me. You perceive my faults only in theory and not in fact, and you do not in your heart wish to see me different from what I am. Is it not so?"

"Yes," the girl said shyly, "I suppose it is. Anyhow, I don't like the thought of your going away from me to that horrid Iberia."

Although defeated for the moment by the popular vote, the party of Hanno were not discouraged. They had suffered a similar check when they had attempted to prevent Hannibal joining Hasdrubal in Spain.

Not a moment was lost in setting to work to recover their lost ground. Their agents among the lower classes spread calumnies against the Barcine leaders. Money was lavishly distributed, and the judges, who were devoted to Hanno's party, set their machinery to work to strike terror among their opponents. Their modes of procedure were similar to those which afterwards made Venice execrable in the height of her power. Arrests were made secretly in the dead of night. Men were missing from their families, and none knew what had become of them.

Dead bodies bearing signs of strangulation were found floating in the shallow lakes around Carthage; and yet, so great was the dread inspired by the terrible power of the judges, that the friends and relations of those who were missing dared make neither complaint nor inquiry. It was not against the leaders of the Barcine party that such measures were taken. Had one of these been missing the whole would have flown to arms. The dungeons would have been broken open, and not only the captives liberated, but their arrest might have been made the pretext for an attack upon the whole system under which such a state of things could exist.

It was chiefly among the lower classes that the agents of Hanno's vengeance operated. Among these the disappearance of so many men who were regarded as leaders among the rest spread a deep and mysterious fear. Although none dared to complain openly, the news of these mysterious disappearances was not long in reaching the leaders of the Barcine party.

These, however, were for the time powerless to act. Certain as they might be of the source whence these unseen blows descended, they had no evidence on which to assail so formidable a body as the judges. It would be a rash act indeed to accuse such important functionaries of the state, belonging, with scarcely an exception, to powerful families, of arbitrary and cruel measures against insignificant persons.

The halo of tradition still surrounded the judges, and added to the fear inspired by their terrible and unlimited power. In such an attack the Barcine party could not rely upon the population to side with them; for, while comparatively few were personally affected by the arrests which had taken place, the fear of future consequences would operate upon all.

Among the younger members of the party, however, the indignation aroused by these secret blows was deep. Giscon, who was continually brooding over the tyranny and corruption which were ruining his country, was one of the leaders of this section of the party; with him were other spirits as ardent as himself. They met in a house in a quiet street in the lower town, and there discussed all sorts of desperate projects for freeing the city of its tyrants.

One day as Giscon was making his way to this rendezvous he met Malchus riding at full speed from the port.

"What is it, Malchus, whither away in such haste?"

"It is shameful, Giscon, it is outrageous. I have just been

down to the port to tell the old fisherman with whom I often go out that I would sail with him to-morrow, and find that four days ago he was missing, and his body was yesterday found by his sons floating in the lagoon. He had been strangled. His sons are as much overpowered with terror as by grief; they believe that he has suffered for the part he took in rousing the fishermen to declare for Hannibal a fortnight since, and they fear lest the terrible vengeance of Hanno should next fall upon them.

"How it happened they know not. A man arrived late in the evening and said that one of their father's best customers wanted a supply of fish for a banquet he was to give next day, and that he wanted to speak to him at once to arrange about the quantity and quality of fish he required. Suspecting nothing the old man left at once, and was never heard of afterwards. Next morning, seeing that he had not returned, one of his sons went to the house to which he had been fetched, but found that its owner knew nothing of the affair, and denied that he had sent any message whatever to him. Fearing that something was wrong they searched everywhere, but it was not until last night that his body was, as I have told you, found.

"They are convinced that their father died in no private feud. He had not, as far as they know, an enemy in the world. You may imagine how I feel this; not only did I regard him as a friend, but I feel that it was owing to his acting as I led him that he has come to his death."

"The tyrants!" Giscon exclaimed in a low voice. "But what can you do, Malchus?"

"I am going to my father," Malchus replied, "to ask him to take the matter up."

"What can he do?" Giscon said with a bitter laugh. "What can he prove? Can he accuse our most noble body of judges, without a shadow of proof, of making away with this unknown old fisherman. No, Malchus, if you are in earnest to revenge your friend come with me, I will introduce you to my friends, who are banded together against this tyranny, and who are sworn to save Carthage. You are young, but you are brave and full of ardour; you are a son of General Hamilcar, and my friends will gladly receive you as one of us."

Malchus did not hesitate. That there would be danger in joining such a body as Giscon spoke of he knew, but the young officer's talk during their expedition had aroused in him a deep sense of the tyranny and corruption which were sapping the power or his country, and this blow which had struck him personally rendered him in a mood to adopt any dangerous move.

"I will join you, Giscon," he said, "if you will accept me. I am young, but I am ready to go all lengths, and to give my life if needs be to free Carthage."

THE YOUNG CARTHAGINIAN

CHAPTER V: THE CONSPIRACY

GISCON led his companion along the narrow lanes until he reached the back entrance of the house where the meetings were held. Knocking in a particular way it was opened at once and closed behind them. As they entered a slave took Malchus' horse without a word and fastened it to a ring in the wall, where four or five other horses were standing.

"I rather wonder you are not afraid of drawing attention by riding on horseback to a house in such a quarter," Malchus said.

"We dare not meet secretly, you know. The city is full of spies, and doubtless the movements of all known to be hostile to Hanno and his party are watched, therefore we thought it best to meet here. We have caused it to be whispered as a secret in the neighbourhood, that the house has been taken as a place where we can gamble free from the presence of our elders. Therefore the only comments we excite is, 'There go those young fools who are ruining themselves.' It is only because you are on horseback that I have come round to this gate; had you come on foot we should have entered by the front. Fortunately there are among us many who are deemed to be mere pleasure-seekers— men who wager fortunes on their horses, who are given to banquets, or whose lives seem to be passed in luxury and indolence, but who at heart are as earnest in the cause of Carthage as I am. The presence of such men among us gives a probability to the tale that this is a gambling house. Were we all of my stamp, men known to be utterly hostile to Hanno and his party, suspicion would fall upon our meetings at once. But here we are."

As he spoke he drew aside some heavy curtains and entered

53

a large room. Some ten or twelve young men were assembled there. They looked up in surprise as Giscon entered followed by his companion.

"I have brought a recruit," Giscon said, "one whom all of you know by repute if not personally; it is Malchus, the son of General Hamilcar. He is young to be engaged in a business like ours, but I have been with him in a campaign and can answer for him. He is brave, ready, thoughtful and trustworthy. He loves his country and hates her tyrants. I can guarantee that he will do nothing imprudent, but can be trusted as one or ourselves. Being young he will have the advantage of being less likely to be watched, and may be doubly useful. He is ready to take the oath of our society."

As Giscon was the leading spirit of the band his recommendation was taken as amply sufficient. The young men rose and formed in a circle round Malchus. All drew their daggers, and one, whom Malchus recognized with a momentary feeling of surprise as Carthalon, whom Adherbal had pointed out at the Barcine Club as one who thought only of horse-racing, said:

"Do you swear by Moloch and Astarte to be true to this society, to devote yourself to the destruction of the oppressors of Carthage, to carry out all measures which may be determined upon, even at the certain risk of your life, and to suffer yourself to be torn to pieces by the torture rather than reveal aught that passes within these walls?"

"That I swear solemnly," Malchus said.

"I need not say," Carthalon said carelessly, "that the punishment of the violation of the oath is death. It is so put in our rules. But we are all nobles of Carthage, and nobles do not break their oaths, so we can let that pass. When a man's word is good enough to make him beggar himself in order to discharge a wager, he can be trusted to keep his word in a matter which concerns the lives of a score of his fellows. And now that this business is arranged we can go on with our talk; but first let us have some wine, for all this talking is thirsty work at best."

The young men threw themselves upon the couches around the room and, while slaves brought round wine, chatted lightly with each other about horses, the play presented the day before, the respective merits of the reigning beauties of Carthage, and other similar topics, and Malchus, who was impressed with the serious nature of the secret conspiracy which he had just sworn to aid, could not help being surprised at the careless gaiety of the young men, although engaged in a conspiracy in which they risked their lives.

It was not until some minutes after the slaves had left the apartment that the light talk and banter ceased, as Giscon rose and said:

"Now to business. Malchus has told me that an old fisherman, who took a lead in stirring up his fellows to declare for Hannibal, has been decoyed away from his home and murdered; his body has been found floating in the lake, strangled. This is the nineteenth in the course of a week. These acts are spreading terror among the working-classes, and unless they are put a stop to we can no longer expect assistance from them.

"That these deeds are the work of the officials of the tribunals we have no doubt. The sooner we strike the better. Matters are getting ripe. I have eight men sworn into my section among the weavers, and need but two more to complete it. We will instruct our latest recruit to raise a section among the fishermen. The sons of the man just murdered should form a nucleus. We agreed from the first that three hundred resolute men besides ourselves were required, and that each of us should raise a section of ten. Malchus brings up our number here to thirty, and when all the sections are filled up we shall be ready for action.

"Failure ought to be impossible. The houses of Hanno and thirty of his party will be attacked, and the tyrants slain before any alarm can be given. Another thirty at least should be slain before the town is fairly aroused. Maybe each section can undertake three if our plans are well laid, and each chooses for attack three living near each other. We have not yet settled whether it will be better to separate when this is done, content with the first blow against our tyrants, or to prepare beforehand for a popular rising, to place ourselves at the head of the populace, and to make a clean sweep of the judges and the leaders of Hanno's party."

Giscon spoke in an ordinary matter-of-fact tone, as if he were discussing the arrangements of a party of pleasure; but

Malchus could scarcely repress a movement of anxiety as he heard this proposal for the wholesale destruction of the leading men of Carthage. The council thus opened was continued for three hours. Most of those present spoke, but, to the surprise of Malchus, there was an entire absence of that gloom and mystery with which the idea of a state conspiracy was associated in his mind.

The young men discussed it earnestly, indeed, but in the same spirit in which they would have agreed over a disputed question as to the respective merits of two horses. They laughed, joked, offered and accepted wagers and took the whole matter with a lightness of heart which Malchus imitated to the best of his power, but which he was very far from feeling; and yet he felt that beneath all this levity his companions were perfectly in earnest in their plans, but they joked now as they would have joked before the commencement of a battle in which the odds against them were overwhelming and great.

Even Giscon, generally grave and gloomy, was as light-hearted as the rest. The aristocracy of Carthage were, like the aristocracy of all other countries, from tradition, training, and habit, brave to excess. Just as centuries later the noblesse of France chatted gaily on the tumbril on their way to execution, and offered each other their snuff-boxes on the scaffold, so these young aristocrats of Carthage smiled and jested, though well aware that they were risking their lives.

No decision was arrived at, for this could only be decided upon at a special meeting, at which all the members of the society would be present. Among those now in council opinions were nearly equally divided. The one party urged that, did they take steps to prepare the populace for a rising, a rumour would be sure to meet the ears of their opponents and they would be on their guard; whereas, if they scattered quickly after each section had slain two of their tyrants, the operation might be repeated until all the influential men of Hanno's faction had been removed.

In reply to these arguments the other party urged that delays were always dangerous, that huge rewards would be offered after the first attempts, that some of the men of the sections might turn traitors, that Hanno's party would be on their guard in future, and that the judges would effect wholesale arrests and executions; whereas, were the populace appealed to in the midst of the excitement which would be caused by the death of Hanno and his principal adherents, the people would rise and finish with their tyrants.

After all who wished to speak on the subject had given their opinions, they proceeded to details; each gave a statement of the number of men enrolled in his section, with a few words as to the disposition of each. Almost without an exception each of these men was animated with a sense of private wrong. Some had lost near relatives, executed for some trifling offence by the tribunals, some had been ruined by the extortion of the tax-gatherers. All were stated to be ready to give their lives for vengeance.

"These agents of ours, you see, Malchus, are not for the most part animated by any feeling of pure patriotism, it is their own wrongs and not the injuries of Carthage which they would avenge. But we must take them as we find them; one cannot expect any deep feeling of patriotism on the part of the masses, who, it must be owned, have no very great reason to feel any lively interest in the glories of the republic. So that they eat and drink sufficiently, and can earn their living, it matters not very greatly to them whether Carthage is great and glorious, or humbled and defeated. But this will not always be so. When we have succeeded in ridding Carthage of her tyrants we must next do all we can so to raise the condition of the common people that they may feel that they too have a common interest in the fate of our country. I should not, of course, propose giving to them a vote; to bestow the suffrage upon the ignorant, who would simply follow the demagogues who would use them as tools, would be the height of madness. The affairs of state, the government of the country, the making of the laws, must be solely in the hands of those fitted for the task–of the men who, by education, by birth, by position, by study and by leisure have prepared their minds for such a charge. But the people should share in the advantages of a good government; they should not be taxed more than they could reasonably pay, and any tax-gatherers who should extort a penny beyond the legal amount should be disgraced and punished.

"The courts should be open to all, the judges should be impartial and incorruptible; every man should have his rights and his privileges, then each man, feeling an interest in the stability of the state, would be ready to bear arms in its defence, and Carthage, instead of being dependent entirely upon her tributaries and mercenaries, would be able to place a great army in the field by her own unaided exertions.

"The barbarian tribes would cease to revolt, knowing that success would be hopeless. And as we should be strong at home we should be respected abroad, and might view without apprehension the rising power of Rome. There is plenty of room for both of us. For us, Africa and Spain; for her all the rest of Europe and as much of Asia as she cares to take. We could look without jealousy at each other's greatness, each secure in his own strength and power. Yes, there may be a grand future before Carthage yet."

The meeting now broke up.

"Where are you going, Malchus?" Giscon asked the lad as they went out into the court-yard; "to see the sacrifices? You know there is a grand function to-day to propitiate Moloch and to pray for victory for our arms."

"No," Malchus said with a shudder. "I don't think I am a coward, Giscon, but these terrible rites frighten me. I was taken once by my father, and I then swore that never again, unless it be absolutely necessary for me in the performance of public office, will I be present at such a scene. For weeks afterwards I scarcely slept; day and night there was before me that terrible brazen image of Moloch. If I fell off to sleep, I woke bathed in perspiration as I heard the screams of the infants as they were dropped into those huge hands, heated to redness, stretched out to receive them. I cannot believe, Giscon, that the gods are so cruel.

"Then there was the slaughter of a score of captives taken in war. I see them now, standing pale and stern, with their eyes directed to the brazen image which was soon to be sprinkled with their blood, while the priests in their scarlet robes, with the sacrificial knives in hand, approached them. I saw no more, for I shut my eyes till all was over. I tell you again, Giscon, I do not believe the gods are so cruel. Why should the gods of Phoenicia and Carthage alone demand blood? Those of Greece and Rome are not so bloodthirsty, and yet Mars gives as many victories to the Roman arms as Moloch does to ours."

"Blaspheme not the gods, Malchus," Giscon said gloomily; "you may be sure that the wreath of a conquering general will never be placed around your brow if you honour them not."

"If honouring them means approval of shedding the blood of infants and captives, I will renounce all hopes of obtaining victory by their aid."

"I would you had spoken so before, Malchus; had I known that you were a scorner of the gods I would not have asked you to join in our enterprise. No good fortune can be expected to attend our efforts unless we have the help of the gods."

"The matter is easily mended, Giscon," Malchus said calmly. "So far I have taken no step towards carrying out your plans, and have but listened to what you said, therefore, no harm can yet have been done. Strike my name off the list, and forget that I have been with you. You have my oath that I will say nought of anything that I have heard. You can well make some excuse to your comrades. Tell them, for example, that though I fear not for myself, I thought that, being the son of Hamilcar, I had no right to involve his name and family in such an enterprise, unless by his orders."

"Yes, it were better so," Giscon said after a pause; "I dare not continue the enterprise with one who condemns the gods among us; it would be to court failure. I did not dream of this; who could have thought that a lad of your age would have been a spurner of the gods?"

"I am neither a condemner nor a spurner," Malchus said indignantly; "I say only that I believe you worship them wrongfully, that you do them injustice. I say it is impossible that the gods who rule the world can have pleasure in the screams of dying infants or the groans of slaughtered men."

59

Giscon placed his hand to his ears as if to shut out such blasphemy, and hurried away, while Malchus, mounting his horse, rode out slowly and thoughtfully to his father's villa. He was not at heart sorry that he was freed from this association into which, without knowing the measures by which it intended to carry out its aims, he had rashly entered. He was ready for armed insurrection against the tyrants of Carthage, but he revolted from the thought of this plan for a midnight massacre–it was not by such means that he would have achieved the regeneration of his country. He felt, too, that the reason which he had given Giscon was a valid one. He had no right, at his age, to involve his family in such a conspiracy. Did it fail, and were he found to be among the conspirators, Hanno and his associates would be sure to seize the fact as a pretext for assailing Hamilcar. They would say that Malchus would never have joined in such a plot had he not known that it had the approval of his father, and that he was in fact but the representative of his family in the design for overthrowing the constitution of the republic.

Fortunately for Malchus, a few days later orders were given for the instant embarkation of a portion of the reinforcements destined for Hannibal. Hamilcar was to proceed in command of them, and, busied with his preparation for the start, Malchus thought little more of the conspiracy which was brewing. Thirty large merchant ships were hired to convey the troops, who numbered six thousand. These were principally Libyan footmen. The main body, with the Numidian horse, were to follow shortly. At last the day for embarkation arrived, and the troops defiled through the temple of Moloch, where sacrifices were offered up for the success of the enterprise.

Malchus, under the pretense that something was not ready, at the last moment lingered at home, and only joined his comrades, a hundred young men of the Carthaginian horse, on the quays. This body, all composed of young men of the best families of Carthage, were to sail in the same ship which carried Hamilcar. The scene was a busy one–the docks of Carthage were extensive, and the ships which were to convey the expedition lay in deep water by the quays, so that the troops could march on board. A great crowd of the populace had assembled to view the embarkation. These were with difficulty kept from crowding the troops and impeding their movement by a cordon of soldiers.

As the troops marched on to the quay they were formed up in parties by the side of the ships which were to convey them. Very different was the demeanour of the men of the different nationalities. The Libyans were stern and silent, they were part of the contingent which their state was bound to furnish to Carthage, and went unwillingly, cursing in their hearts the power which tore them from their homes to fight in a war in which they had neither concern nor interest.

Near them were a body of Garamantes, wrapped in the long bernous which then as now was the garb of the children of the desert. Tall, swarthy figures these, lissome and agile, with every muscle standing out clear through the brown skin. Strange as must have been the scene to them, there was no wonder expressed in the keen glances which they shot, around them from underneath their dark eyebrows. Silent and taciturn, scarce a word was to be heard among them as they stood awaiting the orders to embark; they were there unwillingly, and their hearts were far away in the distant desert, but none the less would they be willing to fight when the time came. Terrible foes these would be in a night attack, with their stealthy tiger-like tread, their gleaming, vengeful eyes, and their cruel mouths.

Very different were the band of Ethiopians from the distant Soudan, with their cloaks of lion skin, and the gaudy feathers fastened in a fillet round their heads. Their black faces were alive with merriment and wonder–everything was new and extraordinary to them. The sea, the ships, the mighty city, the gathered crowd, all excited their astonishment, and their white teeth glistened as they chatted incessantly with a very babel of laughter and noise.

Not less light-hearted were the chosen band of young nobles grouped by the general's ship. Their horses were held in ranks behind them for the last time by their slaves, for in future they would have to attend to them themselves, and as they gathered in groups they laughed and jested over the last scandal in Carthage, the play which had been produced the night before at the theatre, or the horse-race which was to be run on the following day. As to the desperate work on which they were to be engaged–for it was whispered that Hannibal had in preparation some mighty enterprise–it troubled them not at all, nor the thought that many of them might never look on Carthage again. In their hearts perhaps some of them, like Malchus, were thinking sadly of the partings they had just gone through with those they loved, but no signs of such thoughts were apparent in their faces or conversation.

Presently a blast of trumpets sounded, and the babel of voices was hushed as if by magic. The soldiers fell into military order, and stood motionless. Then Hamilcar walked along the quays inspecting carefully each group, asking questions of the captains of the ships as to their store of provisions and water, receiving from the officers charged with that duty the lists of the war-machines and stores which were stored away in the hulls; and, having assured himself that everything was in order, he gave the signal to his trumpeter, who again blew a long and piercing blast.

The work of embarkation at once commenced. The infantry were soon on board, but the operation of shipping the horses of the cavalry took longer. Half of these were stored away in the hold of the general's ship, the rest in another vessel. When the troops were all on board the soldiers who had kept back the crowd were withdrawn, and the Carthaginians thronged down on to the quay. A small space was still kept clear on the wharf by whose side the admiral's ship was lying, and here was gathered a throng of the aristocracy of the city to see the last of their sons and relatives of the guard.

Having seen their horses safely stowed below the young men crowded to the side of the ship to exchange adieus with their friends. The parting was a brief one, for the wind was fair, and the general anxious to be well out of the bay before nightfall. Therefore the signal was hoisted. Numbers of slaves seized the hawsers of the ships and towed them along through the narrow passage which connected the docks with the sea. A shout of adieu rose from the crowd, the sails were hoisted, and the fleet proceeded on its way.

The arrangements for the comfort of the troops at sea were simple and primitive. Each man shifted for himself. The whole space below was occupied by cargo or horses. The troops lived and slept on deck. Here, on wide flat stones, they cooked their meals, whiled away the day by games of chance, and slept at night on skins or thick rugs. Fortunately the weather was fair. It was early in March, but the nights were not cold.

The fleet hugged the coast, anchoring at night, until the northern shores stood out clear and well defined as Spain stretched down towards Africa. Then they crossed and cruised along until they arrived at Carthagena. Short as was the time which had elapsed since the foundation of that city, its aspect was already imposing and extensive. It lay at the head of a gulf facing south, about a mile in depth and nearly double that width. Across the mouth of this bay was an island, with but a narrow passage on each side, protecting it from the southern winds, and forming with it a magnificent harbour.

On a bold hill at the head of the harbour stood the town. This hill rose from a wide lagoon, which communicated on one side with the sea, and was on the other separated from it only by a strip of land, four hundred yards wide. Through this a wide channel had been dug. Thus the hill, which was of considerable extent, rugged and precipitous, was isolated, and could only be attacked by sea.

The town was built in a sort of amphitheatre facing the sea, and was surrounded by a strong fortification two miles and a half in circumference, so that even should an assailant cross the lagoon, which in summer was nearly dry, he would have before him an almost impregnable defence to carry. Here, in buildings whose magnitude surprised the new-comers, acquainted as they were with the buildings of Carthage, were stored the treasures, the baggage, the ammunition of war, and the provisions of the army.

It had been the aim of the great Hamilcar, and of Hasdrubal

after him, to render the army of Spain as far as possible independent of the mother country. They well knew how often the treasury of Carthage was empty owing to the extravagance and dishonesty of her rulers, and how impossible it would be to obtain thence the supplies required for the army. Therefore they established immense workshops, where arms, munitions of war, machines for sieges, and everything required for the use of the army were fabricated.

Vast as were the expenses of these establishments, the revenues of Iberia were amply sufficient not only to defray all the cost of occupation, but to transmit large sums to Carthage. These revenues were derived partly from the tribute paid by conquered tribes, partly from the spoils taken in captured cities, but most of all from the mines of gold and silver, which were at that time immensely rich, and were worked by the labour of slaves taken in war or of whole tribes subdued.

Some idea of the richness of these mines may be formed by the fact that one mine, which Hannibal had inherited from his father, brought in to him a revenue of nearly a thousand pounds a day; and this was but one of his various sources of wealth. This was the reason that Hamilcar, Hasdrubal, and Hannibal were able to maintain themselves in spite of the intrigues of their enemies in the capital. Their armies were their own rather than those of the country.

It was to them that the soldiers looked for their pay, as well as for promotion and rewards for valour, and they were able, therefore, to carry out the plans which their genius suggested untrammelled by orders from Carthage. They occupied, indeed, a position very similar to that of Wallenstein, when, with an army raised and paid from his private means, he defended the cause of the empire against Gustavus Adolphus and the princes of the Protestant league. It is true that the Carthaginian generals had always by their side two commissioners of the senate. The republic of Carthage, like the first republic of France, was ever jealous of her generals, and appointed commissioners to accompany them on their campaigns, to advise and control their movements and to report on their conduct; and many of the defeats of the Carthaginians were due in no small degree to their generals being hampered by the interference of the commissioners. They were present, as a matter of course, with the army of Hannibal, but his power was so great that their influence over his proceedings was but nominal.

The war which was about to break out with Rome is called the second Punic war, but it should rather be named the war of Hannibal with Rome. He conceived and carried it out from his own resources, without interference and almost without any assistance from Carthage. Throughout the war her ships lay idle in her harbour. Even in his greatest need Carthage never armed a galley for his assistance. The pay of the army came solely from his coffers, the material for the war from the arsenals constructed by his father, his brother-in-law, and himself. It was a war waged by a single man against a mighty power, and as such there is, with the exception of the case of Wallenstein, nothing to resemble it in the history of the world.

Passing through the narrow passage into the harbour the fleet sailed up to the end of the bay, and were soon alongside the spacious quays which had been erected. A large quantity of shipping already lay there, for the trade of Carthagena with the mother city and with the ports of Spain, Africa, and the East already rivaled that of Carthage. A group of officers were gathered on the quay as Hamilcar's ship, which was leading the fleet, neared it, and Hamilcar exclaimed, "There is Hannibal himself!"

As the ship moored alongside the quay Hannibal came on board and warmly embraced his cousin, and then bestowed a cordial greeting upon Malchus.

"Why, cousin Malchus," he said, "though it is but a year since I was in Carthage, I should scarce have known you, so much have you grown. I see you have entered the cavalry. That is well. You cannot begin too early to accustom yourself to war."

Then turning, he went among the young men of the guard, to all of whom he was personally known, greeting them with a cordiality and kindness which greatly gratified them. Malchus gazed at him with admiration. Fortunately an accurate description of Hannibal has come down to us. He was one who, even at first sight, won all hearts by his lofty and noble expression, by the kindness and sincerity which his face expressed. The

65

Hannibal welcomes Hamilcar and Malchus

Carthaginians, as a race, were short, but Hannibal was very tall, and his great width of shoulders testified to his immense strength.

The beauty of the Carthaginian race was proverbial, but even among them he was remarkable. His head was well placed on his shoulders; his carriage was upright and commanding; his forehead lofty; his eye, though soft and gentle at ordinary times, was said to be terrible in time of battle. His head was bare. His hair, of a golden brown, was worn long, and encircled by a golden band. His nose was long and straight, forming, with the forehead, a perfect profile. The expression of the mouth was kind but firm. His beard was short. The whole contour of the face was noble in the extreme.

In battle he wore a helmet of bronze closely fitting the head, behind which projected a curved metal plate covering his neck. A band of gold surrounded the helmet; in front were five laurel leaves in steel; at the temples two leaves of the lotus of the same metal. On the crest, rising from an ornament enriched with pearls, was a large plume of feathers, sometimes red and sometimes white. A tuft of white horsehair fell from the plate behind. A coat of mail, made of a triple tissue of chains of gold, covered his body. Above this he wore a shirt of the finest white linen, covered to the waist by a jerkin of leather overlaid with gold plates. A large mantle of purple embroidered with gold hung from his shoulders. He wore sandals and leggings of red morocco leather.

But it was only on special occasions that Hannibal was thus magnificently clad. On the march he dressed generally in a simple blouse like that worn by his soldiers. His arms were borne behind him by an esquire. These consisted of his shield, of Galatian manufacture. Its material was bronze, its shape circular. In the centre was a conical, sharply-pointed boss. The face of the shield was ornamented with subjects taken from the history of Carthage in relief. The offensive arms were a sword, a lance, and a bow with arrows. But it was not to the splendour of his appearance that Hannibal owed the enthusiasm by which he was regarded by his troops. His strength and skill were far superior to those of any man in his army. His food was as simple as that of his soldiers, he was capable of going for days without eating, and it was seldom that he broke his fast until the day's work was over. When he ate it would be sitting on horseback, or as he walked about seeing to the needs of the soldiers.

At night he slept among them, lying on a lion skin without covering. He was indifferent to heat and cold, and in the heaviest tempest of wind and rain would ride bareheaded among his troops, apparently unconscious of the tempest against which he was struggling. So far as was known he was without a vice. He seldom touched wine. His morals were irreproachable. He never gave way to anger. His patience under trials and difficulties of all sorts was illimitable.

In the midst of the greatest trials and dangers he preserved his cheerfulness, and had ever an encouraging word for his soldiers. Various as were the nationalities of the troops who followed him, constrained as most of them had been to enter the service of Carthage, so great was their love and admiration for their commander that they were ready to suffer all hardships, to dare all dangers for his sake. It was his personal influence, and that alone, which welded this army, composed of men of various nationalities and tribes, into one whole, and enabled it to perform the greatest military exploits in the world's history, and for years to sustain a terrible struggle against the whole power of Rome.

THE YOUNG CARTHAGINIAN

CHAPTER VI: A CAMPAIGN IN SPAIN

MONG the young officers who had followed Hannibal on board were some who had left Carthage only a few months before and were known to Malchus. From them he learned with delight that the troops would take the field at once.

"We are going on a campaign against the Vaccæi," one of them said. "The army marched out two days since. Hannibal has been waiting here for your arrival, for a fast-sailing ship which started a few hours after you brought the news that you were on your way, and you will set off to join the rest without delay. It is going to be a hard campaign."

"Where is the country of the Vaccæi?" Malchus asked.

"A long way off," the other replied. "The marches will be long and tiresome. Their country lies somewhat to the north-west of the great plateau in the centre of Iberia. We shall have to ascend the mountains on this side, to cross the plateau, to follow the rivers which flow to the great ocean."

The Vaccæi, in fact, dwelt in the lands bordered by the upper Duero, their country comprising a portion of old Castille, Leon, and the Basque provinces. The journey would indeed be a long and difficult one; and Hannibal was undertaking the expedition not only to punish the turbulent Vaccæi, who had attacked some of the tribes which had submitted to Carthage, but to accustom the troops to fatigues and hardships, and to prepare them for the great expedition which he had in view. No time was indeed lost, for as soon as the troops were landed they were formed up and at once started on their march.

THE YOUNG CARTHAGINIAN

"This is more than we bargained for," Trebon, a young guardsman whose place in the ranks was next to Malchus, said to him. "I thought we should have had at least a month here before we set out. They say the city is as gay as Carthage; and as I have many friends here I have looked forward to a month of jollity before starting. Every night when I lay down on the hard planks of the deck I have consoled myself with the thought that a soft bed awaited me here; and now we have to take at once to the bare ground, with nothing but this skin strapped on the pommel of my saddle to sleep on, and my bernous to cover me. It is colder already a great deal than it was at Carthage; and if that is so here, what will it be on the tops of those jagged mountains we see before us? Why, as I live, that highest one over there is of dazzling white! That must be the snow we have heard of—the rain turned solid by cold, and which they say causes a pain to the naked limbs something like hot iron. Fancy having to sleep in such stuff!"

Malchus laughed at the complaints of his comrade.

"I confess I am glad we are off at once," he said, "for I was sick of doing nothing but idling away my time at Carthage; and I suppose it would be just the same here. How busy are the streets of the town! Except for the sight of the mountains which we see through the breaks of the houses, one might believe one's self still at home."

The aspect of Carthagena, indeed, closely resembled that of the mother city, and the inhabitants were of the same race and blood.

Carthagena had in the first place been formed by a great colony of Libyans. The inhabitants of that province inhabiting the sea-ports and coasts near Carthage were a mixture of Phoenician and native blood. They were ever impatient of the supremacy of Carthage, and their rebellions were frequent and often dangerous. After the suppression of these insurrections, Carthage, sensible of the danger arising from the turbulence of her neighbours, deported great numbers of them to form colonies. Vast numbers were sent up into the Soudan, which was then one of the most important possessions of the republic. The most extensive, however, of these forced emigrations was the great colony sent to found Carthagena, which had thus in a very few years, under the fostering genius of the great Hamilcar, become a great and prosperous city.

Carthage itself had thus suddenly sprung into existence. After many internal troubles the democracy of Tyre had gained the upper hand in that city; and finding their position intolerable, the whole of the aristocracy decided to emigrate, and, sailing with a great fleet under their queen Dido or Elisa–for she was called by both names–founded Carthage. This triumph of the democracy in Tyre, as might be expected, proved the ruin of that city. Very rapidly she fell from the lofty position she had held, and her place in the world and her proud position as Queen of the Seas was very speedily taken by Carthage.

The original Libyan colony of Carthagena had been very largely increased by subsequent emigration, and the populace presented an appearance very similar to that of the mother city, save that instead of the swarthy desert tribesmen, with their passive face and air of proud indifference, mingling with the population of the town, there was in Carthagena a large admixture of native Iberians, who, belonging to the tribes first subdued by Carthage, had either been forced to settle here to supply manual labour needed for the rising city, or who had voluntarily abandoned their wandering life and adopted the more settled habitudes and more assured comforts of existence in a great town.

Skirting the lower part of the city, Hamilcar's force marched along the isthmus and crossed the bridge over the canal cut through it, and was soon in the country beyond. The ground rose gradually, and after marching for six miles the brigade was halted at a spot to which Hannibal had, when the fleet was first discerned approaching along the coast, despatched some bullocks and other provisions for their use. The march was a short one, but after a week's confinement on board ship the men were little fitted for a long journey. The bullocks and other rations were served out to the various companies, and the work of preparing the repast began. Malchus was amused, although rather disgusted at his first experience in a real campaign. When with Hamilcar on the expedition against the Atarantes he had formed part of his father's suite and had lived in luxury. He was now a simple soldier, and was called upon to assist to cut up the bullock which had fallen to the share of the Carthaginian cavalry.

Some of the party went out to cut and bring in wood for the fires and cooking; others moistened the flour and made dough for the flat cakes which would be baked in the hot embers and eaten with the meat. Loud shouts of laughter rose as the young soldiers worked at their unaccustomed tasks, superintended by the officers, who, having all made several campaigns, were able to instruct them as to their duties. From a culinary point of view the meal could not be pronounced a success, and was, indeed, a contrast to the food to which the young nobles were accustomed. The march, however, and the keen bracing air had given them good appetites, and the novelty and strangeness of the experience gave a zest to the food; and in spite of the roughness of the meal, all declared that they had never dined better. Many fires were now lit; and round these, as the evening closed in, the men gathered in groups, all closely wrapped in their bernouses, which were worn alike by officers and men of the whole of the nationalities serving in the Carthaginian army, serving as a cloak by day and a blanket at night. Presently a trampling of horses was heard, and Hannibal and his personal staff rode into the encampment.

He had not started until several hours after them, when, having given his last orders and made all final arrangements for the management of affairs during his absence, he had ridden on to join the army. Dismounting, he went at once on foot among the troops, chatting gaily with them and inquiring how they fared. After visiting all the other detachments he came to the bivouac of the Carthaginian horse, and for an hour sat talking by their fires.

"Ah!" he said as he rose to go, "the others will sleep well enough to-night; but you sybarites, accustomed to your soft couches and your luxuries, will fare badly. I remember my first night on the hard ground, although 'tis now sixteen years back, how my limbs ached and how I longed for morning. Now, let me give you a hint how to make your beds comfortable. Mind, this is not for the future, but till your limbs get accustomed to the ground you may indulge in luxuries. Before you try to go off to sleep note exactly where your hip-bones and shoulders will rest;

take your daggers and scoop out the earth at these points so as to make depressions in which they may lie. Then spread your lion-skins above them and lie down. You will sleep as comfortably as if on a soft couch."

Many of the young soldiers followed Hannibal's advice; others, among whom was Malchus, determined to accustom themselves at once to the hard ground. Malchus was not long in getting to sleep, his last thought being that the precaution advised by Hannibal to ensure repose was altogether unnecessary. But he changed his opinion when, two or three hours later, he woke up with acute pains in his hip and shoulder. After trying vainly, by changing his position, again to go off to sleep, he rose, rolled up the skin, and set to work to make the excavations recommended by the general. Then spreading out the skin again he lay down, and was astonished to find how immense was the relief afforded by this simple expedient.

At daybreak the party were in motion. Their march was a long one; for Hannibal wished to come up with the main army as soon as possible, and no less than thirty miles were encompassed before they halted for the night. They were now far up on the slopes of the Sierras. The latter part of the journey had been exceedingly toilsome. The route was mostly bare rock, which sorely tried the feet of the soldiers, these being in most cases unprotected even by sandals. Malchus and his mounted companions did not of course suffer in their feet. But they were almost as glad as the infantry when the camping-place was reached, for nothing is more fatiguing to a horseman than to be obliged to travel in the saddle for ten hours at the pace of footmen. The halting-place this time was near the upper edge of the forest which then clothed the lower slopes of the mountains.

Enough meat had been killed on the previous evening for three days' rations for the troops, and there was therefore no loss of time in preparing the meal. Wood, of course, was in abundance, and the pots were soon hanging from thick poles placed above the fires. The night was exceedingly cold, and the soldiers were grateful for the shelter which the trees afforded from the piercing wind which blew across the snow-covered peaks of the higher range of mountains.

"What is that noise?" Malchus asked one of the officers as, after the meal was finished and silence began to reign in the camp, a deep sound was heard in the forest.

"That is the howling of a pack of wolves," the officer said. "They are savage brutes, and when in company will not hesitate to attack small parties of men. They abound in the mountains, and are a scourge to the shepherds of the plains, especially in the cold weather, when they descend and commit terrible damage among the flocks."

"I thought I did not know the sound," Malchus said. "The nights were noisy enough sometimes at the southern edge of the desert. The packs of jackals, with their sharp yelping cry, abounded; then there was the deeper note of the hyenas, and the barking cry of troops of monkeys, and the thundering roar of the lions. They were unpleasant enough, and at first used to keep one awake; but none of them were so lugubrious as that mournful howl I hear now. I suppose sometimes, when there is nothing else to do, we get up hunting parties?"

"Yes," the officer replied; "it is the chief amusement of our garrisons in winter among the wild parts of the country. Of course, near Carthagena these creatures have been eradicated; but among the mountains they abound, and the carcass of a dead horse is sure to attract plenty of them. It is a sport not without danger; and there are many instances where parties of five or six have gone out, taking with them a carcass to attract the wolves, and have never returned; and a search has resulted in the discovery of their weapons, injured and perhaps broken, of stains of blood and signs of a desperate struggle, but of them not so much as a bone has remained behind."

"I thought lion-hunting was an exciting sport; but the lions, although they may move and hunt in companies, do not fight in packs, as these fierce brutes seem to do. I hope some day to try it. I should like to send back two of their heads to hang on the wall by the side of that of the lion I killed up in the desert."

"Next winter you may do so," the officer said. "The season is nearly over now, and you may be sure that Hannibal will give us enough to do without our thinking of hunting wolves. The

Vaccæi are fierce enough. Perhaps two of their heads would do instead of those of wolves."

"I do not think my mother and sisters would approve of that," Malchus laughed; "so I must wait for the winter."

The night did not pass so quietly as that which had preceded it. The distant howling of the wolves, as they hunted in the forest, kept the horses in a tremor of terror and excitement, and their riders were obliged over and over again to rise and go among them, and by speaking to and patting them, to allay their fear. So long as their masters were near them the well-trained horses were quiet and tractable, and would at a whispered order lie down and remain in perfect quiet; but no sooner had they left them and again settled to sleep than, at the first howl which told that the pack were at all approaching, the horses would lift their heads, prick their ears in the direction of the sound, and rise to their feet and stand trembling, with extended nostrils snuffing the unknown danger, pawing the ground, and occasionally making desperate efforts to break loose from their picket ropes.

The work of soothing had then to be repeated, until at last most of the riders brought their lions' skins and lay down by the prostrate horses, with their heads upon their necks. The animals, trained thus to sleep with their riders by their side, and reassured by the presence of their masters, were for the most part content to lie quiet, although the packs of wolves, attracted by the scent of the meat that had been cooked, approached close to the camp and kept up a dismal chorus round it until morning.

Day by day the march was continued. The country was wild and rugged, foaming torrents had to be crossed, precipices surmounted, barren tracts traversed. But after a week's hard marching the column had overcome the greater part of the difficulty, had crossed the Sierras and gained the plateau, which with a gradual fall slopes west down to the Atlantic, and was for the most part covered with a dense growth of forests. They now to their satisfaction overtook the main body of the army, and their marches would be somewhat less severe, for hitherto they had each day traversed extra distances to make up for the two days' loss in starting. Here Malchus for the first time saw the bands of Gaulish mercenaries.

The Spanish troops had excited the admiration and astonishment of the Carthaginians by their stature and strength; but the Gauls were a still more powerful race. They belonged to the tribes which had poured down over the Apennines, and occupied the northern portion of Spain long anterior to the arrival of the Carthaginians. Their countenances were rugged, and as it seemed to Malchus, savage. Their colour was much lighter than that of any people he had yet seen. Their eyes were blue, their hair, naturally fair or brown, was dyed with some preparation which give it a red colour.

Some wore their long locks floating over their shoulders, others tied it in a knot on the top of their heads. They wore a loose short trouser fastened at the knee, resembling the baggy trousers of the modern Turks. A shirt with open sleeves came half-way down their thighs, and over it was a blouse or loose tunic decorated with ornaments of every description, and fastened at the neck by a metal brooch. Their helmets were of copper, for the most part ornamented with the horns of stags or bulls. On the crest of the helmet was generally the figure of a bird or wild beast. The whole was surmounted by immense tufts of feathers, something like those of our Highland bonnets, adding greatly to the height and apparent stature of the wearers.

The Gauls had a passion for ornaments, and adorned their persons with a profusion of necklaces, bracelets, rings, baldricks, and belts of gold. Their national arms were long heavy pikes–these had no metal heads, but the points were hardened by fire; javelins of the same description–these before going into battle they set fire to, and hurled blazing at the enemy–lighter darts called *matras saunions*, pikes with curved heads, resembling the halberds of later times; and straight swords. Hannibal, however, finding the inconvenience of this diversity of weapons, had armed his Gaulish troops only with their long straight swords. These were without point, and made for cutting only, and were in the hands of these powerful tribesmen terrible weapons. These swords were not those they had been accustomed to carry, which were made of copper only, and often bent at the first blow, but were especially made for them in Carthage of heavy steel, proof against all accident.

The march was conducted with all military precautions, although they were still traversing a country which had been already subdued. Nevertheless they moved as if expecting an instant attack. The light horse scoured the country. The lithe and active soldiers furnished by the desert tribes formed the advanced guard of the army, and marched also on its flanks, while the heavy-armed soldiery marched in solid column ready for battle. Behind them came the long train of baggage protected by a strong rear-guard.

At last they reached a fertile country, and were now in the land of the Vaccæi and their allies. Arbocala, now called Tordesillas, was captured without much difficulty. The siege was then laid to Salamanca, the chief town of the enemy. In the actual siege operations the Carthaginian horse took no part. The place resisted vigourously, but the machines of Hannibal effected a breach in the walls, and the inhabitants, seeing that further resistance was impossible, offered to capitulate, stipulating that they should be allowed to depart unharmed, leaving behind them all their arms and their treasure.

The Carthaginian army were drawn up in readiness to march into the town as the Vaccæi came out. As they filed past the Carthaginians they were inspected to see that they had carried out the terms of the agreement. It was found that they had done so rigidly–not an arm of any kind was found upon them. Their necklaces, bracelets, and ornaments had all been left behind.

"What a savage-looking race!" Malchus remarked to Trebon; "they look at us as if they would gladly spring on us, unarmed as they are, and tear us with their hands. They are well-nigh as dark skinned as the Numidians."

"Here come their women!" Trebon said; "verily I would as soon fight the men as these creatures. Look how they glare at us! You see they have all had to give up their ornaments, so they have each their private grievance as well as their national one."

THE YOUNG CARTHAGINIAN

When the whole of the population had filed out, the Carthaginian army entered the town, with the exception of a body of light horse who were ordered to remain without and keep an eye on the doings of the late garrison. Malchus was amused at the scene within. The members of the Carthaginian horse disdained to join in the work of plunder, and were, therefore, free to watch with amusement their comrades at work. The amount of booty was large, for the number of gold ornaments found in every house, deposited there by the inhabitants on departing, was very great; but not satisfied with this the soldiers dug up the floors in search of buried treasure, searched the walls for secret hiding-places, and rummaged the houses from top to bottom. Besides the rich booty, the soldiers burdened themselves with a great variety of articles which it would be impossible for them to carry away.

Men were seen staggering under the weight of four or five heavy skins. Some had stuck feathers in their helmets until their heads were scarce visible. Some had great bundles of female garments, which they had collected with a vague idea of carrying them home to their families. The arms had in the first place been collected and placed under a strong guard, and picked troops were placed as sentries over the public treasury, whose contents were allotted to the general needs of the army.

Night fell soon after the sack commenced. Malchus with a number of his comrades took possession of one of the largest houses in the place, and, having cleared it of the rubbish with which it was strewn, prepared to pass the night there. Suddenly a terrible uproar was heard–shouts, cries, the clashing of arms, the yells of the enemy, filled the air. The cavalry charged to watch the Vaccæi, believing that these had departed quietly, had abandoned their post, and had entered the town to join in the work of plunder.

As the garrison had marched out the men had been rigidly searched; but the women had been allowed to pass out without any close inspection. This carelessness cost the Carthaginians dear, for under their garments they had hidden the swords and daggers of the men. Relying upon the disorder which would reign in the city, the Vaccæi had returned, and now poured in through the gates, slaying all whom they met.

For a short time a terrible panic reigned among the Carthaginians, great numbers were cut down, and it seemed as if the whole force would be destroyed. Hannibal and his generals rode about trying to get the scattered men to form and oppose the enemy; but the panic was too general, and had it not been for the Carthaginian legion all would have been lost. The horse and foot, however, of this body, having abstained from joining in the pillage, had, for the most part, kept together in bodies, and these now sallied out in close and regular order, and fell upon the attacking enemy.

The streets were too narrow for cavalry to act, and Malchus and his comrades fought on foot. The enemy, who had scattered on their work of slaughter, were in their turn taken at a disadvantage, and were unable to withstand the steady attack of the solid bodies. These, in the first place, cut their way to the square in the centre of the town, and there united. Hannibal, seeing he had now a solid body of troops under his command, at once broke them up into parties and advanced down all the streets leading from the central square. The hand-to-hand fight which was going on all over the town was soon terminated. The Carthaginians fell in in good order behind the ranks of their comrades, and the small bodies soon became columns which swept the enemy before them.

The enemy fought desperately, firing the houses, hurling stones from the roofs upon the columns, and throwing themselves with reckless bravery upon the spears, but their efforts were in vain. Foot by foot they were driven back, until they were again expelled from the town. Keeping together, and ever showing front to the Carthaginians, the Vaccæi, now reduced to less than half their number, retired to an eminence near the town, and there prepared to sell their lives dearly. The Carthaginians now fell into their regular ranks, and prepared to storm the enemy's position; but Hannibal rode forward alone towards the Vaccæi, being plainly visible to them in the broad blaze of light from the burning city.

From his long residence in Spain he was able to speak the

Iberian tongue with fluency, and indeed could converse with all the troops of the various nationalities under the banner of Carthage in their own language.

"Men of Salamanca," he said, "resist no longer. Carthage knows how to honour a brave enemy, and never did men fight more valiantly in defence of their homes than you have done, and although further resistance would be hopeless, I will press you no further. Your lives are spared. You may retain the arms you know so well how to wield, and to-morrow my army will evacuate your town and leave you free to return to it."

Hannibal's clemency was politic. He would have lost many more men before be finally overcame the desperate band, and he was by no means desirous of exciting a deep feeling of hate among any of the tribes, just as he was meditating withdrawing the greater portion of the army for his enterprise against Rome. With the fall of Salamanca the resistance of the Vaccæi ceased, and Hannibal prepared to march back to Carthagena.

A storm, however, had gathered in his rear. Great numbers of the Vaccæi had sought refuge among the Olcades, who had been subdued the previous autumn, and together they had included the whole of the fierce tribes known as the Carpatans, who inhabited the country on the right bank of the upper Tagus, to make common cause with them against the invaders. As Hannibal approached their neighbourhood they took up their position on the right bank of the river near Toledo. Here the stream is rapid and difficult of passage, its bed being thickly studded with great boulders brought down in time of flood from the mountains. The country on each side of the river is sandy, free from forests or valleys, which would cover the movements of an army.

The host gathered to oppose the Carthaginians were fully one hundred thousand strong, and Hannibal saw at once that his force, weakened as it was with its loss at Salamanca, and encumbered by the great train laden with the booty they had gathered from the Vaccæi, would have no chance whatever in a battle with so vast a body. The enemy separated as he approached the river, their object being evidently to fall upon his rear when engaged in the difficult operation of crossing. The Carthaginians moved in two heavy columns, one on each side of their baggage, and Hannibal's orders were stringent that on no account should they engage with the enemy.

The natives swarmed around the columns, hurling darts and javelins; but the Carthaginians moved forward in solid order, replying only with their arrows and slings, and contenting themselves with beating off the attacks which the bolder of their foes made upon them. Night was falling when they arrived on the bank of the river. The enemy then desisted from their attack, believing that in the morning the Carthaginians would be at their mercy, encumbered by their vast booty on one side and cut off from retreat by a well-nigh impassable river on the other.

As soon as the army reached the river Hannibal caused the tents of all the officers to be erected. The baggage-wagons were arranged in order, and the cattle unharnessed. The troops began to throw up intrenchments, and all seemed to show that the Carthaginians were determined to fight till the last on the ground they held. It was still light enough for the enemy to perceive what was being done, and, secure of their prey in the morning, they drew off to a short distance for the night. Hannibal had learned from a native that morning of a ford across the river, and it was towards this that be had been marching, as soon as it was perfectly dark a number of men entered the river to search for the ford. This was soon discovered.

Then the orders were passed noiselessly round to the soldiers, and these, in regular order and in the most perfect quiet, rose to their feet and marched down to the ford. A portion of the infantry first passed, then the wagons were taken over, the rest of the infantry followed, and the cavalry and the elephants brought up the rear. The point where the river was fordable was at a sharp angle, and Hannibal now occupied its outer side. As daylight approached he placed his archers on the banks of the river where, owing to the sharp bend, their arrows would take in flank an enemy crossing the ford, and would also sweep its approaches.

The cavalry were withdrawn some distance, and were ordered not to charge until the Spaniards had got across the river. The elephants, forty in number, were divided into two bodies.

One of these was allotted to protect each of the bodies of infantry on the bank from attack, should the Spaniards gain a strong footing on the left bank. When day broke the enemy perceived that the Carthaginians had made the passage of the river. Believing that they had been too much alarmed to risk a battle, and were retreating hastily, the natives thronged down in a multitude to the river without waiting for their leaders or for orders to be given, and rushing forward, each for himself, leaped into the river.

Numbers were at once swept away by the stream but the crowd who had struck upon the ford pressed forward. When they were in mid-stream in a tumultuous mass Hannibal launched his cavalry upon them, and a desperate conflict ensued in the river. The combat was too unequal to last long. The Spaniards, waist-deep in the rapid stream, had difficulty in retaining their feet, they were ignorant of the width or precise direction of the ford, and were hampered by their own masses; the cavalry, on the other hand, were free to use their weapons, and the weight and impetus of their charge was alone sufficient to sweep the Spanish from their footing into deep water.

Many were drowned, many more cut down, and the rest driven in disorder back across the river. But fresh hordes had now arrived; Hannibal sounded the retreat, and the cavalry retired as the Spaniards again threw themselves into the stream. As the confused mass poured across the ford the two divisions of infantry fell upon them, while the arrows of the archers swept the struggling mass. Without order or discipline, bewildered at this attack by a foe whom they had regarded as flying, the Spaniards were driven back across the river, the Carthaginians crossing in their rear.

The flying Iberians scattered terror among their comrades still flocking down to the bank, and as the Carthaginian infantry in solid column fell upon them, a panic seized the whole host and they scattered over the plain. The Carthaginian cavalry followed close behind the infantry, and at once dashed forward among the broken masses, until the Spanish army, lately so confident of victory, was but a broken mass of panic stricken fugitives.

The victory of Toledo was followed at once by the submission of the whole of the tribes of Spain south of the

Ebro, and Hannibal, having seen that the country was everywhere pacified, marched back with his army to Carthagena to pass the winter there (220-219 B.C.).

THE YOUNG CARTHAGINIAN

CHAPTER VII: A WOLF HUNT

THE summer's work had been a hard one and the young soldiers of the Carthaginian cavalry rejoiced when they marched into Carthagena again, with the prospect of four months' rest and gaiety. When in the field their discipline was as strict and their work as hard as that of the other corps, but, whereas, when they went into winter quarters, the rest of the army were placed under tents or huts, this *corps d'élite* were for the time their own masters.

Two or three times a week they drilled and exercised their horses, but with these exceptions they were free to do as they chose. Scarce one but had relations or friends in Carthagena with whom they took up their abode, and those who were not so fortunate found a home at the great military club, of which, ranking as they did with the officers of other corps, they were all members.

Hamilcar and Malchus had rooms assigned to them in the splendid mansion of Hannibal, which was the centre of the life and gaiety of the place, for Hannibal had, before starting on his campaign in the spring, married Imilce, the daughter of Castalius, a Spaniard of noble blood, and his household was kept up with a lavish magnificence, worthy alike of his position as virtual monarch of Spain and of his vast private wealth. Fêtes were given constantly for the amusement of the people. At these there were prizes for horse and foot racing, and the Numidian cavalry astonished the populace by the manner in which they maneuvered their steeds; bowmen and slingers entered the lists for prizes of value given by the general; and the elephants exhibited proof of their docility and training.

A WOLF HUNT

In the bay there were races between the galleys and triremes, and emulation was encouraged among the troops by large money prizes to the companies who maneuvered with the greatest precision and activity. For the nobles there were banquets and entertainments of music. The rising greatness of Carthagena had attracted to her musicians and artists from all parts of the Mediterranean. Snake-charmers from the far Soudan, and jugglers from the distant East exhibited their skill. Poets recited their verses, and bards sung their lays before the wealth and beauty of Carthagena. Hannibal, anxious at once to please his young wife and to increase his popularity, spared no pains or expense in these entertainments.

Gay as they were Malchus longed or a more stirring life, and with five or six of his comrades obtained leave of absence for a month, to go on a hunting expedition on the mountains. He had heard, when upon the campaign, the issue of the plot in which he had been so nearly engaged. It had failed. On the very eve of execution one of the subordinates had turned traitor, and Giscon and the whole of those engaged in it had been arrested and put to a cruel death.

Malchus himself had been denounced, as his name was found upon the list of the conspirators, and an order had been sent to Hannibal that he should be carried back a prisoner to Carthage. Hannibal had called the lad before him, and had inquired of him the circumstances of the case. Malchus explained that he had been to their meeting but once, being taken there by Giscon, and being in entire ignorance of the objects of the plot, and that he had refused when he discovered them to proceed in the matter. Hannibal and Hamilcar blamed him severely for allowing himself at his age to be mixed up in any way in public affairs; but they so represented the matter to the two Carthaginian commissioners with the army, that these had written home to say, that having inquired into the affair they found that beyond a boyish imprudence in accompanying Giscon to the place where the conspirators met, Malchus was not to blame in the matter.

The narrow escape that he had had was a lesson which was not lost upon Malchus. Hamilcar lectured him sternly, and pointed out to him that the affairs of nations were not to be settled by the efforts of a handful of enthusiasts, but that grievances, however great, could only be righted when the people at large were determined that a change should be made.

"There would be neither order nor stability in affairs, Malchus, if parties of desperate men of one party or another were ever striving for change, for revolution would be met by counter-revolution. The affairs of nations march slowly; sudden changes are ever to be deprecated. If every clique of men who chance to be supported by a temporary wave of public opinion, were to introduce organic changes, there would be no stability in affairs. Capital would be alarmed; the rich and powerful, seeing their possessions threatened and their privileges attacked by the action of the demagogues of the hour, would do as did our forefathers of Tyre, when the whole of the aristocracy emigrated in a body to Carthage, and Tyre received a blow from which she has never recovered."

For some time after this event Malchus had felt that he was in disgrace, but his steadiness and good conduct in the campaign, and the excellent reports which his officers gave of him, had restored him to favour; and indeed his father and Hannibal both felt that a lad might well be led away by an earnest enthusiast like Giscon.

The hunting-party took with them a hundred Iberian soldiers used to the mountains, together with six peasants acquainted with the country and accustomed to the chase. They took several carts laden with tents, wine, and provisions. Four days' journey from Carthagena took the party into the heart of the mountains, and here, in a sheltered valley through which ran a stream, they formed their camp.

They had good sport. Sometimes with dogs they tracked the bears to their lair, sometimes the soldiers made a wide sweep in the hills, and, having inclosed a considerable tract of forest, moved forward, shouting and clashing their arms until they drove the animals inclosed down through a valley in which Malchus and his companions had taken post.

Very various was the game which then fell before their arrows and javelins. Sometimes a herd of deer would dart past, then two bears with their family would come along growling fiercely as they went, and looking back angrily at the disturbers of their peace. Sometimes a pack of wolves, with their red tongues hanging out, and fierce, snarling barks, would hurry along, or a wild boar would trot leisurely past, until he reached the spot where the hunters were posted. The wolves and deer fell harmlessly before the javelins of the Carthaginians, but the bears and wild boars frequently showed themselves formidable opponents, and there were several desperate fights before these yielded to the spears and swords of the hunters.

Sometimes portions of the animals they had killed were hung up at night from the bough of a tree at a distance from the camp, to attract the bears, and one or two of the party, taking their post in neighbouring trees, would watch all night for the coming of the beasts. The snow was now lying thick on the tops of the mountains, and the wolves were plentiful among the forests.

One day Malchus and two of his companions had followed a wounded deer far up among the hills, and were some miles away from the camp when the darkness began to set in.

"I think we had better give it up," Malchus said; "we shall find it difficult as it is to find our way back; I had no idea that it was so late."

His companions at once agreed, and they turned their faces towards the camp. In another half-hour it was perfectly dark under the shadow of the trees, but the moon was shining, and its position afforded them a means of judging as to the direction where the camp lay. But even with such assistance it was no easy matter making their way. The country was rough and broken; ravines had to be crossed, and hills ascended. After pushing on for two hours, Halcon, the eldest of the party, said:

"I am by no means sure that we are going right after all. We have had a long day's work now, and I do not believe we shall find the camp to-night. I think we had better light a fire here and wrap our selves in our cloaks. The fire will scare wild beasts away, and we shall be easily able to find the camp in the morning."

The proposal was at once accepted; sticks were collected, and, with flint and steel and the aid of some dried fungus which they carried in their pouches, a fire was soon lit, and some choice portions of a deer which they had killed early in the day were soon broiling on sticks over it.

"We must keep watch by turns," Halcon said; "it will not do to let the fire burn low, for likely enough we may be visited by bears before morning."

After eating their meal and chatting for some time, Halcon and his companions lay down to rest, Malchus volunteering to keep the first watch. For some time he sat quietly, occasionally throwing logs on the fire from the store which they had collected in readiness. Presently his attitude changed, he listened intently and rose to his feet. Several times he had heard the howls of wolves wandering in the woods, but he now made out a long, deep, continuous howling; he listened for a minute or two and then aroused his companions.

"There is a large pack of wolves approaching," he said, "and by the direction of the sound I judge they are hunting on the traces of our footsteps. That is the line by which we came down from yonder brow, and it seems to me that they are ascending the opposite slope."

"Yes, and by the sound there must be a very large pack of them," Halcon agreed; "pile up the fire and set yourselves to gather more wood as quickly as possible; these beasts in large packs are formidable foes."

The three men set to work, vigourously cutting down brushwood and lopping off small boughs of trees with their swords.

"Divide the fire in four," Halcon said, "and pile the fuel in the centre; they will hardly dare to pass between the fires."

The pack was now descending the slope, keeping up a chorus of howls and short yelps which sent a shiver of uneasiness through Malchus. As the wolves approached the spot the howling suddenly ceased.

"They see us," Halcon said; "keep a sharp lookout for them, but do not throw away a shot, we shall need all our arrows before daylight."

Standing perfectly quiet, the friends could hear the pattering sound made by the wolves' feet upon the fallen leaves; but the moon had sunk now, and they were unable to make out their figures.

A WOLF HUNT

"It seems to me," Malchus said in a whisper, "that I can see specks of fire gleaming on the bushes."

"It is the reflection of the fire in their eyes," Halcon replied. "See ! they are all round us! There must be scores of them."

For some time the wolves approached no closer; then, encouraged by the silence of the little group standing in the centre of the fire, two or three gray forms showed themselves in the circle of light. Three bows twanged. Two of the wolves fell, and the third, with a howl of pain, fled in the darkness. There was a sound of snarling and growling; a cry of pain, a fierce struggle, and then a long-continued snarling.

"What are they doing?" Malchus asked with a shudder.

"I believe they are eating their wounded comrade," Halcon replied. "I have heard such is the custom of the savage brutes. See, the carcasses of the other two have disappeared already."

Short as had been the time which had elapsed since they had fallen, other wolves had stolen out, and had dragged away the bodies of the two which had been killed. This incident, which showed how extreme was the hunger of the wolves, and how noiseless were their motions, redoubled the vigilance of the party.

Malchus threw a handful of brushwood on to each of the fires.

"We must be careful of the fuel," Halcon said. "I would we had thought of this before we lay down to sleep. If we had collected fuel enough for our fires we should have been safe; but I doubt much if our supply will last now till morning."

As the hours went on the attitude of the wolves became more and more threatening, and in strong bodies they advanced close up to the fires. Every time that they did so armfuls of fuel were thrown on, and as the flames leaped up brightly they each time fell back, losing several of their numbers from the arrows of the little party. But the pile of fuel was now sinking fast, and except when the wolves advanced it was necessary to let the fires burn down.

"It must want four hours yet of daylight," Halcon said, as he threw on the last piece of wood. "Look round as the fire blazes up and see if you can make out any tree which may be climbed. I would that we had taken to them at first instead of trusting to our fires."

Unfortunately they had chosen a somewhat open space of ground for their encampment, for the brushwood grew thick among the trees.

"There is a tree over there," Malchus said, pointing to it, "with a bough but six feet from the ground. One spring on to that and we are safe."

"Very well," Halcon assented; "we will attempt it at once before the fire burns low. Put your swords into your sheaths, sling your bows and arrows behind you, and take each a burning brand. These will be better weapons in such a case than swords or spears. Now, are you ready? Now!"

Waving the burning brands over their heads, the three Carthaginians dashed across the intervening space towards the tree.

It seemed as if the wolves were conscious that their prey were attempting to escape them; for, with a fierce howl, they sprang from the bushes and rushed to meet them; and, undeterred by the blazing brands, sprang upon them.

Malchus scarce knew what passed in the short, fierce struggle. One wolf sprang upon his shield and nearly brought him to the ground; but the sharp boss pierced its body, and he flung it from him, at the same moment that he dashed the brand full in the face of another. A third sprang upon his shoulder, and he felt its hot breath in his face. Dropping his brand, he drove his dagger deep into its side. Then he hurled his heavy shield among the mass of wolves before him, took a bound into their midst, and grasping the bough, swung himself into the tree and sat there with his legs drawn up as a score of wolves leaped up towards him with open mouths.

He gave a cry of horror. His two friends were down, and a confused mass of struggling bodies alone showed where they had fallen. For an instant he hesitated, debating whether he should leap down and strive to rescue them; but a glance below showed him that he would be pulled down long before he could reach the spot where they had fallen.

Shifting himself along the arm until he reached the trunk, he rose to his feet and sent his arrows vengefully into the midst of

The dangers of a wolf hunt

the struggling mass of wolves until he had but three or four shafts left. These he reserved as a last resource.

There was nothing to do now, and he sat down on the branch, and burst into tears over the fate of his comrades. When he looked up again all was quiet. The fierce pack had devoured not only his comrades, but their own fallen companions, and now sat in a circle with their red tongues hanging out and their eyes fixed upon him. As the fire gradually died out their form disappeared; but he could hear their quick breathing, and knew that they were still on the watch.

Malchus climbed the tree until he reached a fork where he could sit at ease, and there waited for morning, when he hoped that his foes would disappear. But as the gray light dawned he saw them still on the watch; nor, as the dawn brightened into day, did they show any signs of moving.

When he saw they had no intention of leaving the place, Malchus began to consider seriously what he had best do. He might still be, for aught he knew, miles away from the camp, and his friends there would have no means of knowing the position in which he was placed. They would no doubt send out all the soldiers in search of the party; but in that broken wilderness of forest and mountain, it was the merest chance whether they would find the spot where he was prisoner. Still, it appeared to him that this was the only possibility of his rescue. The trees grew thickly together, and he could easily have climbed from that in which he was stationed to the next, and might so have made his way for some distance; but as the wolves were watching him, and could see as well by night as by day, there was no advantage in shifting his position.

The day passed slowly. The wolves had for the most part withdrawn from beneath the tree, but a few kept their station there steadily, and Malchus knew that the rest were only lying beneath the bushes round; for he could hear their frequent snarling, and sometimes a gray head was thrust out, and a pair of eager eyes looked hungrily towards him. From time to time Malchus listened breathlessly in hopes of hearing the distant shouts of his comrades; but all was still in the forest, and he felt sure that the wolves would hear anyone approaching before he should.

Once or twice, indeed, he fancied that by their pricked ears and attitude of attention they could hear sounds inaudible to him; but the alarm, if such it was, soon passed away, and it might have been that they were listening only to the distant footsteps of some stag passing through the forest. Night came again with its long, dreary hours. Malchus strapped himself by his belt to the tree to prevent himself from falling and managed to obtain a few hours of uneasy sleep, waking up each time with a start, in a cold perspiration of fear, believing that he was falling into the hungry jaws below. In the morning a fierce desire to kill some of his foes seized him, and he descended to the lowest branch.

The wolves, seeing their prey so close at hand, thronged thickly under it, and strove to leap up at him. Lying down on the bough, and twisting his legs firmly under it to give him a purchase, Malchus thrust his sword nearly to the hilt between the jaws, which snapped fiercely as a wolf sprang to within a few inches of the bough. Several were killed in this way, and the rest rendered cautious, withdrew to a short distance. Suddenly an idea struck Malchus. He took off his belt and formed it into a running noose, and then waited until the wolves should summon up courage to attack again. It was not long. Furious with hunger, which the prey they had already devoured was only sufficient to whet, the wolves again approached and began to spring towards the bough.

Malchus dropped the noose over one of their necks, and with an effort, hauled it to the bough, and despatched it with his dagger. Then he moved along the bough and hung it on a branch some ten feet from the ground, slashing open with his dagger its chest and stomach. Having done this he returned to his place. Six wolves were one after the other so hauled up and despatched, and as Malchus expected, the smell of their blood rendered the pack more savage than ever. They assembled round the foot of the tree, and continued to spring at the trunk, making vain endeavours to get at the supply of food which hung tantalizingly at so short a distance beyond their reach.

So the day passed as before without signs of rescue. When

it became dark Malchus again descended to the lowest trunk, and fired his three remaining arrows among the wolves below him. Loud howls followed each discharge, followed by a desperate struggle below. Then he tumbled from their position the six dead wolves to the ground below, and then as noiselessly as possible made his way along a bough into an adjoining tree, and so into another, till he had attained some distance from the spot where the wolves were fighting and growling over the remains of their companions, far too absorbed in their work for any thought of him.

Then he dropped noiselessly to the ground and fled at the top of his speed. It would be, he was sure, some time before the wolves had completed their feast; and even should they discover that he was missing from the tree, it would probably be some time before they could hit upon his scent, especially, as, having just feasted on blood, their sense of smell would for a time be dulled. His previsions were accurate. Several times he stopped and listened in dread lest he should hear the distant howl, which would tell him that the pack was again on his scent. All was quiet, save for the usual cries and noises in the forest. In two hours he saw a distant glow of light, and was soon in the encampment of his friends.

"Why, Malchus!" his comrades exclaimed as he entered the tent, "where have you been these two days? Why, you are splashed with blood. Where are Halcon and Chalcus?"

"Dead," Malchus said–"devoured by wolves."

A cry of horror broke from the three young guardsmen.

"'Tis too true," Malchus went on; "but give me food and wine. I have neither eaten nor drunk for the last two days, and I have gone through a terrible time. Even now I seem to see all round me countless cruel eyes, and hungry open mouths with their red tongues."

Seeing that Malchus was utterly worn and exhausted his companions hastened to place food and drink before him before asking any further questions.

Malchus drank a cup of wine and took a mouthful of bread; but he was too faint and exhausted at present to eat more. He had supported well the terrible strain for the last forty-eight hours, and as he had run through the forest he had not noticed how it had told upon him; but now that he was safe among his friends he felt as weak as a child. For a time he lay upon the lion skin on which he had thrown himself upon entering the tent, unable to reply to his comrades' questions. Then, as the cordial began to take effect, he roused himself and forced himself to eat more. After that he told his friends what had happened.

"You have indeed had an escape, Malchus; but how was it you did not take to the trees at once?"

"I did not think of it," Malchus said, "nor, I suppose, did the others. Halcon was our leader, and we did as he told us. He thought the fires would keep them off. Who could have thought the beasts would have ventured to attack us!"

"I have always heard they were terrible," one of the others said; "but I should have thought that three armed men would have been a match for any number of them."

"It would have been as much as thirty could have done to withstand them," Malchus replied; "they did not seem to care for their lives, but sought only to slay. There were hundreds and hundreds of them. I would rather march alone to the assault of a walled city than face those terrible beasts."

In the morning the whole party started for the scene of the encounter.

Malchus had some difficulty in discovering it; but at last, after searching a long time he came upon it.

The ground beneath the tree was everywhere trampled and torn by the wolves in their struggles, and was spotted with patches of dry blood. The helmets, shields and arms of Halcon and Chalcus lay there, but not a remnant of their bones remained, and a few fragments of skin and some closely gnawed skulls alone testified to the wolves which had fallen in the encounter. The arms were gathered up, and the party returned to their camp, and the next day started for Carthagena; for, after that experience, none cared for any further hunting.

It was some weeks before Malchus completely recovered from the effects of the strain he had undergone. His nights were disturbed and restless. He would constantly start from his couch, thinking that he heard the howl of the wolves, and any sudden noise made him start and turn pale. Seeing how shaken his young kinsmen was, and what he had passed through, Hannibal sent him several times in ships which were going across to Africa for stores. He did not venture to send him to Carthage; for although his influence with the commissioners had been sufficient to annul the order of the council for the sending of Malchus as a prisoner there, it was probable that were he to return he would be seized and put to death–not for the supposed crime he had committed, but to gratify the hatred of Hanno against himself and his adherents.

The sea voyages soon restored Malchus to his accustomed health. Trained and disciplined as his body had been by constant exercise, his nerves were not easily shaken, and soon recovered their tone, and when, early in March, he rejoined his regiment, he was able to enter with zest and energy into the preparations which Hannibal was making for the siege of Saguntum. Difficult as this operation would be, the preparations which were being made appeared enormous. Every week ships brought over reinforcements of troops and the Iberian contingents were largely increased.

One day Malchus entered an apartment where his father and Hannibal were talking earnestly together with a large map spread out before them. He would have retired at once, but Hannibal called him in.

"Come in, Malchus, I would have no secrets from you. Although you are young I know that you are devoted to Carthage, that you are brave and determined. I see in you what I was myself at your age, but nine years ago, and it may be that some day you will be destined to continue the work which I am beginning. You, too, have commenced early, your training has been severe. As your father's son and my cousin your promotion will naturally be rapid. I will, therefore, tell you my plans. It is clear that Rome and Carthage cannot both exist; one or the other must be destroyed. It is useless to strike at extremities, the blow must be dealt at the heart. Unfortunately our fleet is no longer superior to that of Rome, and victories at sea, however important, only temporarily cripple an enemy.

A WOLF HUNT

"It is by land the blow must be struck. Were the sea ours, I should say, land troops in southern Italy, and continue to pour over reinforcements until all the fighting men of North Africa are at the gates of Rome. But without the absolute command of the sea this cannot be done. Therefore I intend to make Spain our base, and to march through Southern Gaul over the Alps into Italy, and there to fight the Romans on their own ground. Already I have agents at work among the Gauls and the northern tribes of Italy, who will, I trust, join me in the war against our common enemy. The enterprise is a great one, but it is not impossible; if it succeeds, Rome will be destroyed and Carthage will reign, without a rival, mistress of the world. The plan was Hasdrubal's, but it has fallen to me to carry it out."

"It is a grand plan indeed," Malchus exclaimed enthusiastically—"a glorious plan, but the difficulties seem tremendous."

"Difficulties are made to be overcome by brave men," Hannibal said. "The Alps are the greatest barrier, but my agents tell me that the difficulties are not insuperable even for elephants. But before we start we have Spain to subdue. Saguntum is under the protection of Rome, and must be crushed, and all the country north of the Ebro conquered and pacified. This done the passage of reinforcements to my army in Italy will be easy. The Gauls will favour us, the mountains tribes will be crushed or bought over, so that the route for the advance of reinforcements, or for our retreat, if too hardly pressed, will be always open. But all this is for yourself alone.

"My plans must not yet be known. Already our enemies in Carthage are gaining in strength. Many of our adherents have been put to death and the estates of others confiscated; but the capture of Saguntum will restore our supremacy, and the enthusiasm which it will incite among the populace will carry all before it. The spoils which will be taken there will be sufficient to silence every murmur in Carthage. Now leave us, Malchus, we have much to talk over and to arrange, and I have given you plenty to think about for the present."

THE YOUNG CARTHAGINIAN

CHAPTER VIII: A PLOT FRUSTRATED

AFTER leaving Hannibal, Malchus did not rejoin his comrades, but mounted the hills behind the town and sat down there, looking over the sea, and thinking over the vast plan which Hannibal's words had laid before him, and to which his father had once alluded in his presence. Malchus had been brought up by Hamilcar to regard Rome as the deadly enemy of Carthage, but he had not till now seen the truth which Hannibal had grasped, that it was a struggle not for empire only between the two republics, but one of life and death–that Carthage and Rome could not co-exist, and that one or other of them must be absolutely destroyed.

This, indeed, was the creed of the Barcine party, and was, apart from the minor questions of internal reforms, the great point on which they differed from Hanno and the trading portion of the community, who were his chief supporters. These were in favour of Carthage abandoning her colonies and conquests, and devoting herself solely to commerce and the acquisition of wealth. Believing that Rome, who would then have open to her all Europe and Asia to conquer, would not grudge to Carthage the northern sea-board of Africa, they forgot that a nation which is rich and defenceless will speedily fall a victim to the greed of a powerful and warlike neighbour, and that a conqueror never needs excuses for an attack upon a defenceless neighbour.

Hitherto Malchus had thought only of a war with Rome made up of sea-fights and of descents upon Sicily and Sardinia. The very idea of invading Italy and striking at Rome herself had never even entered his mind, for the words of his father had been forgotten in the events which followed so quickly upon them. The prospect which the words opened seemed immense. First Northern Spain was to be conquered, Gaul to be crossed, the terrible mountains of which he had heard from travellers were next to be surmounted, and finally a fight for life and death to be fought out on the plains of Italy. The struggle would indeed be a tremendous one, and Malchus felt his heart beat fast at the thought that he was to be an actor in it. Surely the history of the world told of no greater enterprise than this. Even the first step which was to be taken, a mere preliminary to this grand expedition, was a most formidable one.

Saguntum stood as an outpost of Rome. While Carthage had been advancing from the south Rome had been pressing forward from the east along the shores of the Mediterranean, and had planted herself firmly at Marseilles, a port which gave her a foothold in Gaul, and formed a base whence she could act in Spain. In order to check the rising power of the Carthaginians there she had entered into a firm alliance with the Saguntines, whose country occupied what is now the district of Valencia. By the terms of the last treaty between the two republics each was forbidden to make war upon tribes in alliance with their rivals, and Saguntum being thus under the jurisdiction of Rome, an attack upon it would be almost equivalent to a declaration of war.

The position of the city was one of great strength. It stood on an almost isolated rock at the foot of a spur of the mountains which formed an amphitheatre behind it. Around it extended a rich and fertile country, the sea was less than a mile from its walls, and the Romans could thus quickly send succour to their allies. The rock on which the town stood was well-nigh inaccessible, falling sheer down from the foot of the walls, and was assailable only on the western side, where the rocks sloped gradually down to the plain. Here the walls were extremely strong and lofty, and were strengthened by a great tower which dominated the whole slope. It would be difficult to form approaches, for the rock was bare of soil and afforded no cover of any kind.

Hitherto the Carthaginian generals had scrupulously respected the territory of the Saguntines, but now that the rest of

Spain was subdued it was necessary to reduce this advanced post of Rome–this open door through which Rome, now mistress of the sea, could at any moment pour her legions into the heart of Spain.

The Saguntines were not ignorant of the danger which threatened them. They had again and again sent urgently to Rome to demand that a legion should be stationed there for their protection. But Rome hesitated at despatching a legion of troops to so distant a spot, where, in case of a naval reverse, they would be isolated and cut off.

Hannibal had not far to look for an excuse for an attack upon Saguntum. On the previous year, while he had been engaged in his campaign against the Carpatans, the Saguntines, taking advantage of his critical position, had made war upon the town of Torbola, an ally of Carthage. Torbola had implored the assistance of Hannibal, and he was now preparing to march against Saguntum with his whole force without waiting for the arrival of spring. His preparations had been silently made. The Saguntines, although uneasy, had no idea of any imminent danger, and the Carthaginian army collected in and around Carthagena were in entire ignorance that they were about to be called upon to take the field.

"What say you, Malchus?" Hannibal asked that evening. "It is time now that I gave you a command. As my near relative it is fitting that you should be in authority. You have now served a campaign, and are eligible for any command that I may give you. You have shown yourself prompt in danger and worthy to command men. Which would you rather that I should place under you–a company of these giant Gauls, of the steady Iberians, of the well-disciplined Libyans, or the active tribesmen of the desert? Choose which you will, and they shall be yours."

Malchus thought for some time.

"In the day of battle," he said at last, "I would rather lead Gauls, but, in such a march as you have told me you are meditating, I would rather have a company of Numidian footmen to act as scouts and feel the way for the army. There would not, perhaps, be so much glory to be obtained, but there would be constant work and excitement, and this will be far better than marching in the long column of the army."

A PLOT FRUSTRATED

"I think your choice is a good one," Hannibal replied. "Such a corps will be needed to feel the way as we advance, to examine the roads and indicate that by which the column had best move, and to guard against ambushes and surprises. To-morrow I will inspect the Numidian footmen and will put them through their exercises. We will have foot-races and trials of skill with the bow, and I will bid their officers pick me out two hundred of the most active and vigourous among them; these you shall have under your command. You can choose among your comrades of the guards one whom you would like to have as your lieutenant."

"I will take Trebon," Malchus said; "we fought side by side through the last campaign. He is prompt and active, always cheerful under fatigue, and as brave as a lion. I could not wish a better comrade."

"So be it," Hannibal replied, "henceforth you are captain of the advanced company of the army. Remember, Malchus, that the responsibility is a great one, and that henceforward there must be no more boyish tricks. Your company will be the eyes of the army, and upon your vigilance its safety, when we once start upon our expedition, will in no slight degree depend. Remember, too, that you have by your conduct to justify me in choosing my young kinsman for so important a post."

The next day the Numidians were put through their exercises, and by nightfall the two hundred picked men were chosen from their ranks and were placed by Hannibal under the command of Malchus. Trebon was greatly pleased when he found himself appointed as lieutenant of the company. Although of noble family his connections were much less influential than those of the majority of his comrades, and he had deemed himself exceptionally fortunate in having been permitted to enter the chosen corps of the Carthaginian cavalry, and had not expected to be made an officer for years to come, since promotion in the Carthaginian army was almost wholly a matter of family influence.

"I am indeed obliged to you, Malchus," he said as he joined his friend after Hannibal had announced his appointment to him. "The general told me that he had appointed me at your request.

I never even hoped that such good fortune would befall me. Of course I knew that you would speedily obtain a command, but my people have no influence whatever. The general says that your company are to act as scouts for the army, so there will be plenty of opportunity to distinguish ourselves. Unfortunately I don't see much chance of fighting at present. The Iberian tribesmen had such a lesson last autumn that they are not likely for a long time to give us further trouble."

"Do not make yourself uneasy on that score, Trebon," Malchus said, "I can tell you, but let it go no further, that ere long there will be fighting enough to satisfy even the most pugnacious."

One evening Malchus had left the club early. Full as he was of the thoughts of the tremendous struggle which was soon to begin between the great antagonists, he wearied of the light talk of his gay comrades. The games of chance, to which a room in the club was allotted, afforded him no pleasure; nor had he any interest in the wagering which was going on as to the merits of the horses which were to run in the races on the following day. On leaving the club he directed his footsteps towards the top of the hill on which Carthagena stood, and there, sitting alone on one of the highest points, looked over the sea sparkling in the moonlight, the many vessels in the harbour and the lagoons stretching inland on each side of the city.

He tried to imagine the course that the army was to follow, the terrible journey through the snow-covered passes of that tremendous range of mountains of which he had heard, the descent into the plains of Italy, and the first sight of Rome. He pictured to himself the battles which would have to be fought by the way, and above all, the deadly conflict which would take place before Rome could be carried by assault, and the great rival of Carthage be humbled to the dust. Then he pictured the return of the triumphant expedition, the shouting multitudes who would acclaim Hannibal the sole arbitrator of the destinies of Carthage, and in his heart rejoiced over the changes which would take place – the overthrow of the faction of Hanno, the reform of abuses, the commencement of an era of justice, freedom, and prosperity for all.

For more than three hours he sat thus, and then awoke to

the fact that the night was cold and the hour late. Drawing his bernous tightly round him he descended into the city, which was now for the most part wrapped in sleep. He was passing through the native quarter when a door opened and several men came out. Scarcely knowing why he did so Malchus drew back into a doorway until they had moved on ahead of him, and then followed them at some little distance. At any other time he would have thought nothing of such an incident, but his nerves were highly strung at the moment, and his pause was dictated more by an indisposition to encounter anything which might disturb the current of his thoughts than by any other motive.

In the moonlight he could see that two of the five men ahead of him were members of the Carthaginian horse-guard, for the light glittered on their helmets; the other three were, by their attire, natives. Two of the latter soon separated from the others, and on reaching the better part of the town the two Carthaginians turned down a side street, and in the still night Malchus heard the parting words to their neighbour, "At the same place to-morrow night." The remaining native kept straight along the road which Malchus was following. Still onward he went, and Malchus, to his surprise, saw him go up to one of the side entrances to Hannibal's palace. He must have knocked very quietly, or someone must have been waiting to admit him, for without a sound the door was opened and the man entered.

Malchus went round to the principal entrance, and after a little badinage from the officer on guard as to the lateness of the hour at which he returned, made his way to his apartment.

He was puzzled by what he had seen. It was strange that two of the Carthaginian guard, men necessarily belonging to noble families, should have been at a native gathering of some sort in the upper town. Strange, too, that a man probably an attendant or slave belonging to the palace should also have been present. The more he thought of it the more he was puzzled to account for it, and before he went to sleep he came to the resolution that he would, if possible, on the following night discover the object of such a gathering.

Next evening, therefore, he returned from the Syssite early, exchanged his helmet for a skull-cap, and, wrapping himself in his cloak, made his way to the house from which he had seen the men come forth. It stood at the corner of the street. Thick hangings hung across the openings for the windows, and prevented even a ray of light from finding its way out. Listening attentively Malchus could hear a low hum of voices within. As there were still people about he moved away for half an hour.

On his return the street was deserted. Malchus put his hand through a window opening into the side street and felt that the hanging was composed of rushes tightly plaited together. With the point of his dagger he very cautiously cut a slit in this, and applying his eye to it was able to obtain a glimpse of the apartment within. On low stools by a fire two Carthaginians were sitting, while four natives were seated on the rushes which covered the floor. Malchus recognized the Carthaginians at once, for they were members of the troop in which he had served. Neither of them were men popular among their fellows, for they belonged to families closely related to Hanno. They had always, however, professed the greatest admiration for Hannibal, and had declared that for their part they altogether repudiated the doings of the party to which their family belonged.

The conversation was carried on in low tones, a precaution absolutely necessary in the day when glass windows were unknown, unless the discourse was upon general subjects. Malchus listened attentively, but although he thought he caught the words Hanno and Hannibal repeated several times, he was unable to hear more. At the end of the half hour the conference was apparently at an end, for all rose to their feet. One of the Carthaginians put a bag, which was evidently heavy, into the hands of one of the natives, and the party then went out. Malchus stepped to the corner and caught the words, "To-morrow night, then, without fail."

The party then separated, the Carthaginians passing straight on, the natives waiting until they had gone some little distance ahead before they followed. Malchus remained for some little time in the side street before he sallied out and took his way after them. After he saw two of the natives leave the other, he quickened his steps and passed the man, who proceeded alone towards the palace, a short distance before he arrived there. As he did so he glanced at his face, and recognized him as one of the attendants who waited at Hannibal's table. Malchus did not turn his head, however, but kept straight on his way and entered the palace as usual.

"Malchus," the captain of the guard laughed as he went in, "assuredly I shall have to tell Hamilcar of your doings. Last night you entered an hour after every one had retired to rest, to-night you are back in better time, but assuredly you have not been to the Syssite in that hunting-cap. This savours of a mystery. Do not pretend to me that you have been looking after your company of Numidians at this time of the night, because, did you swear it by Astarte, I should not believe you."

"No; I think I could invent a better story than that if I were put to it," Malchus said with a laugh; "but as I am not obliged to invent one at all, I will leave you to do so for me. In truth I have been about some private business, but what that business is is a profound secret."

"A secret of state, no doubt," the officer rejoined. "Well, I will say nothing this time; but do not let it occur again, or I shall think that some Iberian maiden has captured that susceptible heart of yours."

After Malchus had reached his chamber he sat down for some time in deep thought. It was clear to him that something was wrong. This secret meeting of the two Carthaginians with natives, one of whom was employed in Hannibal's household, could mean no good. Money had passed, too, and, judging from the size and apparent weight of the bag, no inconsiderable amount. What could it mean? It was but a few months before that Hasdrubal had fallen beneath the dagger of a native servant. Could this be a plot against the life of Hannibal?

The two Carthaginians were connected with Hanno, and might well be agents employed to rid him of his great rival. And yet he had heard nothing which would justify his bringing so grave an accusation against these men. The money which he had seen exchanged might be for the price of a horse or of a slave, and he might only make himself ridiculous were he to speak to Hannibal or his father as to what had occurred. He decided, therefore, that any action he might take must be on his own account. If the words he had overheard meant anything, and if a plot were really on hand, it was to be carried out on the following night. Malchus determined to take steps to meet it.

The next day he took Trebon into his counsels and told him of the mysterious meetings which he had accidentally discovered. There was free access to Hannibal's palace; officers were constantly coming in and out, and soldiers arriving and leaving with messages and orders. Malchus, had, therefore, had no difficulty in passing into his apartment, one by one, ten picked men of his company. They had orders to remain there perfectly quiet, and Trebon also took post with them, Malchus telling him to make some excuse or other to prevent any attendant or slave from entering the apartment while he was absent.

There was a concert that evening; the palace was crowded with guests. From time to time Malchus stole away to his room, where the Numidians were seated on the ground silent and immovable as so many bronze statues. At other times he kept near Hannibal, watching closely the movements of every native who passed near him; and ready to spring forward instantly if he saw any signs of an evil intention. However, he did not much apprehend, that even if his suspicions were correct and a plot was on foot against Hannibal, any attempt would be made to assassinate him in the midst of a crowded assembly, where there would be no possibility of escape for the perpetrators of such a deed. At last the guests began to depart, and an hour later all was quiet in the palace. Laying aside his sandals, Malchus stole noiselessly over the marble pavements until he approached the entrance which he had twice seen opened so late. A slave was lying close to it.

Unobserved Malchus stole away again to his chamber and bade the Numidians follow him. Noiselessly the troop of barefooted Arabs moved shadow-like through the lofty halls and corridors. Two of them he placed at the entrance to the chamber where Hannibal slept, with orders to allow no one to pass until he returned, then with the others he proceeded to the entrance. Few lights only were burning in the passages, and it was not until they were close at hand that the slave perceived the approaching figures. He leaped to his feet, but before he could cry out Malchus stepped forward and said:

"Silence, if you value your life. You know me; I am Malchus the son of Hamilcar. Now, tell me the truth, or to-morrow the torture shall wring it from you. Who placed you here, and why?"

"Carpadon, one of the chief attendants, ordered me to remain here to admit him on his return. I knew not there was harm in it," the slave said.

"Is it the first time you have kept watch for such a purpose?"

"No, my lord, some six or seven times he has gone out late." `

"Do you know the cause of his absence?"

"No, my lord, it would not become a slave to question one of the chief attendants of my lord Hannibal as to why he goes or comes."

The man's manner was so natural, and his surprise at the interest which one of the rank of Malchus showed in the doings of an attendant so genuine, that Malchus was convinced he knew nothing of any enterprise in which the man who had placed him there might be engaged.

"Very well," he said, "I will believe what you tell me. Now, do you resume your place at the door, and open it as usual at his signal. Say no word and make no sign which may lead him to know of our presence here. Mind, my eye will be upon you, and your life will pay for any treachery."

Malchus with four of his men now took post on one side of the door, standing well back in the shadow so that their presence would not be noticed by any one entering. Trebon with the remaining four men took up a similar position on the other side of the doorway.

Two hours passed. At length a low tap followed by two others was heard at the door. The slave at once opened it. Carpadon entered, and with a sudden movement threw one arm round the slave's neck and with the other stabbed him to the heart. Then he opened the door wide, and said in a low tone:

"Enter, all is safe."

In a moment a dark mass of men poured in at the door. The matter was more serious than Malchus had expected. He had looked for the entry perhaps of three or four men, and had intended to close in behind them and cut them off; but here were a score at least, and how many more might be outside he knew not. He therefore gave the signal by shouting "Carthage," and at once with his followers fell upon one flank of the natives, for such their dress showed them to be, while Trebon attacked them on the other. There was a shout of surprise and alarm at the unexpected onslaught, and several were cut down at once. The others, drawing their swords, began to defend themselves, trying at the same time to retreat to the door, through which, however, many others were still pressing in. For a few minutes a severe fight went on, and the numbers and desperation of Carpadon's followers began to tell, and, in spite of the efforts of Malchus and the Numidians, they would have been forced to fall back and allow the others to pass out, had not help been at hand.

The shouting and clashing of weapons had awakened the palace, and the officer of the guard with ten of his men, some of them bearing torches, came running at full speed from their post at the chief entrance. As the guard came up and stood gazing uncertain what to do, or among whom the conflict was raging, Malchus for a moment drew out from the fray.

"Seize and disarm all the natives," he said; "the Numidians are here by my orders."

The instant the soldiers understood the situation they fell to, and the natives whose retreat was cut off by the Numidians, were speedily disarmed; those nearer to the door had, the instant they saw the torches approaching, taken to flight.

A moment later Hannibal, Hamilcar, and many other officers resident at the palace came running up.

"What means this fray, Malchus?"

"It means an attempt upon your life, Hannibal, which I have been fortunate enough to discover and defeat."

A PLOT FRUSTRATED

"Who are these men?" Hamilcar asked.

"So far as I know they are natives," Malchus replied. "The chief of the party is that man who lies bleeding there; he is one of your attendants."

One of the soldiers held a torch close to the man's face.

"It is Carpadon," Hannibal said. "I believed him honest and faithful."

"He is the tool of others, Hannibal; he has been well paid for this night's work."

Hannibal gave orders for the prisoners to be strictly guarded, and then, with Hamilcar and Malchus, returned to his private study. The lamps were lighted by the attendants, who then withdrew.

"Now, Malchus, tell us your story," Hannibal said. "It seems strange to me that you should have said nought to your father or me of what you had learned, and left us to take such measures as might seem fit to us, instead of taking the matter into your own hands."

"Had I had certainties to go upon I should assuredly have done so, but, as you will see when I tell you all I had learned, I had nothing but suspicions, and those of the vaguest, and for aught I knew I might be altogether in the wrong."

Malchus then gave the full details of the manner in which his suspicions had been first excited, and in which on the previous night he had taken steps to ascertain whether there were any foundation for them.

"You see," he concluded, "there was no sort of certainty, nothing to prove that the money was not paid for the purchase of a horse or slave. It was only the one fact that one of the party was a servant here that rendered what I discovered serious. Had it not been for the fate of Hasdrubal I should never have given the matter a second thought; but, knowing that he was assassinated by a trusted servant, and seeing two men whose families I knew belonged to Hanno's faction engaged in secret talk with one of your attendants, the suspicion struck me that a similar deed might again be attempted. The only words I had to go upon were, 'To-morrow night, then, without fail.' This was not enough for me to bring an accusation against two men of noble family; and, had I told you the tale without the confirmation it has now received, you would probably have treated it but lightly. I resolved, therefore, to wait and see, taking such precaution that no harm could come of my secrecy. I concealed in my room ten of my Numidians, with my lieutenant Trebon—an ample force whatever might betide.

"If, as I suspected, this man intended, with two or three others, to steal into your chamber and slay you while you slept, we could at once have stopped the attempt; should he come with a larger force, we could, as is proved, resist them until the guard arrived on the spot. If, on the other hand, night passed off quietly and my suspicions proved to be altogether erroneous, I should escape the ridicule which would certainly have been forthcoming had I alarmed you without cause."

"You have acted very wisely and well, my son," Hamilcar said, "and Carthage owes you the life of our beloved Hannibal. You indeed reasoned with great wisdom and forethought. Had you informed us of what you had discovered we should have taken precautions which would doubtless have effected the object; but they would probably have become known to the plotters, and the attempt would have been postponed and attempted some other time, and perhaps with success. What say you, Hannibal, have I not reason to be proud of this young son of mine?"

"You have indeed, Hamilcar, and deeply am I indebted to him. It is not my life I care for, although that now is precious to me for the sake of my beloved Imilce, but had I fallen now all the plans which we have thought of together would have been frustrated, and the fairest chance which Carthage ever had of fighting out the quarrel with her rival would have been destroyed. Truly it has been a marvellous escape, and it seems to me that the gods themselves must have inspired Malchus to act as he did on such slight grounds as seeing two Carthaginians of the guard in company with three or four natives at a late hour of the evening.

"What do you think will be best to do with the traitors who have plotted against your life, Hannibal? Shall we try and execute them here, or send them to Carthage to be dealt with?"

Hannibal did not answer for a minute.

"I think, Hamilcar, the best plan will be to keep silent

altogether as to the danger I have run. The army would be furious but would at the same time be dispirited were it known in Carthage that two of her nobles had been executed for an attempt on my life. It would only cause a fresh outbreak of animosity and an even deadlier feud than before between Hanno's friends and ours. Therefore, I say, let the men taken to-night be executed in the morning without question asked, and let no word be said by them or by us that they were bribed by Carthaginians. All in the palace now know that a party of natives have broken in, and will guess that my life was their object; there is no need that they should know more. As to the two men, I will call them before me to-morrow, with none but you present, and will let them know that I am aware that they are the authors of this attempt, and will bid them resign their places in the guard and return at once to Carthage."

"It grieves me that they should go unpunished," Hamilcar said; "but doubtless your plan is the wisest."

"Then," Hannibal said, rising, "we will to bed again. Malchus, acquaint Trebon of our determination that silence is to be kept; tell him that I shall bear him in mind, and not forget his share in this night's work. As for you, Malchus, henceforth you are more than my cousin; you have saved my life, and I shall never forget it. I shall tell Imilce in the morning of the danger which has passed, for it is sure to come to her ears, and she will know better than I do how to thank you."

Accordingly in the morning Hannibal's orders were carried out; the twelve natives taken prisoners were beheaded without any of the usual tortures which would have been inflicted upon a similar occasion. No less than fourteen others had been killed in the fight. The two Carthaginian nobles were sent for by Hannibal. They came prepared to die, for they knew already by rumour that the attempt had failed, and doubted not when the summons reached them that Carpadon had denounced them as his accomplices. But they went to their certain doom with the courage of their class—pale, perhaps, but otherwise unmoved. Hannibal was alone with Hamilcar when they entered.

"That assassination is not an altogether unknown crime in Carthage," he said quietly, "I was well aware, but I did not before think that nobles in the Carthaginian horse would stoop to it. I know that it was you who provided the gold for the payment of the men who made an attempt upon my life, that you personally paid my attendant Carpadon to hire assassins, and to lead them to my chamber. Were I to denounce you, my soldiers would tear you in pieces. The very name of your families would be held accursed by all honest men in Carthage for all time. I do not ask you whether I have given you cause for offence, for I know that I have not done so; you acted simply for the benefit of Hanno. Whether you were instructed by him I do not deign to ask. I shall not harm you. The tale of your infamy is known to but four persons, and none others will ever know it. I am proud of the honour of the nobles of Carthage, and would not that the scum of the people should bandy the name of your families on their lips as guilty of so foul an act of treason. You will, of course, at once resign your positions in the Carthaginian horse. Make what pretext you will—illness or private affairs. To-morrow sail for Carthage, and there strive by efforts for the good of your country to efface the remembrance of this blow which you would have struck her."

So saying, with a wave of the hand he dismissed them.

They went without a word too astonished at his clemency, too humiliated by their own disgrace even to utter a word of thanks. When they were fairly beyond the palace they looked at each other as men awakened from a dream.

"What a man!" one of them exclaimed. "No wonder the soldiers adore him! He has given us our lives—more, he has saved our names from disgrace. Henceforth, Pontus, we, at least, can never again take part against him."

"It is almost too much to bear," the other said; "I feel that I would rather that he had ordered us to instant execution."

"Ay, for our own sakes, Pontus, but not for those of others. For myself I shall retire to the country; it seems to me that never again shall I be able to mix with others; they may know nothing of it, but it will be ever on my mind. How they would shrink back in horror were what we have done whispered to them! Truly, were it not for my family, I would prefer death with the worst torture to life as it will be now."

A PLOT FRUSTRATED

The excitement in the army was intense when it became known that a body of Iberians had attempted to break into Hannibal's palace with the design of murdering him, and many of the soldiers, seizing their arms, hurried towards the city, and had not an officer ridden with the news to Hannibal, they would assuredly have fallen upon the native inhabitants, and a general massacre would have taken place.

Hannibal at once mounted and rode out to meet the soldiers. He was received with enthusiastic acclamations; at length he raised his arm to restore silence, and then addressed the troops, telling them how deeply he valued the evidence of their affection, but that he prayed them to return to their camps and lay by their arms.

"We must not," he said, "confound the innocent with the guilty. Those who were concerned in the attempt have paid the penalty with their lives; it is not because a handful of Spaniards have plotted against me that you are to swear hatred against the whole race; were you to punish the innocent for the guilty you would arouse the fury of the Iberians throughout the whole peninsula, and all our work would have to be done over again. You know that above all things I desire the friendship and good-will of the natives. Nothing would grieve me more than that, just as we are attaining this, our efforts should be marred by a quarrel between yourselves and the people here. I pray you, therefore, as a personal favour to me, to abstain from all tumult, and go quietly back to your camp. The attack upon my palace was made only by some thirty or forty of the scum of the inhabitants, and the attempt was defeated by the wisdom and courage of my young cousin Malchus, whom you must henceforth regard as the saviour of my life."

The soldiers at once acceded to the request of their general, and after another outburst of cheering they returned quietly to their camp.

The result of this affair was to render Malchus one of the most popular personages in the army, and the lad was quite abashed by the enthusiastic reception which the soldiers gave him when he passed among them. It removed, too, any feeling of jealousy which might have existed among his former comrades of the Carthaginian horse, for although it was considered as a matter of course in Carthage that generals should appoint their near relatives to posts of high command, human nature was then the same as now, and men not possessed of high patronage could not help grumbling a little at the promotion of those more fortunate than themselves. Henceforth, however, no voice was ever raised against the promotion of Malchus, and had he at once been appointed to a command of importance none would have deemed such a favour undeserved by the youth who had saved the life of Hannibal.

THE YOUNG CARTHAGINIAN

CHAPTER IX: THE SIEGE OF SAGUNTUM

A FEW days later the Carthaginian army were astonished by the issue of an order that the whole were to be in readiness to march upon the following day. The greatest excitement arose when the news got abroad. None knew against whom hostilities were to be directed. No one had heard aught of the arrival of messengers announcing fresh insurrection among the recently conquered tribes, and all sorts of surmises were indulged in as to the foe against whom this great force, the largest which had ever been collected by Carthage, were about to get in motion.

The army now gathered around Carthagena amounted, indeed, to a hundred and fifty thousand men, and much surprise had for some time existed at the continual arrival of reinforcements from home, and at the large number of troops which had during the winter been raised and disciplined from among the friendly tribes.

Simultaneously with the issue of the order long lines of wagons, laden with military stores, began to pour out from the arsenals, and all day long a procession of carts moved across the bridge over the canal in the isthmus to the mainland. The tents were struck at daylight, the baggage loaded up into the wagons told off to accompany the various bodies of soldiers, and the troops formed up in military order.

When Hannibal rode on to the ground, surrounded by his principal officers, a shout of welcome rose from the army; and he proceeded to make a close inspection of the whole force. The officers then placed themselves at the head of their respective commands, the trumpets gave the signal, and the army set out on a march, as to whose direction and distance few present had any idea, and from which few, indeed, were ever destined to return.

There was no longer any occasion for secrecy as to the object of the expedition. The generals repeated it to their immediate staffs, these informed the other officers, and the news speedily spread through the army that they were marching against Saguntum. The importance of the news was felt by all. Saguntum was the near ally of Rome, and an attack upon that city could but mean that Carthage was entering upon another struggle with her great rival.

Saguntum lay about 140 miles north of Carthagena, and the army had to cross the range of mountains now known as the Sierra Morena, which run across the peninsula from Cape St. Vincent on the west to Cape St. Martin on the east. The march of so large an army, impeded as it was by a huge train of wagons with stores and the machines necessary for a siege, was toilsome and arduous in the extreme. But all worked with the greatest enthusiasm and diligence; roads were made with immense labour through forests, across ravines, and over mountain streams.

Hannibal himself was always present, encouraging the men by his praises, and sharing all their hardships.

At last the mountains were passed, and the army poured down into the fertile plains of Valencia, which town, however, was not then in existence. Passing over the site where it is now situated they continued their march north until Saguntum, standing on its rocky eminence, came into view.

During the march Malchus and his company had led the way, guided by natives, who pointed out the easiest paths. As there were no enemies to be guarded against, they had taken their full share in the labours of the army.

The Saguntines were already aware of the approach of the expedition. No sooner had it crossed the crest of the mountains than native runners had carried the news of its approach, and the inhabitants had spent the intervening time in laying in great stores of provisions, and in making every preparation for defence. The garrison was small in comparison with the force marching against it, but it was ample for the defence of the walls, for its position rendered the city well-nigh impregnable against the machines in use at the time, and was formidable in the extreme even against modern artillery, for 2000 years afterwards Saguntum, with a garrison of 3000 men, resisted for a long time all the efforts of a French army under General Suchet. As soon as his force arrived near the town Hannibal rode forward, and, in accordance with the custom of the times, himself summoned the garrison to surrender. Upon their refusal he solemnly declared war by hurling his javelin against the walls. The troops at once advanced to the assault, and poured flights of arrows, masses of stones from their machines, javelins, and missiles of all descriptions into the city, the defenders replying with equal vigour from the walls. At the end of the first day's fighting Hannibal perceived that his hopes of carrying the place by assault were vain–for the walls were too high to be scaled, too thick to be shaken by any irregular attack–and that a long siege must be undertaken.

This was a great disappointment to him, as it would cause a long delay that it would be scarce possible to commence the march which he meditated that summer. As to advancing, with Saguntum in his rear, it was not to be thought of, for the Romans would be able to land their armies there and to cut him off from all communication with Carthagena and Carthage. There was, then, nothing to be done but to undertake the siege in regular order.

The army formed an encampment in a circle round the town. A strong force was left to prevent the garrison from making a sortie, and the whole of the troops were then marched away in detachments to the hills to fell and bring down the timber which would be required for the towers and walls, the bareness of the rock rendering it impossible to construct the approaches as usual with earth. In the first place, a wall, strengthened by numerous small towers, was erected round the whole circumference of the rock; then the approaches were begun on the western side, where attack was alone possible.

This was done by lines of wooden towers, connected one with another by walls of the same material; movable towers were constructed to be pushed forward against the great tower which

Hannibal's assault on Saguntum

formed the chief defence of the wall, and on each side the line of attack was carried onward by portable screens covered with thick hide. In the mean time the Saguntines were not idle. Showers of missiles of all descriptions were hurled upon the working parties, great rocks from the machines on the walls crashed through the wooden erections, and frequent and desperate sorties were made, in which the Carthaginians were almost always worsted. The nature of the ground, overlooked as it was by the lofty towers and walls, and swept by the missiles of the defenders, rendered it impossible for any considerable force to remain close at hand to render assistance to the workers, and the sudden attacks of the Saguntines several times drove them far down the hillside, and enabled the besieged, with axe and fire, to destroy much of the work which had been so labouriously carried out.

In one of these sorties Hannibal, who was continually at the front, overlooking the work, was seriously wounded by a javelin in the thigh. Until he was cured the siege languished, and was converted into a blockade, for it was his presence and influence alone which encouraged the men to continue their work under such extreme difficulties, involving the death of a large proportion of those engaged. Upon Hannibal's recovery the work was pressed forward with new vigour, and the screens and towers were pushed on almost to the foot of the walls. The battering-rams were now brought up, and–shielded by massive screens, which protected those who worked them from the darts and stones thrown down by the enemy, and by lofty towers, from whose tops the Carthaginian archers engaged the Saguntines on the wall–began their work.

The construction of walls was in those days rude and primitive, and they had little of the solidity of such structures in succeeding ages. The stones were very roughly shaped, no mortar was used, and the displacement of one stone consequently involved that of several others. This being the case it was not long before the heavy battering-rams of the Carthaginians produced an effect on the walls, and a large breach was speedily made. Three towers and the walls which connected them fell with a mighty crash, and the besiegers, believing that the place was won, advanced to the assault. But the Saguntines met them in the breach, and for hours a desperate battle raged there.

The Saguntines hurled down upon the assailants trunks of trees bristling with spear-heads and spikes of iron, blazing darts and falariques–great blocks of wood with projecting spikes, and covered thickly with a mass of pitch and sulphur which set on fire all they touched. Other species of falariques were in the form of spindles, the shaft wrapped round with flax dipped in pitch. Hannibal fought at the head of his troops with desperate bravery, and had a narrow escape of being crushed by an enormous rock which fell at his feet; but in spite of his efforts and those of his troops they were unable to carry the breach, and at nightfall fell back to their camp, having suffered very heavy losses.

Singularly enough the French columns were repulsed in an effort to carry a breach at almost the same spot, the Spaniards hurling among them stones, hand-grenades of glass bottles and shells, and defending the breach with their long pikes against all the efforts of Suchet's troops.

Some days passed before the attack was renewed, as the troops were worn out by their labours. A strong guard in the meantime held the advanced works against any sorties of the Saguntines.

These, on their side, worked night and day, and by the time the Carthaginians again advanced the wall was rebuilt and the breach closed. But Hannibal had also been busy. Seeing that it was impossible for his troops to win an entrance by a breach, as long as the Saguntines occupied every point commanding it, he cause a vast tower to be built sufficiently lofty to overlook every point of the defences, arming each of its stages with catapults and balistas. He also built near the walls a great terrace of wood higher than the walls themselves, and from this and from the tower he poured such torrents of missiles into the town that the defenders could no longer remain upon the walls. Five hundred Arab miners now advanced, and these, setting to work with their implements, soon loosened the lower stones of the wall, and this again fell with a mighty crash and a breach was opened.

The Carthaginians at once swarmed in and took possession

of the wall; but while the besiegers had been constructing their castle and terrace, the Saguntines had built an interior wall, and Hannibal saw himself confronted with a fresh line of defences.

As preparations were being made for the attack of the new defences messengers arrived saying that the Carpatans and Orotans, furious at the heavy levies of men which had been demanded from them for the army, had revolted. Leaving Maharbal to conduct the siege in his absence, Hannibal hurried away with a portion of his force, and returned in two months, having put down the revolt and severely punished the tribesmen.

While the siege had been continuing the Romans had been making vain efforts to induce the Carthaginians to desist. No sooner had the operations commenced than agents from the Roman senate waited on Hannibal and begged him to abandon the siege. Hannibal treated their remonstrance with disdain, at the same time writing to Carthage to say that it was absolutely necessary that the people of Saguntum, who were insolent and hostile, relying on the protection of Rome, should be punished. The envoys then went to Carthage, where they made an animated protest against what they regarded as an unprovoked attack upon their allies. Rome, in fact, was anxious at this moment to postpone the struggle with Carthage for the same reason that Hannibal was anxious to press it on.

She had but just finished a long struggle with the Gaulish tribes of Northern Italy, and was anxious to recover her strength before she engaged in another war. It was for this very reason that Hannibal desired to force on the struggle. His friends at Carthage persuaded the senate to refuse to listen to the envoys of Rome. Another embassy was sent to Hannibal, but the general would not give them an interview, and, following the instructions they had received, the ambassadors then sailed to Carthage to make a formal demand for reparation, and for the person of Hannibal to be delivered over to them for punishment.

But the Barcine party were for the moment in the ascendancy; long negotiations took place which led to nothing, and all this time the condition of the Saguntines was becoming more desperate. Five new ambassadors were therefore sent from

Rome to ask in the name of the republic whether Hannibal was authorized by the Carthaginians to lay siege to Saguntum, to demand that he should be delivered to Rome, and, in case of refusal, to declare war. The Carthaginian senate met in the temple of Moloch and there received the Roman ambassadors. Q. Fabius, the chief man of the embassy, briefly laid the demands of Rome before the senate. Gestar, one of the Barcine leaders, replied, refusing the demands. Fabius then rose.

"I give you the choice—peace or war?"

"Choose yourself," the Carthaginians cried.

"Then I choose war," Fabius said.

"So be it," the assembly shouted.

And thus war was formally declared between the two Republics. But Saguntum had now fallen. The second wall had been breached by the time Hannibal had returned from his expedition, and an assault was ordered. As before, the Saguntines fought desperately, but after a long struggle the Carthaginians succeeded in winning a footing upon the wall.

The Saguntines, seeing that further resistance was vain, that the besiegers had already won the breach, that there was no chance of assistance from Rome, and having, moreover, consumed their last provisions, sought for terms. Halcon, the Saguntine general, and a noble Spaniard named Alorcus, on the part of Hannibal, met in the breach. Alorcus named the conditions which Hannibal had imposed—that the Saguntines should restore to the Torbolates the territory they had taken from them, and that the inhabitants, giving up all their goods and treasures, should then be permitted to leave the town and to found a new city at a spot which Hannibal would name.

The Saguntines, who were crowding round, heard the terms. Many of the principal senators at once left the place, and hurrying into their houses carried the gold and silver which they had there, and also some of that in the public treasury, into the forum, and piling up a vast heap of wood set it alight and threw themselves into the flames. This act caused a tremendous commotion in the city. A general tumult broke out, and Hannibal, seeing that his terms were refused, poured his troops across the breach, and after a short but desperate fight captured the city. In accordance with the cruel customs of the times, which, however, were rarely carried into effect by Hannibal, the male prisoners were all put to the sword, as on this occasion he considered it necessary to strike terror into the inhabitants of Spain, and to inflict a lesson which would not be forgotten during his absence in the country.

The siege had lasted eight months. The booty taken was enormous. Every soldier in the army had a rich share of the plunder, and a vast sum was sent to Carthage; besides which the treasure chests of the army were filled up. All the Spanish troops had leave given them to return to their homes for the winter, and they dispersed highly satisfied with the booty with which they were laden. This was a most politic step on the part of the young general, as the tribesmen, seeing the wealth with which their countrymen returned, no longer felt it a hardship to fight in the Carthaginian ranks, and the levies called out in the spring went willingly and even eagerly.

Hannibal returned with his African troops to spend the winter at Carthagena. He was there joined by the emissaries he had sent to examine Southern Gaul and the passes of the Alps, to determine the most practicable route for the march of the army, and to form alliances with the tribes of Southern Gaul and Northern Italy. Their reports were favourable, for they had found the greatest discontent existing among the tribes north of the Apennines, who had but recently been conquered by the Romans.

Their chiefs, smarting under the heavy yoke of Rome, listened eagerly to the offers of Hannibal's agents, who distributed large sums of money among them, and promised them, in return for their assistance, not only their freedom from their conqueror, but a full share in the spoils of Rome. The chiefs replied that they would render any assistance to the Carthaginians as soon as they passed the Alps, and that they would then join them with all their forces. The reports as to the passes of the Alps were less satisfactory. Those who had examined them found that the difficulties they offered to the passage of an army were enormous, and that the tribes who inhabited the lower passes, having suffered in no way yet at the hands of Rome, would probably resist any army endeavouring to cross.

THE YOUNG CARTHAGINIAN

By far the easiest route would be to follow the sea-shore, but this was barred against the Carthaginians by the fact that the Massilians (the people of Marseilles) were the close allies of Rome. They had admitted Roman colonists among them, and carried on an extensive trade with the capital. Their town was strong, and their ports would be open to the Roman fleets. The tribes in their neighourhood were all closely allied with them.

Hannibal saw at once that he could not advance by the route by the sea without first reducing Marseilles. This would be an even more difficult operation than the siege of Saguntum, as Rome would be able to send any number of men by sea to the aid of the besieged, and the great struggle would be fought out in Southern Gaul instead of, as he wished, in Italy. Thus he decided to march by a route which would take him far north of Marseilles, even although it would necessitate a passage through the terrible passes of the Alps.

During the winter Hannibal laboured without intermission in preparing for his expedition. He was ever among his soldiers, and personally saw to everything which could conduce to their comfort and well-being. He took a lively interest in every minute detail which affected them; saw that their clothing was abundant and of good quality, inspected their rations, and saw that these were well cooked.

It was this personal attention to the wants of his soldiers which, as much as his genius as a general, his personal valour, and his brilliant qualities, endeared him to his troops. They saw how anxious he was for their welfare; they felt that he regarded every man in his army as a friend and comrade, and in return they were ready to respond to every appeal, to make every sacrifice, to endure, to suffer, to fight to the death for their beloved leader. His troops were mercenaries– that is, they fought for pay in a cause which in no way concerned them–but personal affection for their general supplied in them the place of the patriotism which inspires modern soldiers, and transformed these semi-barbarous tribesmen into troops fit to cope with the trained legionaries of Rome.

Hannibal was far in advance of any of the generals of his

time in all matters of organization. His commissariat was as perfect as that of modern armies. It was its duty to collect grain from the country through which the army marched, to form magazines, to collect and drive with the troops herds of cattle, to take over the provisions and booty brought in by foraging parties, and, to see to the daily distribution of rations among the various divisions.

Along the line of communication depots were formed, where provisions, clothing, and arms were stored in readiness for use, and from which the whole army could, in case of necessity, be supplied with fresh clothing and shoes. A band of surgeons accompanied the army, at the head of whom was Synhalus, one of the most celebrated physicians of the time. So perfect were the arrangements that it is said that throughout the long campaign in Italy not a single day passed but that the troops, elephants, and animals of all descriptions accompanying the army received their daily rations of food.

THE YOUNG CARTHAGINIAN

CHAPTER X: BESET

DURING the winter Hannibal made every preparation to ensure the tranquillity of Spain while he was absent. In order to lessen the number of possible enemies there he raised a body of twelve hundred horse and fourteen thousand infantry from among the most turbulent tribes, and sent them across to Africa to serve as garrisons in Carthage and other points, while an equal number of African troops were brought over to garrison Spain, of which Hasdrubal, Hannibal's brother, was to have the government during his absence.

Hanno, an able general, was to command the force which was to be left in southern Gaul to keep open the communications between the Pyrenees and the Alps, while the youngest brother, Mago, a youth of about the same age as Malchus, was to accompany him to Italy. Hannibal's wife and a child which had been born in the preceding spring, were sent by ship to Carthage.

In the early spring the march commenced, the army following the coast line until it reached the mouth of the Ebro. The mountainous and broken country lying between this river and the Pyrenees, and now known as Catalonia, was inhabited by fierce tribes unconquered as yet by Roman or Carthaginian. Its conquest presented enormous difficulties. There was no coherence between its people; but each valley and mountain was a stronghold to be defended desperately until the last. The inhabitants, accustomed to the mountains, were hardy, active, and, vigourous, ready to oppose a desperate resistance so long as resistance was possible, and then to flee across their hills at a speed which defied the fleetest of their pursuers.

Every man was a soldier, and at the first alarm the inhabitants of the villages abandoned their houses, buried their grain, and having driven away their cattle into almost inaccessible recesses among the hills, returned to oppose the invaders. The conquest of such a people was one of the most difficult of undertakings, as the French generals of Napoleon afterwards discovered, to their cost. The cruelty of the mountaineers was equal to their courage, and the lapse of two thousand years change them but little, for in their long struggle against the French they massacred every detachment whom they could surprise among the hills, murdered the wounded who fell into their hands, and poisoned wells and grain.

The army which Hannibal had brought to the foot of this country through which he had to pass, amounted to 102,000 men, of which 12,000 were cavalry and 90,000 infantry. This force passed the Ebro in three bodies of equal strength. The natives opposed a desperate resistance, but the three columns pressed forward on parallel lines. The towns were besieged and captured, and after two months of desperate fighting Catalonia was subdued, but its conquest cost Hannibal twenty-one thousand men, a fifth of his whole army. Hanno was for the time left here with ten thousand infantry and a thousand cavalry. He was to suppress any fresh rising, to hold the large towns, to form magazines for the army, and to keep open the passes of the Pyrenees. He fixed his headquarters at Burgos. His operations were facilitated by the fact that along the line of the sea-coast were a number of Phoenician colonies who were natural allies of the Carthaginians, and aided them in every way in their power. Before advancing through the passes of the Pyrenees Hannibal still further reduced the strength of his force by weeding out all those who had in the conflict among the mountains shown themselves wanting in personal strength or in military qualities. Giving these leave to return home he advanced at the head of fifty thousand picked infantry and nine thousand cavalry.

The company under Malchus had rendered good service during the campaign of Catalonia. It had accompanied the column marching by the sea-shore; with this were the elephants, the treasure, and the heavy baggage of the army. It had throughout been in advance of the column, feeling the way, protecting it from ambushes, and dispersing any small bodies of tribesmen who might have placed themselves on heights, whence with arrows and slings they could harass the column on its march. The company had lost comparatively few men in the campaign, for it had taken no part in the various sieges. Its duties, however, were severe in the extreme. The men were ever on the watch, scouting the country round, while the army was engaged in siege operations, sometimes ascending mountains whence they could command views over the interior or pursuing bands of tribesmen to their refuges among the hills.

Severely as Malchus had trained himself in every exercise, he found it at first difficult to support the fatigues of such a life; but every day his muscles hardened, and by the end of the campaign he was able to keep on foot as long as the hardest of his men.

One day he had followed a party of the tribesmen far up among the mountains. The enemy had scattered, and the Arabs in their hot pursuit had also broken up into small parties. Malchus kept his eye upon the man who appeared to be the chief of the enemy's party, and pressing hotly upon him brought him to bay on the face of a steep and rugged gorge. Only one of the Numidians was at hand, a man named Nessus, who was greatly attached to his young leader, and always kept close to him in his expeditions. The savage, a bulky and heavy man, finding he could no longer keep ahead of his fleet-footed pursuers, took his post at a narrow point in the path where but one could oppose him; and there, with his heavy sword drawn, he awaited the attack. Malchus advanced to meet him, sword in hand, when an arrow from Nessus whizzed past him and struck the chief in the throat, and his body fell heavily down the rocks.

"That is not fair," Malchus said angrily. "I would fain have fought him hand to hand."

The Arab bowed his head.

"My lord," he said, "the combat would not have been even; the man had the upper ground, and you would have fought at a grievous disadvantage. Why should you risk your life in a fight with the swords, when my arrow has answered all purposes? What should I have said if I had gone back without you? What satisfaction would it have been to me to avenge your fall? What would they have said to me when I told them that I looked on idly while you engaged in such a struggle? Valour is valour, and we all know that my lord is the bravest among us; but the life of the cousin of our general is too valuable to be risked for nought when we are embarked upon a great enterprise."

"Look, Nessus ! what is there?" Malchus exclaimed, his attention attracted by a dark object which was crossing the narrow path some distance ahead and ascending the steep side of the gorge. "It is a bear, let us follow him; his flesh will form a welcome change for the company to-night."

The bear, who had been prowling in the bottom of the ravine, had been disturbed by the fall of the body of the savage near him, and started hastily to return to its abode, which lay high up on the face of the cliff. Malchus and his companion hurried forward to the spot where it had crossed the path. The way was plain enough; there were scratches on the rock, and the bushes growing in the crevices were beaten down. The path had evidently been frequently used by the animal.

"Look out, my lord!" Nessus exclaimed as Malchus hurried along. "These bears of the Pyrenees are savage brutes. See that he does not take you unawares."

The rocks were exceedingly steep; and Malchus, with his bow in his hand and the arrow fitted and ready to draw, climbed on, keeping his eyes on every clump of bush lest the bear should be lurking there. At last he paused. They had reached a spot now but a short distance from the top. The cliff here fell almost perpendicularly down, and along its face was a narrow ledge scarcely a foot wide. Along this it was evident the bear had passed.

"I should think we must be near his den now, Nessus. I trust this ledge widens out before it gets there. It would be an awkward place for a conflict, for a stroke of his paw would send one over the edge."

"I shall be close behind you, my lord," said Nessus, whose blood was now up with the chase. Should you fail to stop him, drop on one knee that I may shoot over you."

Malchus and Nessus are suddenly stopped.

For some fifty yards the ledge continued unbroken. Malchus moved along cautiously, with his arrow in the string and his shield shifted round his shoulder, in readiness for instant action. Suddenly, upon turning a sharp corner of the cliff, he saw it widened ten feet ahead into a sort of platform lying in the angle of the cliff, which beyond it again jutted out. On this platform was a bear, which with an angry growl at once advanced towards him. Malchus discharged his arrow; it struck the bear full on the chest, and penetrated deeply. With a stroke of his paw the animal broke the shaft asunder and rushed forward. Malchus threw forward the point of his spear, and with his shield on his arm awaited the onset. He struck the bear fairly on the chest, but, as before, it snapped the shaft with its paw, and rising to its feet advanced.

"Kneel, my lord!" Nessus exclaimed.

Malchus dropped on one knee, bracing himself as firmly as he could against the rock, and, with his shield above his head and his sword in his hand, awaited the attack of the enraged animal. He heard the twang of the bow behind him; then he felt a mighty blow, which beat down his shield and descended with terrible force upon his helmet, throwing him forward on to his face. Then there was a heavy blow on his back; and it was well for him that he had on backpiece as well as breastplate, or the flesh would have been torn from his shoulder to his loins. As the blow fell there was an angry roar. For a moment he felt crushed by a weight which fell upon him. This was suddenly removed, and he heard a crash far below as the bear, pierced to the heart by the Arab's spear, fell over the precipice. Nessus hastened to raise him.

"My lord is not hurt, I hope?"

"In no way, Nessus, thanks to you; but my head swims and my arm is well-nigh broken with that blow. Who would have thought a beast like that could have stuck so hard? See, he has dented in my helmet and has bent my shield! Now, before we go back and search for the body, let us see what its den is like."

"Do you take my spear, my lord; your own is broken, and your bow has gone over the precipice. It may be that there is another bear here. Where one is, the other is seldom far off."

They advanced on to the platform, and saw in the corner of the angle a cave entering some distance into the hill. As they approached the entrance a deep growl was heard within.

"We had best leave it alone, my lord," Nessus said as they both recoiled a step at the entrance. "This is doubtless the female, and these are larger and fiercer than the males."

"I agree with you, Nessus," Malchus said. "Were we on other ground I should say let us attack it, but I have had enough of fighting bears on the edge of a precipice. There is as much meat as we can carry ready for us below. Besides, the hour is late and the men will be getting uneasy. Moreover, we are but half armed; and we cannot get at her without crawling through that hole, which is scarce three feet high. Altogether, we had best leave her alone."

While they were speaking the bear began to roar angrily, the deeper notes being mingled with a chorus of snarls and whinings which showed that there was a young family with her.

"Do you go first, Nessus," Malchus said. "The rear is the post of honour here, though I fancy the beast does not mean to come out."

Nessus without a word took the lead, and advanced across the platform towards the corner.

As he was in the act of turning it he sprang suddenly back, while an arrow flew past, grazing the corner of the rock.

"There are a score of natives on the path!" he exclaimed. "We are in a trap."

Malchus looked round in dismay. It was evident that some of the natives must have seen the fall of their leader and watched them pursue the bear, and had now closed in behind them to cut off their retreat. The situation was a most unpleasant one. The ledge extended no further than the platform; below, the precipice fell away sheer down a hundred feet; above, it rose as high. The narrow path was occupied with numerous foes. In the den behind them was the angry bear.

For a moment the two men looked at each other in consternation.

"We are fairly caught, Nessus," Malchus said. "There is one thing, they can no more attack us than we can attack them.

Only one can come round this corner at a time, and we can shoot or spear them as they do so. We are tolerably safe from attack, but they can starve us out."

"They can shoot over from the other side of the ravine," Nessus said; "their arrows will carry from the opposite brow easily enough."

"Then," Malchus said firmly, "we must dispose of the bear; we must have the cave. We shall be safe there from their arrows, while, lying at the entrance, we could shoot any that should venture past the corner. First, though, I will blow my horn. Some of our men may be within hearing."

Malchus pulled forth the horn which he carried. It was useless, being completely flattened with the blow that the bear had struck him.

"That hope is gone, Nessus," he said. "Now let us get the bear to come out as soon as possible, and finish with her. Do you stand at the corner with your arrow ready, in case the natives should try to surprise us, and be ready to aid me when she rushes out."

Malchus went to the mouth of the den struck his spear against the side, and threw in some pieces of stone; but, although the growling was deep and continuous, the bear showed no signs of an intention of coming out.

The Arab was an old hunter, and he now asked Malchus to take his place with the bow while he drove the bear out. He first took off his bernous, cut off several strips from the bottom, knotted them together, and then twisted the strip into a rope. Growing out from a crevice in the rock, some three feet above the top of the cave, was a young tree; and round this, close to the root, Nessus fastened one end of his rope, the other he formed into a slip-knot and let the noose fall in front of the cave, keeping it open with two twigs placed across it. Then he gathered some brushwood and placed it at the entrance, put a bunch of dried twigs and dead leaves among it, and, striking a light with his flint and steel on some dried fungus, placed this in the middle of the sticks and blew upon it. In a minute a flame leaped up. "Now, my lord," he said, "be ready with your sword and spear. The beast will be out in a minute; she cannot stand the smoke."

Malchus ran to the corner and looked round. The natives were at a distance along the ledge, evidently with no intention of attacking a foe of whom they felt sure. A taunting shout was raised and an arrow flew towards him, but he instantly withdrew his head and ran back to the platform.

A minute later there was a fierce growl and the bear rushed out. The brushwood was scattered as, checked suddenly in its rush by the noose, the animal rose on its hind-legs. In an instant the spear of Nessus was plunged deeply into it on one side, while Malchus buried his sword to the hilt in its body under the fore-shoulder of the other. Stabbed to the heart, the beast fell prostrate. Nessus repeated his blow, but the animal was dead. Five young bears rushed out after their mother, growling and snapping; but as these were only about a quarter grown they were easily despatched.

"There is a supply of food for a long time," Malchus said cheerfully; "and as there is a drip of water coming down in this angle we shall be able to quench our thirst. Ah! we are just in time."

As he spoke an arrow struck the rock close to them and dropped at their feet. Others came in rapid succession; and, looking at the brow of the opposite side of the ravine, they saw a number of natives.

"Pull the bear's body across the mouth of the cave," Malchus said, "it will prevent the arrows which strike the rock in front from glancing in. The little bears will do for food at present."

They were soon in the cave, which opened beyond the entrance and extended some distance into the mountain; it was seven or eight feet wide and lofty enough to stand upright in. Nessus lay down behind the bear, with his bow and arrow so as to command the angle of the rock. Malchus seated himself further in the cave, sheltered by the entrance from the arrows which from time to time glanced in at the mouth. Only once did Nessus have to shoot. The natives on the ledge, informed by their comrades on the opposite side of the gorge that their foes had sought refuge in the cave, ventured to advance; but the moment the first turned the corner he fell over the precipice, transfixed by an arrow from the bow of Nessus, and the rest hastily retreated.

"Hand me your flint and steel, Nessus, and a piece of fungus. I may as well have a look round the cave."

A light was soon procured, and Malchus found that the cave extended some fifty feet back, narrowing gradually to the end. It had evidently been used for a long time by wild animals. The floor was completely covered with dry bones of various sizes.

As soon as he saw that this was the case Malchus tore off a strip of his linen shirt, and rolling it into a ball set it on fire. On this he piled up small bones, which caught readily, and he soon had a bright and almost smokeless fire. He now took the place of Nessus. The latter skinned and cut up one of the small bears, and soon had some steaks broiling over the fire. By this time it was getting dusk without.

When the meat was cooked Nessus satisfied his hunger and then sallied out from the cave and took his post as sentry with his spear close to the angle of the rock, as by this time the natives on the opposite side, being no longer able to see in the gathering darkness, had ceased to shoot. Malchus ate his food at his leisure, and then joined his companion.

"We must get out of here somehow, Nessus. Our company will search for us to-morrow; but they might search for a week without finding us here; and, as the army is advancing, they could not spare more than a day; so, if we are to get away, it must be by our own exertions."

"I am ready to fight my way along this ledge, my lord, if such is your wish. They cannot see us to fire at, and as only one man can stand abreast, their numbers would be of no avail to them."

"Not on the ledge, Nessus; but they would hardly defend that. No doubt they are grouped at the further end, and we should have to fight against overwhelming numbers. No, that is not to be thought of. The only way of escape I can think of would be to let ourselves down the precipice; but our bernouses would not make a rope long enough."

"They would not reach a third of the distance," Nessus replied, shaking his head. "They have been worn some time, and the cloth is no longer strong. It would need a broad strip to support us."

"That is so, Nessus, but we have materials for making the rope long enough, nevertheless."

"I do not understand you, my lord. Our other garments would be of but little use."

"Of no use at all, Nessus, and I was not thinking of them; but we have the skins of the bears—the hide of the old bear at least is thick and tough—and a narrow strip would bear our weight."

"Of course," Nessus said. "How stupid of me not to think of it, for in the desert we make all our rope of twisted slips of hide. If you will stand sentry here, my lord, I will set about it at once."

Malchus took the spear, and Nessus at once set to work to skin the bear, and when that was done he cut long strips from the hide, and having fastened them together, twisted them into a rope.

The bernouses—which when on the march were rolled up and worn, over one shoulder like a scarf, as the German and Italian soldiers carry their blankets in modern times—were also cut up and twisted, and in three hours Nessus had a rope which he assured Malchus was long enough to reach to the bottom of the precipice and sufficiently strong to bear their weight.

One end was fastened to the trunk of the young tree, and the rope was then thrown over the edge of the platform. One of the young bear's skins was fastened round and round it at the point where it crossed the edge of the rocky platform, to prevent it from being cut when the weight was put upon it, and they then prepared for their descent.

"Do you go first," Malchus said. "As soon as I feel that the rope is loose, I will follow you."

The Arab swung himself off the edge, and in a very short time Malchus felt the rope slacken. He followed at once. The first twenty feet the descent was absolutely perpendicular, but after that the rock inclined outward in a steep but pretty regular slope. Malchus was no longer hanging by the rope; but throwing the principal portion of his weight still upon it, and placing his feet on the inequalities of the rock, he made his way down without difficulty. Presently he stood by Nessus at the foot of the slope.

"We had better make up the ravine. There will be numbers of them at its mouth. We can see the glow of their fires from here."

"But we may not be able to find a way up," Nessus said; "the sides seem to get steeper and steeper, and we may find ourselves caught in a trap at the end of this gorge."

"At any rate we will try that way first. I wish the moon was up; it is as black as a wolf's mouth here, and the bottom of the gorge is all covered with boulders. If we stumble, and our arms strike a stone, it will be heard by the natives on the opposite heights."

They now set forward, feeling their way with the greatest care; but in the dense darkness the task of making their way among the boulders was difficult in the extreme. They had proceeded but a short distance when a loud yell rose from the height above them. It was repeated again and again, and was answered by shouts from the opposite side and from the mouth of the ravine.

"By Astarte!" Malchus exclaimed, "they have found out that we have escaped already."

It was so. One of the natives had crept forward along the path, hoping to find the sentry asleep, or to steal up noiselessly and stab him. When he got to the angle of the rock he could see no form before him, nor hear the slightest sound. Creeping forward he found the platform deserted. He listened attentively at the entrance to the cave, and the keen ear of the savage would have detected had any been slumbering there; but all was still.

He rose to his feet with the intention of creeping into the cave, when his head struck against something. He put up his hand and felt the rope, and saw how the fugitives had escaped. He at once gave the alarm to his comrades. In a minute or two a score of men with blazing brands came running along the path. On seeing the rope, they entered the cave, and found that their prey had really escaped.

Malchus and his companion had not moved after the alarm was given.

"We had better be going, my lord," the Arab said as be saw the men with torches retracing their steps along the brow. "They will soon be after us."

"I think not, Nessus. Their chance of finding us among these boulders in the dark would be small, and they would offer such good marks to our arrows that they would hardly enter upon it. No, I think they will wait till daybreak, planting a strong force at the mouth of the ravine, and along both sides of the end, wherever an ascent could be made. Hark, the men on the heights there are calling to others along the brow."

"Very well, my lord," Nessus said, seating himself on a rock, "then we will sell our lives as dearly as possible."

"I hope it has not come to that, Nessus. There is a chance of safety for us yet. The only place they are not likely to look for us is the cave, and as we have climbed down from above with the rope, there will be no difficulty in ascending."

Nessus gave an exclamation, which expressed at once admiration of his leader's idea and gratification at the thought of escape. They began without delay to retrace their steps, and after some trouble again found the rope.

Nessus mounted first; his bare feet enabled him to grip any inequality of the surface of the rock. Whenever he came to a ledge which afforded him standing room he shook the rope, and waited until Malchus joined him.

At last they stood together at the foot of the perpendicular rock at the top. The lightly armed Arab found no difficulty whatever in climbing the rope; but it was harder work for Malchus, encumbered with the weight of his armour. The numerous knots however, helped him, and when he was within a few feet of the top, Nessus seized the rope and hauled it up by sheer strength until Malchus was level with the top. Then he gave him his hand, and assisted him to gain his feet. They entered the cave and made their way to the further end, and there threw themselves down. They had not long been there when they saw a flash of light at the mouth of the cave and heard voices.

Malchus seized his spear and would have leaped to his feet, but Nessus pressed his hand on his shoulder.

"They are come for the she-bear," he said. "It is not likely they will enter."

Lying hidden in the darkness the fugitives watched the natives roll the bear over, tie its legs together, and put a stout pole through them. Then four men lifted the pole on their shoulders and started.

Another holding a brand entered the cave. The two fugitives held their breath, and Nessus sat with an arrow in the string ready to shoot. The brand, however, gave but a feeble light, and the native, picking up the bodies of three of the young bears, which lay close to the entrance, threw them over his shoulder, and crawled back out of the cave again. As they heard his departing footsteps the fugitives drew a long breath of relief.

Nessus rose and made his way cautiously out of the cave. He returned in a minute.

"They have taken the rope with them," he said, "and it is well, for when they have searched the valley to-morrow, were it hanging there, it might occur to them that we have made our way up. Now that it is gone they can never suspect that we have returned here."

"There is no chance of our being disturbed again to-night, Nessus. We can sleep as securely as if were in our camp."

So saying, Malchus chose a comfortable place, and was soon asleep.

Nessus, however, did not lie down, but sat watching with unwearied eyes the entrance to the cave. As soon as day had fairly broken, a chorus of loud shouts and yells far down the ravine told that the search had begun. For hours it continued. Every bush and boulder in the bottom was searched by the natives.

Again and again they went up and down the gorge, convinced that the fugitives must be hidden somewhere; for, as Nessus had anticipated, the cliffs at the upper end were so precipitous that an escape there was impossible, and the natives had kept so close a watch all night along the slopes at the lower end, and at the mouth, that they felt sure that their prey could not have escaped them unseen. And yet at last they were forced to come to the conclusion that in some inexplicable way this must have been the case, for how else could they have escaped? The thought that they had reascended by the rope before it was removed, and that they were hidden in the cave at the time the bodies of the bear and its cubs were carried away, never occurred to them.

All day they wandered about in the bottom of the ravine searching every possible place, and sometimes removing boulders with great labour, where these were piled together in such a manner that any one could be hidden beneath them.

THE YOUNG CARTHAGINIAN

At night-fall they feasted upon the body of the bear first killed, which had been found where it had fallen in the ravine. The body of one of the young bears which lay far up the cave, had escaped their search, and a portion of this furnished a meal to the two prisoners, who were, however, obliged to eat it raw, being afraid to light a fire, lest the smoke, however slight, should be observed coming out at the entrance.

The next morning, so far as they could see, the place was deserted by the natives. Lying far back in the cave they could see that the men on the opposite side of the ravine had retired; but as it was quite possible that the natives, feeling still convinced that the fugitives must be hidden somewhere, had set a watch at some spot commanding a view of the whole ravine, they did not venture to show themselves at the entrance.

After making another meal of the bear, they sallied out, when it again became dark, and made their way along the path. When they neared the end they saw a party of the enemy sitting round a great fire at the mouth of the ravine below them. They retired a short distance, and sat down patiently until at last the fire burned low, and the natives, leaving two of the party on watch, lay down to sleep. Then Malchus and his companion rose to their feet, and made their way along the path. When they were nearly abreast of the fire, Malchus happened to tread upon a loose stone, which went bouncing down the side of the hill.

The scouts gave a shout, which called their companions to their feet, and started up the hillside towards the spot where the stone had fallen.

Nessus discharged an arrow, which struck full on the chest of the leader of the party, and then followed Malchus along the hillside.

A shout of rage broke from the natives as their comrade fell; but without pausing they pushed on. Malchus did not hurry. Silence now was of more importance than speed. He strode along, then, with a rapid but careful step, Nessus following closely behind him. The shouts of the savages soon showed that they were at fault. Malchus listened attentively as he went. Whenever the babel of tongues ceased for a moment he stopped perfectly still, and only ventured on when they were renewed.

BESET

At last they had placed a long gap between them and their pursuers, and came out on a level shoulder of the hill. They continued their way until they found themselves at the edge of the forest. It was so dark under the trees that they could no longer advance, and Malchus therefore determined to wait till the dawn should enable them to continue their journey. Whether they were in a clump of trees or in the forest, which covered a large portion of the mountain side, they were unable to tell; nor, as not a single star could be seen, had they any indication of the direction which they should take. Retiring then for some little distance among the trees, they lay down and were soon asleep.

When the first dawn of day appeared they were on their way again, and soon found that the trees under which they had slept formed part of the forest. Through occasional openings, formed by trees which had fallen from age or tempest, they obtained a view of the surrounding country, and were enabled to form an idea where lay the camp which they had left two days before.

They had not proceeded far when they heard in the distance behind them the shouting of men and the barking of dogs, and knew that the enemy were upon their track. They ran now at the top of their speed, convinced, however, that the natives, who would have to follow the track, could not travel as fast as they did. Suddenly Malchus stopped.

"Listen!" he said. They paused, and far down the hillside heard the distant sound of a horn. "Those must be our men," Malchus exclaimed, they are searching for us still; Hannibal must have allowed them to stay behind when the army proceeded on its way."

In another half-hour the horn sounded close at hand and they were speedily among a body of Malchus' own followers, who received them with shouts of delight. The men were utterly worn out, for they had searched continuously day and night from the time they had missed their leader, sometimes high up among the hills, sometimes among the lower valleys. The party which he met comprised but a fourth of the band, for they had divided into four parties, the better to range the country.

They were now ascending the hills again at a distance of two miles apart, and messengers were at once sent off to the other bodies to inform them that Malchus had returned. Malchus quickly recounted to his men the story of what had befallen them, and then bade them lie down to rest while he and Nessus kept watch.

The natives who had been in pursuit did not make their appearance, having doubtless heard the horn which told of the approach of a body of the Carthaginians. In two hours the whole of the band were collected, and after a few hours' halt, to enable the men to recover from their long fatigue and sleeplessness, Malchus put himself at their head and they marched away to join the main body of their army, which they overtook two days later.

Malchus was received with great delight by his father and Hannibal, who had given him up for lost. Nessus had over and over again recounted all the details of their adventure to his comrades, and the quickness of Malchus at hitting upon the stratagem of returning to the cave, and so escaping from a position where escape seemed well-nigh impossible, won for him an even higher place than before in the admiration of his followers.

THE YOUNG CARTHAGINIAN

CHAPTER XI: THE PASSAGE OF THE RHONE

THE army was now moving through the passes of the Pyrenees. The labour was great; no army had ever before crossed this mountain barrier; roads had to be made, streams bridged, and rocks blasted away, to allow the passage of the elephants and baggage wagons. Opinions have differed as to the explosives used by the Carthaginian miners, but it is certain that they possessed means of blasting rocks. The engineers of Hannibal's force possessed an amount of knowledge and science vastly in excess of that attained by the Romans at that time, and during the campaign the latter frequently endeavoured, and sometimes with success, by promises of high rewards, to induce Hannibal's engineers to desert and take service with them. A people well acquainted with the uses of sulphur and niter, skilled in the Oriental science of chemistry, capable of manufacturing Greek fire—a compound which would burn under water—may well have been acquainted with some mixture resembling gunpowder.

The art of making this explosive was certainly known to the Chinese in very remote ages, and the Phoenicians, whose galleys traversed the most distant seas to the east, may have acquired their knowledge from that people.

The wild tribes of the mountains harassed the army during this difficult march, and constant skirmishes went on between them and Hannibal's light-armed troops. However, at last all difficulties were overcome, and the army descended the slopes into the plains of Southern Gaul.

Already Hannibal's agents had negotiated for an unopposed passage through this country; but the Gauls, alarmed at the appearance of the army, and at the news which had reached them of the conquest of Catalonia, assembled in arms. Hannibal's tact and a lavish distribution of presents dissipated the alarm of the Gauls, and their chiefs visited Hannibal's camp at Elne, and a treaty was entered into for the passage of the army.

A singular article of this treaty, and one which shows the esteem in which the Gauls held their women, was that all complaints on the part of the natives against Carthaginian troops should be carried to Hannibal himself or the general representing him, and that all complaints of the Carthaginians against the natives should be decided without appeal by a council composed of Gaulish women. This condition caused much amusement to the Carthaginians, who, however, had no cause to regret its acceptance, for the decisions of this singular tribunal were marked by the greatest fairness and impartiality. The greater part of the tribes through whose country the army marched towards the Rhone observed the terms of the treaty with good faith; some proved troublesome, but were wholly unable to stand against the Carthaginian arms.

The exact route traversed by the army has been a subject of long and bitter controversy; but, as no events of very great importance occurred on the way, the precise line followed in crossing Gaul is a matter of but slight interest. Suffice that, after marching from the Pyrenees at a high rate of speed, the army reached the Rhone at the point where Roquemaure now stands, a short distance above Avignon.

This point had been chosen by Hannibal because it was one of the few spots at which the Rhone runs in a single stream, its course being for the most part greatly broken up by islands. Roquemaure lies sixty-five miles from the sea, and it was necessary to cross the Rhone at some distance from its mouth, for Rome was now thoroughly alarmed, and Scipio, with a fleet and powerful army, was near Marseilles waiting to engage Hannibal on the plains of Gaul.

During the last few days' march no inhabitants had been

encountered. The Arecomici, who inhabited this part of the country, had not been represented at the meeting, and at the news of the approach of the Carthaginians had deserted their country and fled across the Rhone, where, joined by the tribes dwelling upon the further bank, they prepare to offer a desperate opposition to the passage of the river. The appearance of this mass of barbarians, armed with bows and arrows and javelins, on the further side of the wide and rapid river which had to be crossed, was not encouraging.

"It was bad enough crossing the Pyrenees," Malchus said to Trebon, "but that was nothing to this undertaking; it is one thing to climb a precipice, however steep, to the assault of an enemy, another to swim across at the head of the army under such a shower of missiles as we shall meet with on the other side."

Hannibal, however, had prepared to overcome the difficulty. Messengers had been sent up and down the river to all the people living on the right bank, offering to buy from them at good prices every barge and boat in their possession, promising them freedom from all exactions and hard treatment, and offering good pay to those who would render assistance to the army in the passage. Hannibal's offers were accepted without hesitation. That the army, which could, had it chosen, have taken all their boats by force and impressed their labour, should offer to pay liberally for both, filled them with admiration, and they were, moreover, only too glad to aid this formidable army of strangers to pass out of their country.

The dwellers upon the Rhone at this period carried on an extensive commerce, not only with the tribes of the upper river, but with Marseilles and the ports of Spain and Northern Italy, consequently a large number of vessels and barges of considerable tonnage were at once obtained.

To add to the means of transport the whole army were set to work, and, assisted by the natives, the soldiers cut down trees, and, hollowing them out roughly, formed canoes capable of carrying two or three men. So industriously did the troops work that in two days enough canoes were made to carry the army across the river; but there was still the opposition of the natives to be overcome, and when the canoes were finished Hannibal ordered Hanno, one of his best generals, to start with a division at nightfall up the bank of the river.

Hanno marched five miles, when he found a spot where the river was smooth and favourable for the passage. The troops set to at once to cut trees; rafts were formed of these, and the troops passed over. The Spanish corps, accustomed to the passage of rivers, simply stripped, and putting their broad shields of hides beneath them, passed the river by swimming. Once across Hanno gave his men twenty-four hours' rest, and then, calculating that Hannibal's preparations would be complete, he marched down the river until he reached a hill, whose summit was visible from Hannibal's camp at daybreak. Upon this he lit a signal fire.

The moment the smoke was seen in the camp Hannibal gave orders for the troops to embark. The light infantry took to their little canoes, the cavalry embarked in the larger vessels, and, as these were insufficient to carry all the horses, a great many of the animals were made to enter the river attached by ropes to the vessels. The heavier craft started highest up, in order that they might to some extent break the roughness of the waves and facilitate the passage of the canoes.

The din was prodigious. Thousands of men tugged at the oars, the roughly made canoes were dashed against each other and often upset, while from the opposite bank rose loudly the defiant yells of the natives, prepared to dispute to the last the landing of the flotilla. Suddenly these cries assumed a different character. A mass of smoke was seen to rise from the tents of the enemy's camp, and Hanno's division poured down upon their rear. The Arecomici, taken wholly by surprise, were seized with a panic, and fled hastily in all directions, leaving the bank clear for the landing of Hannibal. The whole of the army were brought across at once and encamped that night on the river.

In the morning Hannibal sent off five hundred Numidian horse to reconnoitre the river below, and ascertained what Scipio's army, which was known to have landed at its mouth, was doing. He then assembled his army and introduced to them some chiefs of the tribes beyond the Alps, who had a day or two before arrived in the camp with the agents he had sent to their country. They harangued the soldiers, an interpreter translating their speeches, and assured them of the welcome they would meet in the rich and fertile country beyond the Alps, and of the alacrity with which the people there would join them against the Romans.

Hannibal himself then addressed the soldiers, pointed out to them that they had already accomplished by far the greatest part of their journey, had overcome every obstacle, and that there now remained but a few days' passage over the mountains, and that Italy, the goal of all their endeavours, would then lie before them.

The soldiers replied with enthusiastic shouts, and Hannibal, after offering up prayers to the gods on behalf of the army, dismissed the soldiers, and told them to prepare to start on the following day. Soon after the assembly had broken up the Numidian horse returned in great confusion, closely pressed by the Roman cavalry, who had been sent by Scipio to ascertain Hannibal's position and course. The hostile cavalry had charged each other with fury. A hundred and forty of the Romans and two hundred of the Numidians were slain.

Hannibal saw that there was no time to be lost. The next morning, at daybreak, the whole of his cavalry were posted to the south to cover the movements of the army and to check the Roman advance. The infantry were then set in motion up the bank of the river and Hannibal, with a small party, remained behind to watch the passage of the elephants, which had not yet been brought across.

The elephants had not been trained to take to the water, and the operation was an extremely difficult one. Very strong and massive rafts were joined together until they extended two hundred feet into the river, being kept in their place by cables fastened to trees on the bank above them. At the end of this floating pier was placed another raft of immense size, capable of carrying four elephants at a time. A thick covering of earth was laid over the whole, and on this turf was placed. The elephants were then led forward.

So solid was the construction that they advanced upon it without hesitation. When four had taken their place on the great raft at the end, the fastenings which secured it to the rest of the structure were cut, and a large number of boats and barges filled with rowers began to tow the raft across the river. The elephants were seized with terror at finding themselves afoot, but seeing no way of escape remained trembling in the centre of the raft until they reached the other side. When it was safely across, the raft and towing boats returned, and the operation was repeated until all the elephants were over.

Some of the animals, however, were so terrified that they flung themselves from the rafts into the river and made their way to shore, keeping their probosces above the surface of the water. The Indians who directed them were, however, all swept away and drowned. As soon as the elephants were all across Hannibal called in his cavalry, and with them and the elephants followed the army.

The Romans did not arrive at the spot until three days after the Carthaginians had left. Scipio was greatly astonished when he found that Hannibal had marched north, as he believed that the Alps were impassable for an army, and had reckoned that Hannibal would certainly march down the river and follow the sea-shore. Finding that the Carthaginians had left he marched his army down to his ships again, re-embarked them, and sailed for Genoa, intending to oppose Hannibal as he issued from the defiles of the Alps, in the event of his succeeding in making the passage.

Four days' march up the Rhone brought Hannibal to the point where the Isére runs into that river. He crossed it, and with his army entered the region called by Polybius "The Island," although the designation is an incorrect one, for while the Rhone flows along one side of the triangle and the Isére on the other, the base is formed not by a third river, but by a portion of the Alpine chain.

Malchus and his band had been among the first to push off from the shore when the army began to cross the Rhone. Malchus was in a roughly-constructed canoe, which was paddled by Nessus and another of his men. Like most of the other canoes, their craft soon became water-logged, for the rapid and angry current of the river, broken and agitated by so large a number of boats, splashed over the sides of the clumsy canoes, which were but a

148

few inches above the water. The buoyancy of the wood was sufficient to float them even when full, but they paddled slowly and heavily.

The confusion was prodigious. The greater part of the men, unaccustomed to rowing, had little control over their boats. Collisions were frequent, and numbers of the boats were upset and their occupants drowned. The canoe which carried Malchus was making fair progress, but, to his vexation, was no longer in the front line. He was urging the paddlers to exert themselves to the utmost, when Nessus gave a sudden cry.

A horse which had broken loose from its fastenings behind one of the barges was swimming down, frightened and confused at the din. It was within a few feet of them when Nessus perceived it, and in another moment it struck the canoe broadside with its chest. The boat rolled over at once, throwing its occupants into the water. Malchus grasped the canoe as it upset, for he would instantly have sunk from the weight of his armour. Nessus a moment later appeared by his side.

"I will go to the other side, my lord," he said, "that will keep the tree from turning over again."

He dived under the canoe, and came up on the opposite side, and giving Malchus his hand across it, there was no longer any fear of the log rolling over. The other rower did not reappear above the surface. Malchus shouted in vain to some of the passing boats to pick him up, but all were so absorbed in their efforts to advance and their eagerness to engage the enemy that none paid attention to Malchus or the others in like plight. Besides, it seemed probable that all, if they stuck to their canoes, would presently gain one bank or other of the river. Malchus, too, had started rather low down, and he was therefore soon out of the flotilla.

The boat was nearly in mid-stream when the accident happened.

"The first thing to do," Malchus said when he saw that there was no chance of their being picked up, "is to rid myself of my armour. I can do nothing with it on, and if the tree turns over I shall go down like a stone. First of all, Nessus, do you unloose your sword-belt. I will do the same. If we fasten them together they are long enough to go round the canoe, and if we take off our helmets and pass the belts through the chin chains they will, with our swords, hang safely."

This was with some difficulty accomplished.

"Now," Malchus continued, "let us make our way to the stern of the canoe. I will place my hand on the tree there, and do you unfasten the shoulder and waist-straps of my breast and backpieces. I cannot do it myself."

This was also accomplished, and the two pieces of armour laid on the tree. They were now free to look round. The rapid stream had already taken them half a mile below the point where the army were crossing, and they were now entering a spot where the river was broken up by islands, and raced along its pent-up channel with greater velocity than before, its surface broken with short angry waves, which rendered it difficult for them to retain their hold of the tree.

For a time they strove by swimming to give the canoe an impetus towards one bank or the other; but their efforts were vain. Sometimes they thought they were about to succeed, and then an eddy would take the boat and carry it into the middle of the stream again.

"It is useless, Nessus," Malchus said at last. "We are only wearing ourselves out, and our efforts are of no avail whatever. We must be content to drift down the river until our good luck throws us into some eddy which may carry us near one bank or the other."

It was a long time, indeed, before that stroke of fortune befell them, and they were many miles down the river before the current took them near the eastern bank at a point where a sharp curve of the river threw the force of the current over in that direction; but although they were carried to within a few yards of the shore, so numbed and exhausted were they by their long immersion in the cold water that it was with the greatest difficulty that they could give the canoe a sufficient impulsion to carry it to the bank.

At last, however, their feet touched the bottom, and they struggled to shore, carrying with them the arms and armour; then, letting the canoe drift away again, they crawled up the bank, and threw themselves down, utterly exhausted. It was some time before either of them spoke. Then Malchus said:

"We had best strip off our clothes and wring them as well as we can; after that they will soon dry on us. We have no means of drying them here, so we must lie down among some bushes to shelter us from this bitter wind which blows from the mountains."

The clothes were wrung until the last drop was extracted from them and then put on again. They were still damp and cold, but Malchus and his companion had been accustomed to be drenched to the skin, and thought nothing of this. They were still too exhausted, however, to walk briskly, and therefore lay down among some thick bushes until they should feel equal to setting out on the long tramp to rejoin their companions. After lying for a couple of hours Malchus rose to his feet, and issuing from the bushes looked round. He had resumed his armour and sword. As he stepped out a sudden shout arose, and he saw within a hundred yards of him a body of natives some hundred strong approaching. They had already caught sight of him.

"Nessus," he exclaimed, without looking round, "lie still. I am seen, and shall be taken in a minute. It is hopeless for me to try to escape. You will do me more good by remaining hid and trying to free me from their hands afterwards."

So saying, and without drawing his sword, Malchus quietly advanced towards the natives, who were rushing down towards him with loud shouts. Flight or resistance would be, as he had at once seen, hopeless, and it was only by present submission he could hope to save his life.

The natives were a portion of the force which had opposed Hannibal's landing, and had already killed several Carthaginians who had, like Malchus, struggled to the bank after being upset in the passage. Seeing that he attempted neither to fly nor to defend himself, they rushed upon him tumultuously, stripped him of his arms and armour, and dragged him before their leader. The latter briefly ordered him to be brought along, and the party continued their hurried march, fearing that the Carthaginian horse might at any moment pursue them. For the rest of the afternoon they marched without a halt, but at nightfall stopped in a wood.

No fires were lit, for they knew not how close the Carthaginians might be behind them. Malchus was bound hand and foot and thrown down in their midst. There was no sleep that night; half the party remained on watch, the others sat together round the spot where Malchus lay and discussed the disastrous events of the day—the great flotilla of the Carthaginians, the sudden attack in their rear, the destruction of their camp, the capture of the whole of their goods, and the slaughter and defeat which had befallen them.

As their dialect differed but little from that of the Gauls in the Carthaginian service, Malchus was enabled to understand the greater part of their conversation, and learned that the only reason why he was not put to death at once was that they wished to keep him until beyond the risk of pursuit of the Carthaginians, when he could be sacrificed to their gods formally and with the usual ceremonies.

All the time that they were talking Malchus listened anxiously for any sudden outbreak which would tell that Nessus had been discovered. That the Numidian had followed on their traces and was somewhere in the neighbourhood Malchus had no doubt, but rescue in his present position was impossible, and he only hoped that his follower would find that this was so in time and would wait for a more favourable opportunity. The night passed off quietly, and in the morning the natives continued their march. After proceeding for three or four hours a sudden exclamation from one of them caused the others to turn, and in the distance a black mass of horsemen was seen approaching. At a rapid run the natives started off, for the shelter of a wood half a mile distant. Malchus was forced to accompany them. He felt sure that the horsemen were a party of Hannibal's cavalry, and he wondered whether Nessus was near enough to see them, for if so he doubted not that he would manage to join them and lead them to his rescue.

Just before they reached the wood the natives suddenly stopped, for, coming from the opposite direction was another body of cavalry. It needed not the joyous shouts of the natives to tell Malchus that these were Romans, for they were coming from the south and could only be a party of Scipio's cavalry. The natives halted at the edge of the wood to watch the result of the conflict, for the parties evidently saw each other, and both continued to advance at full speed. The Roman trumpets were sounding, while the wild yells which came up on the breeze told Malchus that Hannibal's cavalry were a party of the Numidians.

The Romans were somewhat the most numerous; but, had the cavalry opposed to them consisted of the Carthaginian horse, Malchus would have had little doubt as to the result; he felt, however, by no means certain that the light-armed Numidians were a match for the Roman cavalry. The party had stopped but a quarter of a mile from the spot where the rival bands met, and the crash of bodies driven violently against each other and the clash of steel on armour could be plainly heard.

For a few minutes it was a wild confused mêlée, neither party appearing to have any advantage. Riderless steeds galloped off from the throng, but neither party seemed to give way a foot. The whole mass seemed interlaced in conflict. It was a moving struggling throng of bodies with arms waving high and swords rising and falling. The Romans fought in silence, but the wild yells of the Numidians rose shrill and continuous.

At last there was a movement, and Malchus gave a groan while the natives around him shouted in triumph as the Numidians were seen to detach themselves from the throng and to gallop off at full speed, hotly followed by the Romans, both, however, in greatly diminished numbers, for the ground on which the conflict had taken place was thickly strewn with bodies; nearly half of those who had engaged in that short but desperate strife were lying there.

No sooner had the pursuers and pursued disappeared in the distance than the natives thronged down to the spot. Such of the Numidians as were found to be alive were instantly slaughtered, and all were despoiled of their clothes, arms, and ornaments. The Romans were left untouched, and those among them who were found to be only wounded were assisted by the natives, who unbuckled their armour, helped them into a sitting position, bound up their wounds, and gave them water.

Highly satisfied with the booty they obtained, and having no longer any fear of pursuit, the natives halted to await the return of the Romans. Malchus learned from their conversation that they had some little doubt whether the Romans would approve of their appropriating the spoils of the dead Numidians, and it was finally decided to hand over Malchus, whose rich armour proclaimed him to be a prisoner of importance, to the Roman commander.

The main body of the natives, with all the spoil which had been collected, moved away to the wood, while the chief, with four of his companions and Malchus, remained with the wounded Romans. It was late in the evening before the Romans returned, after having, as has been said, followed the Numidians right up to Hannibal's camp. There was some grumbling on the part of the Roman soldiers when they found that their allies had forestalled them with the spoil; but the officer in command was well pleased at finding that the wounded had been carefully attended to, and bade the men be content that they had rendered good service to the public, and that Scipio would be well satisfied with them. The native chief now exhibited the helmet and armour of Malchus, who was led forward by two of his men.

"Who are you?" the commander asked Malchus in Greek, a language which was understood by the educated both of Rome and Carthage.

"I am Malchus, and command the scouts of Hannibal's army."

"You are young for such a post," the officer said; "but in Carthage it is interest not valour which secures promotion. Doubtless you are related to Hannibal."

"I am his cousin," Malchus said quietly.

"Ah!" the Roman said sarcastically, that accounts for one who is a mere lad being chosen for so important a post. However, I shall take you to Scipio, who will doubtless have questions to ask of you concerning Hannibal's army."

Many of the riderless horses on the plain came in on hearing the sound of the Roman trumpets and rejoined the troop.

Malchus was placed on one of these. Such of the wounded Romans as were able to ride mounted others, and a small party being left behind to look after those unable to move, the troops started on their way.

They were unable, however, to proceed far; the horses had been travelling since morning and were now completely exhausted; therefore, after proceeding a few miles the troop halted. Strong guards were posted, and the men lay down by their horses, ready to mount at a moment's notice, for it was possible that Hannibal might have sent a large body of horsemen in pursuit. As on the night before, Malchus felt that even if Nessus had so far followed him he could do nothing while so strong a guard was kept up, and he therefore followed the example of the Roman soldiers around him and was soon fast asleep.

At daybreak next morning the troops mounted and again proceeded to the south. Late in the afternoon a cloud of dust was seen in the distance, and the party presently rode into the midst of the Roman army, who had made a day's march from their ships and were just halting for the night. The commander of the cavalry at once hastened to Scipio's tent to inform him of the surprising fact that Hannibal had already, in the face of the opposition of the tribes, forced the passage of the Rhone, and that, with the exception of the elephants, which had been seen still on the opposite bank, all the army were across.

Scipio was greatly mortified at the intelligence, for he had deemed it next to impossible that Hannibal could carry his army across so wide and rapid a river in the face of opposition. He had little doubt now that Hannibal's intention was to follow the Rhone down on its left bank to its mouth, and he prepared at once for a battle. Hearing that a prisoner of some importance had been captured, he ordered Malchus to be brought before him. As the lad, escorted by a Roman soldier on each side, was led in, Scipio, accustomed to estimate men, could not but admire the calm and haughty self-possession of his young prisoner. His eye fell with approval upon his active sinewy figure, and the knotted muscles of his arms and legs.

"You are Malchus, a relation of Hannibal, and the commander of the scouts of his army, I hear," Scipio began.

Malchus bowed his head in assent.

"What force has he with him, and what are his intentions?"

"I know nothing of his intentions," Malchus replied quietly; "as to his force, it were better that you inquired of your allies, who saw us pass the river. One of them was brought hither with me, and can tell you what he saw."

"Know you not," Scipio said, "that I can order you to instant execution if you refuse to answer my questions?"

"Of that I am perfectly well aware," Malchus replied; "but I nevertheless refuse absolutely to answer any questions."

"I will give you until to-morrow morning to think the matter over, and if by that time you have not made up your mind to give me the information I require, you die."

So saying he waved his hand to the soldiers, who at once removed Malchus from his presence. He was taken to a small tent a short distance away, food was given to him, and at nightfall chains were attached to his ankles, and from these to the legs of two Roman soldiers appointed to guard him during the night, while a sentry was placed at the entrance. The chains were strong, and fitted so tightly round the ankles that escape was altogether impossible. Even had he possessed arms and could noiselessly have slain the two soldiers, he would be no nearer getting away, for the chains were fastened as securely round their limbs as round his own. Malchus, therefore, at once abandoned any idea of escape, and lying quietly down meditated on his fate in the morning.

CHAPTER XII: AMONG THE PASSES

IT was not until long after the guards to who he was chained had fallen asleep that Malchus followed their example. It seemed to him he had been asleep a long time when a pressure by a hand on his shoulder woke him; at the same moment another hand was placed over his mouth.

"Hush, my lord!" a voice said. It was Nessus. "Arise and let us go. There is no time to be lost, for it is nigh morning. I have been the whole night in discovering where you were."

"But the guards, Nessus?"

"I have killed them," Nessus said in a tone of indifference.

"But I am chained to them by the ankles."

Nessus gave a little exclamation of impatience, and then in the darkness felt the irons to discover the nature of the fastenings. In a minute there was a sound of a dull crashing blow, then Nessus moved to the other side and the sound was repeated. With two blows of his short heavy sword the Arab had cut off the feet of the dead Romans at the ankle, and the chains were free.

"Put on the clothes of this man, my lord, and take his arms; I will take those of the other."

As soon as this was done Nessus wrapped some folds of cloth round each of the chains to prevent their clanking, then passing a band through the ends he fastened them to Malchus' waist.

"Quick, my lord," he said as he finished the work; "daylight is beginning to break."

They stepped over the dead sentry at the door of the tent and were going on when Malchus said:

"Best lift him inside, Nessus; it may be some little time before it is noticed that he is missing from his post."

This was quickly done, and they then moved away quietly among the tents till they approached the rear of the camp. It was now light enough to enable them to see dimly the figures of the Roman sentries placed at short intervals round the camp.

"We cannot get through unseen," Malchus said.

"No, my lord," Nessus replied; "I have wasted too much time in finding you."

"Then we had best lie down quietly here," Malchus said; "in a short time the men will be moving about, and we can then pass through the sentries without remark."

As the light spread over the sky sounds of movement were heard in the camp, and soon figures were moving about, some beginning to make fires, others to attend to their horses. The two Carthaginians moved about among the tents as if similarly occupied, secure that their attire as Roman soldiers would prevent any observation being directed towards them. They were anxious to be off, for they feared that at any moment they might hear the alarm raised on the discovery that the sentry was missing.

It was nearly broad daylight now, and when they saw two or three soldiers pass out between the sentries unquestioned they started at once to follow them. The morning was very cold, and the soldiers who were about were all wearing their military cloaks. Malchus had pulled the irons as high up as he could possibly force them, and they did not show below his cloak.

Walking carelessly along they passed through the sentries, whose duties, now that morning had dawned, related only to discovering an enemy approaching the camp, the soldiers being now free to enter or leave as they pleased.

"It is of no use to go far," Malchus said; "the nearer we hide to the camp the better. We are less likely to be looked for there than at a distance, and it is impossible for me to travel at any speed until I get rid of these heavy irons. As soon as we get over that little brow ahead we shall be out of sight of the sentries, and will take to the first hiding-place we see."

The little rise was but a short distance from camp, the country beyond was open but was covered with low brushwood. As soon as they were over the brow and were assured that none of those who had left the camp before them were in sight, they plunged into the brushwood, and, making their way on their hands and knees for a few hundred yards, lay down in the midst of it.

"They are not likely to search on this side of the camp," Malchus said. "They will not know at what hour I escaped, and will naturally suppose that I started at once to regain our camp. Listen, their trumpets are blowing. No doubt they are about to strike their camp and march; by this time my escape must be known. And now tell me, Nessus, how did you manage to follow and discover me?"

"It was easy to follow you, my lord," Nessus said. "When I heard your order I lay still, but watched through the bushes your meeting with the Gauls. My arrow was in the string, and had they attacked you I should have loosed it among them, and then rushed out to die with you, but when I saw them take you a prisoner I followed your orders. I had no difficulty in keeping you in sight until nightfall. Then I crept up to the wood and made my way until I was within a few yards of you and lay there till nearly morning; but, as the men around you never went to sleep, I could do nothing and stole away again before daylight broke. Then I followed again until I saw our horsemen approaching. I had started to run towards them to lead them to you when I saw the Roman horse, and I again hid myself.

"The next night again the Romans kept too vigilant a watch for me to do anything, and I followed them all yesterday until I saw them enter the Roman camp. As soon as it was dark I entered, and, getting into the part of the camp occupied by the Massilians, whose Gaulish talk I could understand a little, I gathered that a Carthaginian prisoner who had been brought in was to be executed in the morning. So I set to work to find you; but the night was too dark to see where the sentries were placed, and I had to crawl round every tent to see if one stood at the entrance on guard, for I was sure that a sentry would be placed over you. I entered seven tents, at whose doors sentries were placed, before I found yours, but they were all those of Roman generals or persons of importance. I entered each time by cutting a slit in the back of the tent. At last when I was beginning to despair, I found your tent.

"It was the smallest of any that had been guarded, and this made me think I was right. When I crawled in I found feeling cautiously about, that two Roman soldiers were asleep on the ground and that you were lying between them. Then I went to the entrance. The sentry was standing with his back to it. I struck a blow on his neck from behind, and he died without knowing he was hurt. I caught him as I struck and lowered him gently down, for the crash of his arms as he fell would have roused everyone near. After that it was easy to stab the two guards sleeping by you, and then I woke you."

"You have saved my life, Nessus, and I shall never forget it," Malchus said gratefully.

"My life is my lord's," the Arab replied simply. "Glad am I indeed that I have been able to do you a service."

Just as he spoke they saw through the bushes a party of Roman horse ride at a gallop over the brow between them and the camp. They halted, however, on passing the crest, and an officer with them gazed long and searchingly over the country. For some minutes he sat without speaking, then be gave an order and the horsemen rode back again over the crest."

"I think we shall see no more of them," Malchus said. "His orders were, no doubt, that if I was in sight they were to pursue, if not, it would be clearly useless hunting over miles of brushwood in the hope of finding me, especially as they must deem it likely that I am far away in the opposite direction."

An hour later Nessus crept cautiously forward among the bushes, making a considerable detour until he reached the spot whence he could command a view of the Roman camp. It had gone, not a soul remained behind, but at some distance across the plain he could see the heavy column marching north. He rose to his feet and returned to the spot where he had left Malchus, and told him that the Romans had gone.

"The first thing, Nessus, is to get rid of these chains."

"It is easy as to the chains," Nessus said, "but the rings around your legs must remain until we rejoin the camp, it will need a file to free you from them."

The soil was sandy, and Nessus could find no stone sufficiently large for his purpose. They, therefore, started in the direction which the Romans had taken until, after two hours' slow walking, they came upon the bed of a stream in which were some boulders sufficiently large for the purpose.

The rings were now pushed down again to the ankles, and Nessus wound round them strips of cloth until he had formed a pad between the iron and the skin to lessen the jar of the blow, then he placed the link of the chain near to the leg upon the edge of the boulder, and, drawing his sharp heavy sword, struck with all his force upon the iron.

A deep notch was made; again and again he repeated the blow, until the link was cut through, then, with some difficulty, he forced the two ends apart until the shackle of the ring would pass between them. The operation was repeated on the other chain, and then Malchus was free, save for the two iron rings around his ankles. The work had taken upwards of an hour, and when it was done they started at a rapid walk in the direction taken by the column. They had no fear now of the natives, for should any come upon them they would take them for two Roman soldiers who had strayed behind the army.

Scipio made a long day's march, and it was not until nightfall that his army halted. Malchus and his companion made a long detour round the camp and continued their way for some hours, then they left the track that the army would follow, and, after walking for about a mile, lay down among some bushes and were soon asleep.

In the morning they agreed that before proceeding further it was absolutely necessary to obtain some food. Malchus had been fed when among the Romans, but Nessus had had nothing from the morning when he had been upset in the Rhone four days before, save a manchet of bread which he had found in one of the tents he had entered. Surveying the country round carefully, the keen eye of the Arab perceived some light smoke curling up at the foot of the hills on their right, and they at once directed their course towards it. An hour's walking brought them within sight of a native village.

As soon as they perceived it they dropped on their hands and knees and proceeded with caution until within a short distance of it. They were not long in discovering a flock of goats browsing on the verdure in some broken ground a few hundred yards from the village. They were under the charge of a native boy, who was seated on a rock near them. They made their way round among the brushwood until they were close to the spot.

"Shall I shoot him?" Nessus asked, for he had carried his bow and arrows concealed in his attire as a Roman soldier.

"No, no," Malchus replied, "the lad has done us no harm; but we must have one of his goats. His back is towards us, and, if we wait, one of them is sure to come close to us presently."

They lay quiet among the bushes until, after a delay of a quarter of an hour, a goat, browsing upon the bushes, passed within a yard or two of them.

Nessus let fly his arrow; it passed almost through the animal, right behind its shoulder, and it fell among the bushes. In an instant Nessus was upon it, and, grasping its mouth tightly to prevent it from bleating, cut its throat. They dragged it away until a fall in the ground hid them from the sight of the natives, then they quickly skinned and cut it up, devoured some of the meat raw, and then, each taking a leg of the animal, proceeded upon their way.

They now walked without a halt until, late in the evening, they came down upon the spot where the Carthaginian army had crossed. It was deserted. Going down to the edge of the river they saw the great rafts upon which the elephants had crossed.

"We had best go on a mile or two ahead," Nessus said, "the Roman cavalry may be here in the morning, though the column will be still a day's march away. By daylight we shall have no difficulty in finding the traces of the army."

Malchus took the Arab's advice, and the next morning followed on the traces of the army, which were plainly enough to be seen in the broken bushes, the trampled ground, and in various useless articles dropped or thrown away by the troops. They were forced to advance with caution, for they feared meeting any of the natives who might be hanging on the rear of the army.

AMONG THE PASSES

After three days' travelling with scarce a pause they came upon the army just as the rear-guard was crossing the Isére, and Malchus received a joyous welcome from his friends, who had supposed him drowned at the passage of the Rhone. His account of his adventure was eagerly listened to, and greatly surprised were they when they found that he had been a prisoner in the camp of Scipio, and had been rescued by the fidelity and devotion of Nessus. Hannibal asked many questions as to the strength of Scipio's army, but Malchus could only say that, not having seen it except encamped, he could form but a very doubtful estimate as to its numbers, but considered it to be but little superior to that of the Carthaginian.

"I do not think Scipio will pursue us," Hannibal said. "A defeat here would be as fatal to him as it would be to us, and I think it more likely that, when he finds we have marched away north, he will return to his ships and meet us in Italy."

Malchus learned that everything had progressed favourably since the army had crossed the Rhone, the natives having offered no further opposition to their advance. A civil war was going on in the region the army had now entered, between two rival princes, brothers, of the Allobroges. Hannibal was requested to act as umpire in the quarrel, and decided in favour of the elder brother and restored order. In return he received from the prince whom he reseated on his throne, provisions, clothing, and other necessaries for the army, and the prince, with his troops, escorted the Carthaginians some distance up into the Alps, and prevented the tribes dwelling at the foot of the mountains from attacking them.

The conquest of Catalonia, the passage of the Pyrenees, and the march across the south of Gaul, had occupied many months. Summer had come and gone, autumn had passed, and winter was at hand. It was the eighteenth of October when Hannibal led his army up the narrow valleys into the heart of the Alps. The snow had already fallen thickly upon the upper part of the mountains, and the Carthaginians shuddered at the sight of these lofty summits, these wild, craggy, and forbidding wastes.

The appearance of the wretched huts of the inhabitants, of the people themselves, unshaved and unkempt and clad in sheepskins, and of the flocks and herds gathering in sheltered spots and crowding together to resist the effects of the already extreme cold, struck the Carthaginian troops with dismay. Large bodies of the mountaineers were perceived posted on the heights surrounding the valleys, and the column, embarrassed by its length and the vast quantity of baggage, was also exposed to attack by hordes who might at any moment rush out from the lateral ravines. Hannibal, therefore, ordered his column to halt.

Malchus was now ordered to go forward with his band of scouts, and to take with him a party of Gauls, who, their language being similar to that of the natives, could enter into conversation with them. The mountaineers, seeing but a small party advancing, allowed them to approach peaceably and entered freely into conversation with them. They declared that they would on no account permit the Carthaginian army to pass forward, but would oppose every foot of their advance.

The Gauls learned, however, that, believing the great column could only move forward in the daytime, the natives were in the habit of retiring from their rocky citadels at nightfall. Malchus returned with this news to Hannibal, who prepared to take advantage of it. The camp was at once pitched, and the men set to work to form an intrenchment round it as if Hannibal meditated a prolonged halt there. Great fires were lit and the animals unloaded. The natives, seeing from above everything that was being done, deserted their posts as usual at nightfall, confident that the Carthaginians had no intention of moving forward.

Malchus with his scouts crept on along the path, and soon sent down word to Hannibal that the heights were deserted. The general himself now moved forward with all his light troops, occupied the head of the pass, and posted strong parties of men upon the heights commanding it. As soon as day broke the rest of the army got into motion and proceeded up the pass. The natives were now seen approaching in great numbers, but they halted in dismay on seeing that the Carthaginians had already gained possession of the strong places.

The road by which the column was ascending wound along the face of a precipice, and was so narrow that it was with difficulty that the horses, snorting with fright, could be persuaded to proceed. The natives, seeing the confusion which the fright of the animals created in the column, at once took to the mountains, climbing up rugged precipices which appeared to the Carthaginians absolutely inaccessible, and presently made their appearance far up on the mountain side above the column.

Here, sending up the most piercing yells, they began to roll rocks and stones down upon the column. The confusion below became terrible. The horses, alarmed by the strange wild cries, echoed and re-echoed a score of times among the mountains, and struck by the falling stones, plunged and struggled wildly to escape. Some tore along the path, precipitating those in front of them over the precipice, others lost their footing, and, dragging with them the carts to which they were attached, fell into the valley below. All order was lost. Incapable of defence or of movement the column appeared to be on the verge of destruction.

"Come, my men," Malchus exclaimed to his Arabs, "where these men can climb we can follow them; the safety of the whole column is at stake."

Slinging their weapons behind them the scouts began to climb the crags. Sure-footed and hardy as they were, it was with the greatest difficulty that they could make their way up. Many lost their footing, and rolling down were dashed to pieces; but the great majority succeeded in climbing the heights, and at once became engaged in desperate battle with the natives.

Every narrow ledge and crag was the scene of a conflict. The natives from the distant heights encouraged their companions with their shouts, and for a time the confusion in the column below was heightened by the combat which was proceeding far above them. Every stone dislodged by the feet of the combatants thundered down upon them, and the falling bodies of those hit by arrow or javelin came crushing down with a dull thud among the mass.

At last the bravery and superior weapons of the Arabs prevailed. The precipice was cleared of the natives, and as the uproar ceased and the missiles ceased to fall, the column recovered its order, and again moved forward until the whole army gained the top of the pass. Here Hannibal took possession of a rough fort erected by the natives, captured several villages, and enough flocks and herds to feed his army for three days. Then descending from the top of the pass, which is now known as the Col-du-Chat, he entered the valley of Chambery, and marched forward for three days without opposition.

Malchus and his scouts received the warmest congratulations for their conduct at the pass, for they had undoubtedly saved the army from what had at one time threatened to be a terrible disaster. On arrival at a town supposed to be identical with the modern Conflans, the inhabitants came out with green boughs and expressed their desire for peace and friendship. They said that they had heard of the fate which had befallen those who ventured to oppose the Carthaginians, and that they were anxious to avoid such misfortunes. They offered to deliver hostages as a proof of their good intentions, to supply sheep and goats for the army, and to furnish guides through the difficult country ahead.

For two days the march continued. The route the army was passing was that now known as the Little St. Bernard. Fortunately Hannibal had from the first entertained considerable doubt as to the good faith of his guides, and never relaxed his vigilance. The scouts and light infantry, with the cavalry, preceded the great column of baggage, the heavy cavalry defended the rear.

The track, which had for the last five days' march proceeded along a comparatively level valley, now mounted rapidly, and turning aside from the valley of the Isére it led up the deep bed of the mountain torrent known as the Reclus; this stream ran in a deep trough hollowed out in a very narrow valley. The bed is now so piled with rocks and stones as to be impassable, and the Romans afterwards cut a road along on the side of the mountain. But at this time it was possible for men and animals to proceed along the bed of the torrent.

Suddenly while struggling with the difficulties of the ascent, a vast number of the natives appeared on the hills on either side, and began to hurl down stones and rocks upon the column below, while at the same time a still stronger force attacked them in the rear. The instant the natives made their appearance the treacherous guides, who were proceeding with the scouts at the head of the column, attempted to make their escape by climbing the mountain side. The Arabs were starting off in pursuit, but Malchus checked them.

"Keep together," he shouted, "and on no account scatter; the enemy are upon us in force, and it behoves us all to be steady and deliberate in our action."

A flight of arrows was, however, sent after the traitors, and most of them rolled lifeless down the slope again.

Hannibal's first care was to extricate his cavalry from the gorge. This was performed with great difficulty, and they were drawn up in good order on the narrow piece of level ground between the gorge in which the river ran and the mountains bordering the side of the pass.

The light troops now ascended the hills on both sides, and speedily became engaged with the enemy. The confusion in the bed of the torrent was tremendous. Great numbers of men and animals were killed by the rocks and missiles from above, but more of the soldiers were trampled to death by the frightened horses. The heavy infantry in the rear remained steady, and repulsed every effort of the main body of the enemy to break in upon the column.

As night fell the combat ceased, but Hannibal and the troops in advance of the column passed the night under arms at the foot of a certain white rock standing above the ravine, and which still marks the exact site of the conflict. The natives had suffered heavily both from their conflict with the light troops upon the hillside, and from the repulse of their assaults upon the rear-guard, and in the morning they did not venture to renew the attack, and the column moved forward out of the ravine and continued its march, the natives from time to time dashing down to attack it.

The elephants were placed on the flank of the line of march, and the appearance of these strange beasts so terrified the enemy that they desisted from their attack, and by evening the army encamped on the summit of the pass.

The snow had already fallen deeply, the army were worn out and dispirited by the exertions and dangers through which they had passed, and had suffered great losses in men and animals in the nine days which had elapsed since they first entered the mountains. Hannibal gave them two days' rest, in which time they were joined by many stragglers who had fallen behind, and by beasts of burden which, in the terror and confusion of the attack, had got rid of their loads and had escaped, but whose instinct led them to follow the line of march.

At the end of the second day Hannibal assembled his troops and addressed them in a stirring speech. He told them that the worst part of their journey was now over. He pointed to them the plains of Italy, of which a view could be obtained through the pass ahead, and told them that there they would find rest and friends, wealth and glory. The soldiers as usual responded to the words of their beloved general with shouts of acclamation, and with renewed spirits prepared to meet the difficulties which still lay before them.

The next morning the march was renewed. The snow lay deep on the track, and the soldiers found that, great as had been the difficulties of the ascent, those of the descent were vastly greater, for the slopes of the Alps on the Italian side are far steeper and more abrupt than are those on the French. Every step had to be made with care; those who strayed in the slightest from the path found the snow gave way beneath their feet and fell down the precipice beside them.

Many of the baggage animals thus perished; but at last the head of the column found itself at the foot of the steep descent in a ravine with almost perpendicular walls, amid whose foot was in summer occupied by a mountain stream. Into the depth of this ravine the rays of the sun never penetrated, and in it lay a mass of the previous year's snow which had never entirely melted, but which formed with the water of the torrent a sheet of slippery ice.

The newly formed snow prevented the troops from seeing the nature of the ground, and as they stepped upon it they fell headlong, sliding in their armour down the rapidly sloping bed of ice, many dashing out their brains or breaking their limbs against the great boulders which projected through it. The cavalry next attempted the passage, but with even less success, for the hoofs of the horses broke through the hard upper crust of the old snow and the animals sank in to their bellies. Seeing that it was impossible to pass this obstacle, Hannibal turned back the head of the column until they reached the top of the ascent down which they had just come. There he cleared away the snow and erected a camp; all the infantry were then brought down into the pass and set to work to build up a road along the side of the ravine.

The engineers with fire and explosives blasted away the foot of the cliffs; the infantry broke up the rocks and formed a level track. All night the work continued, the troops relieving each other at frequent intervals, and by the morning a path which could be traversed by men on foot, horses, and baggage animals was constructed for a distance of three hundred yards, beyond which the obstacle which had arrested the advance of the army did not continue.

The cavalry, baggage animals, and a portion of the infantry at once continued their way down the valley, while the rest of the infantry remained behind to widen the road sufficiently for the elephants to pass along. Although the work was pressed on with the greatest vigour it needed three days of labour in all before the elephants could be passed through. The animals were by this time weak with hunger, for from the time when they had turned aside from the valley of the Isére the Alps had been wholly bare of trees, and the ground being covered with snow, no foliage or forage had been obtainable to eke out the store of flour which they carried for their consumption. Nor was any wood found with which to manufacture the flat cakes into which the flour was formed for their rations.

The elephants once through, the march was continued, and, joining the troops in advance, who had halted in the woods below the snow level, the column continued its march. On the third day after passing the gorge they issued out on to the plain of the Po, having lost in the fifteen days' passage of the Alps great numbers of men from the attacks of the enemy, from the passage of the rapid torrents, from falls over the precipices, and from cold, and having suffered still more severely in horses and baggage animals.

THE YOUNG CARTHAGINIAN

Of the 59,000 picked troops with which he had advanced after the conqest of Catalonia, Hannibal reached the plains of Italy with but 12,000 African infantry, 8,000 Spanish and Gaulish infantry, and 6,000 cavalry—in all 26,000 men. A small force indeed with which to enter upon the struggle with the might and power of Rome. Of the 33,000 men that were missing, 13,000 had fallen in the passes of the Pyrenees and the march through Gaul, 20,000 had died in the passage of the Alps.

THE YOUNG CARTHAGINIAN

CHAPTER XIII: THE BATTLE OF THE TREBIA

WELL was it for the Carthaginians that Hannibal had opened communications with the Gaulish tribes in the plains at the foot of the Alps, and that on its issue from the mountain passes his army found itself among friends, for had it been attacked it was in no position to offer a vigorous resistance, the men being utterly broken down by their fatigues and demoralized by their losses. Many were suffering terribly from frost-bites, the cavalry were altogether unable to act, so worn out and enfeebled were the horses. Great numbers of the men could scarce drag themselves along owing to the state of their feet; their shoes and sandals, well enough adapted for sandy plains, were wholly unfitted for traversing rocky precipices, and the greater part of the army was almost barefoot.

So long as they had been traversing the mountains they had struggled on doggedly and desperately; to lag behind was to be slain by the natives, to lie down was to perish of cold; but with the cessation of the absolute necessity for exertion the power for exertion ceased also. Worn-out, silent, exhausted, and almost despairing, the army of Hannibal presented the appearance of one which had suffered a terrible defeat, rather than that of a body of men who had accomplished a feat of arms unrivalled in the history of war.

Happily they found themselves among friends. The Insubres, who had been looking forward eagerly to their coming, flocked in great numbers to receive them as they issued out into the plain, bringing with them cattle, grain, wine, and refreshments of all kinds, and inviting the army to take up their quarters among them until recovered from their fatigues. This offer Hannibal at once accepted. The army was broken up and scattered among the various towns and villages, where the inhabitants vied with each other in attending to the comforts of the guests. A fortnight's absolute rest, an abundance of food, and the consciousness that the worst of their labours was over, did wonders for the men.

Malchus had arrived in a state of extreme exhaustion, and had, indeed, been carried for the last two days of the march on the back of one of the elephants. The company which he commanded no longer existed; they had borne far more than their share of the fatigues of the march; they had lost nearly half their number in the conflict among the precipices with the natives, and while the rest of the army had marched along a track where the snow had already been beaten hard by the cavalry in front of them, the scouts ahead had to make their way through snow knee-deep. Inured to fatigue and hardship the Arabs were unaccustomed to cold, and every day had diminished their numbers, until, as they issued out into the plain, but twenty men of the company remained alive.

Hannibal committed his young kinsman to the care of one of the chiefs of the Insubres. The latter caused a litter to be constructed by his followers, and carried the young Carthaginian away to his village, which was situated at the foot of the hills on the banks of the river Orcus.

Here he was handed over to the care of the women. The wounds and bruises caused by falls on the rocks and ice were bathed and bandaged, then he was placed in a small chamber and water was poured on to heated stones until it was filled with hot steam, and Malchus began to think that he was going to be boiled alive. After being kept for an hour in this vapour bath, he was annointed with oil, and was rubbed until every limb was supple, he was then placed on a couch and covered with soft skins, and in a few more minutes was sound asleep.

It was late next day before he woke, and on rising he found himself a new man. A breakfast of meat, fresh cheese formed from goats' milk, and flat cakes was set before him, and, had it not been that his feet were still completely disabled from the effects

The Insurbrian chief's daughters nurse Malchus

of the frost-bites, he felt that he was fit again to take his place in the ranks. The chief's wife and daughters waited upon him. The former was a tall, majestic-looking woman. She did not belong to the Insubres, but was the daughter of a chief who had, with a portion of his tribe, wandered down from their native home far north of the Alps and settled in Italy.

Two of the daughters were young women of over twenty, tall and robust in figure like their mother, the third was a girl of some fifteen years of age. The girls took after their German mother, and Malchus wondered at the fairness of their skins, the clearness of their complexion, and the soft light brown of their hair, for they were as much fairer than the Gauls as these were fairer than the Carthaginians. Malchus was able to hold little converse with his hosts, whose language differed much from that of the Transalpine Gauls.

His stay here was destined to be much longer than he had anticipated, for his feet had been seriously frost-bitten, and for some time it was doubtful whether he would not lose them. Gradually, however, the inflammation decreased, but it was six weeks after his arrival before he was able to walk. From time to time messengers had arrived from Hannibal and his father to inquire after him, and from them he learned that the Carthaginians had captured the towns of Vercella, Valentinum, and Asta, and the less important towns of Ivrea, Chivasso, Bodenkmag, and Carbantia.

By the time be was cured he was able to talk freely with his hosts, for he soon mastered the points of difference between their language and that of the Gauls, with which he was already acquainted. The chief, with the greater part of his followers, now started and joined the army of Hannibal, which laid siege to the town of Turin, whose inhabitants were in alliance with Rome. It was strongly fortified. Hannibal erected an intrenchment at a distance of sixty yards from the wall, and under cover of this sank a well, and thence drove a wide gallery, the roof above being supported by props.

Divided in brigades, each working six hours, the troops laboured night and day, and in three days from its commencement the gallery was carried under the walls. It was then driven right and left for thirty yards each way, and was filled with wood, combustibles, and explosives. The workers then retired and the wood was fired, the props supporting the roof were soon burned away, the earth above fell in bringing down the walls, and a great breach was made, through which the besiegers, drawn up in readiness, rushed in and captured the town.

On the same day that Hannibal captured Turin, Scipio entered Piacenza. After finding that Hannibal had escaped him on the Rhone, he had despatched the principal part of his army, under his brother Cneius, to Spain, their original destination, and with the rest sailed to Pisa and landed there. Marching with all haste north he enlisted 10,000 troops from among the inhabitants of the country, many of them having already served in the Roman army. He then marched north to Tenneto, where he was joined by the prætors Manlius and Attilius with over 20,000 men, with whom he marched to Piacenza.

Hannibal, after, as usual, rousing the enthusiasm of his soldiers by an address, marched towards Scipio. The latter, with his cavalry, had crossed the Ticino and was within five miles of Vercella, when Hannibal, also with his cavalry, came within sight. Scipio's front was covered with a swarm of foot skirmishers mixed with irregular Gaulish horsemen; the Roman cavalry and the cavalry of the Italian allies formed his main body.

Hannibal ordered the Carthaginian horse to charge full upon the centre of the enemy, and the Numidians to attack them on both flanks. The Romans, in those days, little understood the use of cavalry, the troops frequently dismounting and fighting on foot; Hannibal's soldiers were, on the other hand, trained to fight in tactics resembling those of modern days. No sooner was the word given to charge than the Carthaginian horse, delighted at being at last, after all their toils and sufferings, within striking distance of their foes, gave a mighty shout, and setting spurs to their splendid horses flung themselves at the enemy.

The charge of this solid mass of picked cavalry was irresistible. They swept before them the skirmishers and Gaulish horse, and fell with fury upon the main body, cleaving a way far into its ranks. Before the Romans could recover from their confusion the Numidian horse burst down upon their flanks. The charge was irresistible; large numbers of the Romans were killed and the rest fled in panic, hotly pursued by the Carthaginians, until they reached the shelter of the Roman infantry, which was advancing behind them. Scipio, who had been wounded in the fight, at once led his army back to Piacenza.

The news of this battle reached Malchus just as he was preparing to depart; the messenger who brought it brought also a lead horse, which Hamilcar had sent for his son's use. Resuming his armour Malchus mounted and rode off at once, after many warm thanks to his friends, whom he expected to see again shortly, as they, with the rest of that section of the tribe, were about to join the chief—the Gaulish women frequently accompanying their husbands in their campaigns.

Malchus was delighted to rejoin the army, from which he had now been separated more than two months. He saw with pleasure that they had now completely recovered from the effects of their hardships, and presented as proud and martial an appearance as when they had started from Carthagena.

The issue of their first fight with the Romans had raised their spirits and confidence, and all were eager to enter upon the campaign which awaited them. Malchus, upon his arrival, was appointed to the command of the company of Gauls who formed the body-guard of the general. Hannibal moved up the Po and prepared to cross that river at Cambio, two days' easy march above its junction with the Ticino. The army was accompanied by a considerable number of the Insubres. The work of constructing a bridge was at once commenced.

Malchus, riding through the camp, came upon the tents of his late host, who had been joined that day by his family. To them Malchus did the honours of the camp, took them through the lines of the Carthaginian cavalry, showed them the elephants, and finally conducted them to Hannibal, who received them most kindly, and presented them with many presents in token of his thanks for their care of his kinsman. The next day the bridge was completed and the troops began to pass over, the natives crowding to the banks and even venturing on the bridge to witness the imposing procession of the troops.

Malchus remained with Hannibal in the rear, but seeing

that there was a delay as the elephants crossed, he was ordered to ride on to the bridge and see what was the matter. Finding the crowd too great to enable him to pass on horseback, Malchus gave his horse to a soldier and pressed forward on foot. When he reached the head of the column of elephants he found that one of the leading animals, entertaining a doubt as to the stability of the bridge at this point, obstinately refused to move further. Ordering the mahout to urge the animal forward, and telling some soldiers to prick the beast with a spear from behind, Malchus entered into conversation with the wife and daughters of the Insubrian chief, who had received from Hannibal a special order allowing them to take up their position on the bridge to witness their crossing.

While he was speaking to them the elephant suddenly wheeled round and, trumpeting loudly, tried to force his way back. A scene of wild confusion ensued. The crowd gave way before him, several soldiers were thrust off the bridge into the river, and Malchus and his companions were borne along by the crowd; there was a little cry, and Malchus saw the youngest of the girls pushed off the bridge into the river.

He flung off his helmet, unbuckled the fastenings of his breastplate and back-piece, undid the belt of his sword, and leaped in. As he rose to the surface he heard a merry laugh beside him, and saw the girl swimming quietly close by. Although mortified at having so hastily assumed that she was unable to take care of herself he joined in her laugh, and swam by her side until they reached the bank some distance down. Encumbered by the trappings which he still retained, Malchus had far more difficulty than the girl in gaining the shore.

"What, did you think," she asked, laughing as he struggled up the bank, "that I, a Gaulish maiden, could not swim?"

"I did not think anything about it," Malchus said; "I saw you pushed in and followed without thinking at all."

Although they imperfectly understood each other's words the meaning was clear; the girl put her hand on his shoulder and looked frankly up in his face.

"I thank you," she said, "just the same as if you had saved my life. You meant to do so, and it was very good of you, a great chief of this army, to hazard your life for a Gaulish maiden. Clotilde will never forget."

By the time they reached the bridge the column had moved on. A more docile elephant had been placed in front, and this having moved across the doubtful portion of the bridge, the others had quickly followed. Just as Malchus and his companion reached the end of the bridge they met her mother and sisters coming to meet them.

There was a smile of amusement on their faces as they thanked Malchus for his attempt at rescue, and Clotilde's sisters whispered some laughing remarks into her ear which caused the girl to flush hotly, and to draw her slight figure indignantly to its full height. Malchus retired to his tent to provide himself with fresh armour and sword, for he doubted not that those thrown aside had been carried over the bridge in the confusion. The soldier had returned with his horse, and in a few minutes he took his place at the head of the Gauls who were drawn up near Hannibal's tent.

The general himself soon appeared, and mounting his horse rode forward. Malchus followed with his command, waving an adieu to the party who stood watching the departure, and not ill-pleased that those who had before known him only as a helpless invalid, should now see him riding at the head of the splendid body-guard of the great commander.

Hannibal was marching nearly due east, with the intention of forcing Scipio to give battle south of the Po. A strong Roman fortress, Casteggio (Clastidium), lying at the foot of the hills, should have barred his way; but Hannibal, by the medium of one of his native allies, bribed the Roman commander to abstain from interrupting his march. Then he pressed forward until on the third day after crossing the Po he came within sight of Piacenza, under whose walls the Roman army were ranged.

Scipio, after his disastrous cavalry conflict, had written to Rome urging his inability, with the force under his command, to give battle single-handed to Hannibal, and begging that he might be at once reinforced by the army under Sempronius, then lying at Ariminum (Rimini). The united consular armies, he represented, should take up their position on the river Trebia.

THE BATTLE OF TREBIA

This river rose in the Apennines but a short distance from Genoa, and flowed nearly due north into the Po at Piacenza. The Roman army there would therefore effectually bar Hannibal's march into the rich plains to the east, and would prevent him from making across the Apennines and following the road by the coast, as they would, should he undertake such a movement, be able to fall on his rear.

Hannibal pitched his camp on the Nure, about five miles from Piacenza, but Scipio remained immovable in his lines waiting for the arrival of his colleague. Hannibal's position was a difficult one. He had traversed the Pyrenees and the Alps that he might attack Rome; but between him and Southern Italy lay yet another barrier, the Apennines. Scipio had missed him after he had crossed the Pyrenees, had been too late to attack him when, exhausted and worn out, his army emerged from the Alps; but now, united with Sempronius, he hoped to crush him at the foot of the Apennines. Hannibal wished, if possible, to prevent a junction of the two Roman armies, but if that could not be done he determined to fight them together.

Scipio perceived the danger of his position; and in order to be able the better to join Sempronius he left Piacenza under cover of night, and took up a strong position on the banks of the Trebia. Here he could maintain his communications direct with Rome, and, if absolutely necessary, fall back and join his colleague advancing towards him. Hannibal, when he perceived Scipio's change of position, broke up his camp and took post on the Trebiola, a little stream running into the Trebia and facing the Roman camp at a distance of four miles.

He was now powerless to prevent the junction of the two Roman armies, and for nearly a month Scipio and Hannibal lay watching each other. By that time Sempronius was within a day's march of Scipio. Hannibal had not been idle during this time of rest. He had been occupied in cementing his alliance with the Gaulish tribes inhabiting the Lombard plains. These, seeing how rapidly Hannibal had cleared the province of the Romans, believed that their deliverance would be accomplished, and for the most part declared for the Carthaginians.

Hannibal's agents had also been at work at Clastidium, and

the prefect of the garrison was induced by a bribe to surrender the place to him. This was of enormous advantage to Hannibal, and a corresponding blow to the Romans, for Clastidium was the chief magazine north of the Apennines. The news of the fall of this important place filled Sempronius, an energetic and vigorous general, with fury. He at once rode down from his camp to that of Scipio and proposed that Hannibal should be attacked instantly.

Scipio, who was still suffering from the wound he had received in the cavalry engagement, urged that the Roman army should remain where they were, if necessary, through the coming winter. He pointed out that Hannibal's Gaulish allies would lose heart at seeing him inactive, and would cease to furnish him with supplies, and that he would be obliged either to attack them at a disadvantage or to retire from the position he occupied. But Sempronius was an ambitious man, the time for the consular election was approaching, and he was unwilling to leave for his successor the glory of crushing Hannibal.

The fact, too, that Scipio was wounded and unable to take part in the battle added to his desire to force it on, since the whole glory of the victory would be his. He therefore told his colleague that although he saw the force of his arguments, public opinion in Rome was already so excited at Hannibal having been allowed, without a battle, to wrest so wide a territory from Rome, that it was absolutely necessary that an action should be fought. The two armies were now united on the Trebia; and opinion was among the officers and troops, as between the consuls, widely divided as to the best course to be pursued.

Hannibal's spies among the natives kept him acquainted with what was going on in the Roman camp, and he determined to provoke the Romans to battle. He therefore despatched two thousand infantry and a thousand cavalry to ravage the lands of some Gaulish allies of the Romans. Sempronius sent off the greater part of his cavalry, with a thousand light infantry, to drive back the Carthaginians.

In the fight which ensued the Romans were worsted. Still more furious, Sempronius marched to support them with his army. Hannibal called in his troops and drew them off before

Sempronius would arrive. The disappointment and rage of the Roman general were great, and Hannibal felt that he could now bring on a battle when he would. He determined to fight in the plain close to his own position. This was flat and bare, and was traversed by the Trebiola. This stream ran between steep banks below the level of the plain; its banks were covered with thick bushes and reeds, and the narrow gap across the plain was scarce noticeable.

On the evening of the twenty-fifth of December Hannibal moved his army out from the camp and formed up on the plain facing the Trebia, ordering the corps commanded by his brother Mago to enter the bed of the Trebiola, and to conceal themselves there until they received his orders to attack. The position Mago occupied would bring him on the left rear of an army which had crossed the Trebia, and was advancing to attack the position taken up by Hannibal. Having thus prepared for the battle, Hannibal proceeded to provoke it.

At daybreak on the twenty-sixth he despatched a strong body of horsemen across the river. Crossing the Trebia partly by ford and partly by swimming, the Carthaginian horse rode up to the palisade surrounding the Roman camp, where, with insulting shouts and the hurling of their javelins, they aroused the Roman soldiers from their slumber. This insult had the desired effect, Sempronius rushed from his tent, furious at what he deemed the insolence of the Carthaginians, and called his troops to arms. With their accustomed discipline the Romans fell into their ranks. The light cavalry first issued from the palisade, the infantry followed, the heavy cavalry brought up the rear. The insulting Numidians had already retired, but Sempronius was now determined to bring on the battle. He marched down the river and crossed at a ford.

The water was intensely cold, the river was in flood, the ford waist-deep as the soldiers marched across it. Having gained the opposite bank, the Roman general formed his army in order of battle. His infantry, about forty-five thousand strong, was formed in three parallel lines; the cavalry, five thousand strong, was on the flanks. The infantry consisted of sixteen thousand Roman legionary or heavy infantry, and six thousand light infantry. The Italian tribes, allied to Rome, had supplied twenty thousand infantry; the remaining three thousand were native allies. The infantry occupied a front of two and a half miles in length; the cavalry extended a mile and a quarter on each flank. Thus the Roman front of battle was five miles in extent.

Hannibal's force was inferior in strength; his infantry of the line were twenty thousand strong. He had eight thousand light infantry and ten thousand cavalry. The Carthaginian formation was much deeper than the Roman, and Hannibal's line of battle was less than two miles long. In front of it were the elephants, thirty-six in number, divided in pairs, and placed in intervals of a hundred yards between each pair.

While the Romans, exposed to a bitterly cold wind, chilled to the bone by their immersion in the stream, and having come breakfastless from camp, were forming their long order of battle, Hannibal's troops, gathered round blazing fires, were eating a hearty breakfast; after which, in high spirits and confidence, they prepared for the fight.

Hannibal called the officers together and addressed them in stirring words, which were repeated by them to the soldiers. The Roman preparations had occupied a long time, and it was afternoon before they advanced in order of battle. When within a short distance of the Carthaginians they halted, and the trumpets and musical instruments on both sides blew notes of defiance. Then the Carthaginian slingers stole out between the ranks of their heavy infantry, passed between the elephants, and commenced the battle.

Each of these men carried three slings, one of which was used for long distances, another when nearer to the foe, the third when close at hand. In action one of these slings was wound round the head, one round the body, the third carried in hand. Their long-distance missiles were leaden bullets, and so skilful were they that it is said they could hit with certainty the face of a foe standing at slinging distance.

Naked to the waist they advanced, and with their long-distance slings hurled the leaden bullets at the Roman infantry. When closer they exchanged their slings and discharged from them egg-shaped pebbles which they had gathered from the bed

THE BATTLE OF TREBIA

of the Trebia. When within still closer distance with the third slings they poured in volleys of much larger and heavier stones, with such tremendous force that it seemed as though they were sent from catapults. Against such a storm of missiles the Roman skirmishers could make no stand, and were instantly driven back.

Their Cretan archers, after shooting away their arrows with but small effect, for the strings had been damped in crossing the river, also fled behind the heavy troops; and these in turn were exposed to the hail of stones. Disorganized by this attack, the like of which they had never experienced before, their helmets crushed in, their breastplates and shields battered and dinted, the front line of the Romans speedily fell into confusion. Sempronius ordered up his war machines for casting stones and javelins, but these too had been injured in their passage across the river.

The hail of Carthaginian missiles continued until the Roman light infantry were forced to fall back; and the slingers were then recalled, and the heavy infantry of the two armies stood facing each other. The Carthaginians took up close order, and, shoulder to shoulder, their bodies covered with their shields, they advanced to meet the legions of Rome. As they moved, their music—flute, harp, and lyre—rose on the air in a military march, and keeping step the long line advanced with perfect order and regularity. In the centre were the Carthaginian foot soldiers and their African allies, clothed alike in a red tunic, with helmet of bronze, steel cuiras and circular shield, and carrying, besides their swords, pikes of twenty feet in length. On the left were the Spaniards, in white tunics bordered with purple, with semicircular shields four feet in length and thirty-two inches in width, armed with long swords used either for cutting or thrusting.

On the left were the native allies, naked to the waist, armed with shields and swords similar to those of the Gauls, save that the swords were used only for cutting.

Sempronius brought up his second line to fill the intervals in the first, and the Romans advanced with equal steadiness to the conflict; but the much greater closeness of the Carthaginian formation served them in good stead. They moved like a solid wall, their shields locked closely together, and pressed steadily

183

forward in spite of the desperate efforts of the Roman centre in its more open order to resist them; for each Roman soldier in battle was allowed the space of a man's width between him and his comrade on either side, to allow him the free use of his weapon. Two Carthaginians were therefore opposed to each Roman, in addition to which the greater depth of the African formation gave them a weight and impetus which was irresistible.

While this fight was going on the Numidian horsemen, ten thousand strong, charged the Roman cavalry. These, much more lightly armed than their opponents and inferior in numbers, were unable for a moment to withstand the shock, and were at once driven from the field. Leaving the elephants to pursue them and prevent them from rallying, the Numidian horsemen turned and fell on the flanks of the long Roman line; while at the same moment the Carthaginian slingers, issuing out again from behind the main body, opened a tremendous fire with stones heated in furnaces brought to the spot.

Although taken in flank, crushed under a storm of missiles, with their cavalry defeated and their centre broken, the Romans fought steadily and well. Hannibal now launched against their ranks the elephants attached to the infantry, which, covered in steel armour and trumpeting loudly, carried death and confusion into the Roman ranks. But still the legions fought on obstinately and desperately until the sound of wild music in their rear filled them with dismay, as Mago, with his division of Numidian infantry, emerged from his hiding-place and fell upon the Romans from behind.

Struck with terror at the sudden appearance of these wild soldiers, of whose ferocity they had heard so much, the Romans lost all heart and strove now only to escape. But it was in vain. The Carthaginian infantry were in their front, the cavalry on their flank, the Numidians in their rear.

Some ten thousand Roman soldiers only, keeping in a solid body, cut their way through the cavalry and reached Piacenza.

Thirty thousand were slaughtered on the plain. Many were drowned in trying to swim the Trebia, and only the legion which had remained to guard the camp, the broken remains of the cavalry, and the body which had escaped from Piacenza remained of the fifty thousand men whom Sempronius commanded.

The exultation of the victors was unbounded. The hitherto invincible legions of Rome had been crushed. The way to Rome was clear before them. All the fatigues and hardships they had undergone were forgotten in the hour of triumph, and their native allies believed that their freedom from Rome was now assured.

The verdict of great commanders of all ages has assigned to the battle of the Trebia the glory of being the greatest military exploit ever performed. The genius of Hannibal was shown not only in the plan of battle and the disposition of his troops, but in the perfection with which they were handled, in the movements which he had himself invented and taught them, and the marvellous discipline with which he had inculcated them.

Napoleon the First assigned to Hannibal the leading place among the great generals of the world, and the Trebia was his masterpiece. But the Carthaginians, exulting in their victory, did not gauge the extent of the stubbornness and resources of Rome. Sempronius himself set the example to his countrymen. At Piacenza he rallied the remnants of his army, and wrote to Rome, saying that he had been victorious, but that a sudden storm had saved the enemy from destruction.

The senate understood the truth, but acted in the spirit in which he had written. They announced to the people that a victory had been won, and ordered the consular election to take place as usual, at the same time issuing orders to all parts of the Roman dominion for the enrolment of fresh troops.

Hannibal attempted to surprise Piacenza, but Scipio issued out with his cavalry and inflicted a check upon him, Hannibal himself being slightly wounded. The Carthaginians then marched away and stormed the town of Vicumvæ, and during their absence the two consuls evacuated Piacenza and marched south. Scipio led his portion of the little army to Ariminum (Rimini), Sempronius took his command to Arretium (Arezzo), where they both speedily received reinforcements. Hannibal made an attempt to cross the Apennines, but the snow lay deep among the mountains, and, unable to effect his purpose, he fell back again to winter in the plain.

In the meantime Cneius Servilius Geminus and Caius Flaminius had been elected consuls. Flaminius succeeded Sempronius in command of the Roman army at Arretium, while Geminus took the command of that at Rimini. Between these consuls, as was usually the case in Rome, a bitter jealousy existed. Geminus was the nominee of the aristocratic party, while Flaminius was the idol of the populace, and, as has often been the case in war, this rivalry between two generals possessing equal authority wrought great evil to the armies they commanded.

THE YOUNG CARTHAGINIAN

CHAPTER XIV: THE BATTLE OF LAKE TRASIMENE

THE battle of Trebia cost Malchus the loss of his father. It was against the portion of the force headed by Hamilcar that the Romans, who cut their way through the circle of foes which Hannibal had thrown round them, flung themselves. Hamilcar had in vain attempted to stem the torrent. Surrounded by his bravest officers, he had cast himself in the way of the Roman legion; but nothing could withstand the rush of the heavy armed spearmen, who, knowing that all was lost, and that their only hope was in cutting their way through the Carthaginians, pressed forward, shoulder to shoulder, and swept aside the opposition of their more lightly-armed foes. Hamilcar and most of his officers fell, striving to the last to stem the current.

It was a grievous blow to Malchus, when, as he was exulting in the great victory which had been gained, the news came to him that his father had fallen. Hamilcar was very dear to him. He had been his companion and his friend, his guide and adviser. He had encouraged him in his aspirations, and had from his earliest years urged him to make the sacrifices and exertions necessary to qualify him to bear a prominent part under his cousin Hannibal.

He had been his tutor in arms, and had striven to inspire him with the noblest sentiments. Since they had reached Spain he had seen less of him than before, for Hamilcar felt that it was best for his son to depend upon himself alone. He was proud of the name which Malchus was already winning for himself, and knew that it was better for him that his advancement should be considered due to his own exertions and gallantry and not to the influence of his father.

When, however, they were thrown together, their relations were unchanged. Malchus was as affectionate, as respectful, and as eager to listen to his father's advice, as he had been as a boy, while Hamilcar was glad in the society of his son to forget the cares and toils of the expedition in which they had embarked and to talk of the dear ones at home.

It was only three days before the battle that they had rejoiced together over the news which had reached them by a messenger from Gaul that Thyra had married Adherbal, and had immediately set out with him for Carthagena, where Adherbal had been offered a command by Hannibal's brother Hasdrubal, the governor of Spain, in his absence.

Father and son had rejoiced at this for several reasons. Hanno's faction had now gained the upper hand, and the friends of Hannibal were subjected to persecution of all kinds. The very life of Adherbal as a prominent member of the Barcine party had been menaced. And it was only by embarking secretly for Spain that he had succeeded in avoiding arrest. The property of many of Hannibal's friends had been confiscated. Several had been put to death under one pretext or another, and although Hamilcar did not think that Hanno's faction would venture to bring forward any accusation against him while he was fighting the battles of his country, he experienced a sense of relief at the knowledge that, should the worst happen, his wife and Anna would find a refuge and asylum with Adherbal in Spain. Hamilcar and Malchus had discussed the matter long and seriously, and had talked, Hamilcar with sorrow, Malchus with indignation and rage, of the state of Carthage.

"It makes one hate one's country," Malchus exclaimed passionately, "when one hears of these things. You taught me to love Carthage, father, and to be proud of her. How can one be proud of a country so misgoverned, so corrupt, so base as this? Of what use are sacrifices and efforts here, when at home they think of nothing but luxury and ease and the making of money, when the best and bravest of the Carthaginians are disgraced and dishonoured, and the people bow before these men whose wealth has been gained solely by corruption and robbery? It makes one wish one had been born a Roman."

"Did not one hope that a better time would come, Malchus, when Carthage will emancipate herself from the rule of men like Hanno and his corrupt friends, I should, indeed, despair of her, for even the genius of Hannibal and the valour of his troops cannot avail alone to carry to a successful conclusion a struggle between such a state as Carthage now is and a vigourous, patriotic, and self-reliant people like those of Rome.

"We may win battles, but, however great the victories may be, we can never succeed in the long run against the power of Rome unless Carthage proves true to herself. Our army is not a large one. Rome and her Latin allies can, if need be, put ten such in the field. If Carthage at this crisis of her fate proves worthy of the occasion, if she by a great effort again wins the sovereignty of the sea, and sends over armies to support us in our struggle, we may in the end triumph. If not, glorious as may be our success for a time, we are in the end doomed to failure, and our failure will assuredly involve the final destruction of Carthage.

"Rome will not be slow to profit by the lesson which Hannibal is teaching her. His genius perceives that only by striking at Rome in Italy could a vital blow be given to her. The Romans in turn will perceive that only by an invasion of Africa can Carthage be humbled. Her task will then be far easier than ours is now, for not only is Rome fresh, strong, and vigourous, but she has had the wisdom to bind the Latin peoples around her closely to her by bestowing upon them the rights of citizenship, by making them feel that her cause is theirs.

"Upon the other hand, Carthage has throughout her history been paving the way for her fall. She fights, but it is with foreign mercenaries. She stamps under foot the people she has conquered, and while her tax-collectors grind them to the earth, and she forces them to send their sons to fight her battles, she gives them no share in her privileges, no voice in her councils.

"I had hoped, Malchus, that at such a moment as this faction would have been silent at Carthage, and a feeling of patriotism would once again have asserted itself. I find that it is not so, and my heart sinks for my country. Were it not for my wife and family, Malchus, I would gladly die in the coming battle."

The words recurred to Malchus as he sat in his tent by the side of his father's body on the night after the battle of the Trebia, and a deep bitterness mingled with his sorrow.

"Giscon was right," he exclaimed. "All means are justifiable to rid one's country of those who are destroying her. It makes one mad to think that while men like my father are fighting and dying for their country, the tribunes of the democracy, who fatten on our spoils, are plotting against them at home. Henceforth, I fight not as a Carthaginian, but as a soldier of Hannibal, and will aid him in his endeavour to humble Rome; not that Carthage, with her blood-stained altars, her corrupt officials, and her indolent population, may continue to exist, but that these manly and valiant Gauls who have thrown in their lot with us may live free and independent of the yoke of Rome. These people are rude and primitive, but their simple virtues, their love of freedom, their readiness to die rather than to be slaves, put the sham patriotism of Carthage to shame."

When the army went into winter quarters, and Hannibal dismissed his Gaulish allies, with many rich presents, to their homes, Malchus obtained leave from Hannibal to depart with Allobrigius–the chief of the Insubrian tribe living on the Orcus– who had, with his fighting men, accompanied Hannibal through the campaign. The chief's wife and daughters had returned after seeing the army across the Po. Malchus had sought the society of his late host during the campaign, had often ridden beside him on the march, and had spent the evening in his tent talking either of the civilization of Carthage, which seemed wonderful indeed to the simple Gaulish chieftain, or of the campaign on which they were engaged.

Malchus had by this time mastered the differences between the dialect of the Cisalpine Gauls and that of those in Gaul itself and Iberia, with which he was already acquainted. The chief was gratified by the friendship of Hannibal's kinsman, and liked the frank simplicity of his manner. He had laughed loudly when his wife had told him how Malchus had leaped from the bridge to save the life of Clotilde when she fell into the river. But the act had proved that Malchus was grateful for the kindness which had been shown him, and had cemented the friendship between them. Therefore, when the campaign came to a close, he had offered a hearty invitation to Malchus to spend the time, until the army should again assemble, with him in his village on the banks of the Orcus. Hannibal had smiled when Malchus had asked for leave of absence.

"Those daughters of the chief whom you presented to me on the day when we crossed the Po are the fairest I have seen in Gaul. Malchus, are you thinking of keeping up the traditions of our family? My father wedded all my sisters, as you know, to native princes in Africa, and I took an Iberian maiden as my wife. It would be in every way politic and to be desired that one so nearly related to me as yourself should form an alliance by marriage with one of these Gaulish chiefs."

Malchus laughed somewhat confusedly.

"It will be time to talk about marriage some years hence, Hannibal; I am scarce twenty yet, and she is but a girl."

"Oh ! there is a she in the case," Hannibal laughed; "and my arrow drawn at a venture has struck home. Ah ! yes, there were three of them, two tall and stately maidens and one still a slim and unformed girl. Indeed, I remember now having heard that you lost your armour and helmet in jumping off the bridge across the Po to fish out one of the daughters of Allobrigius, who turned out to be able to swim much better than you could. I had a hearty laugh over it with your poor father, but with the Romans at Piacenza and a great battle before us the matter passed from my mind. So that is how the wind lies. Well, as you say, you are both young, and there is no saying what the next two or three years may bring forth. However, bear in mind that such an alliance would please me much, and remember also that the Gaulish maidens marry young, and in times like ours, Malchus, it is never well to delay long."

Malchus took with him Nessus, who had, from the day when they escaped together from Scipio's camp, been always near his person, had carried his helmet on the line of march, slept next to him by the campfire, and fought by his side in battle, ready at any moment to give his life to avert harm from his leader.

The return of Allobrigius and his tribesmen was celebrated by great rejoicings on the Orcus. The women and old men and boys met them some miles from the village, raising loud cries of welcome and triumph as they returned from their successful campaign against their former oppressors. Among no people were family ties held more precious than among the Gauls, and the rough military order which the tribesmen had preserved upon their march was at once broken up when the two parties met.

Wives rushed into the arms of husbands, mothers embraced their sons, girls hung on the necks of their fathers and brothers. There was nothing to mar the joy of the meeting, for messengers had from time to time carried news from the army to the village, and the women who had lost those dearest to them in the campaign remained behind in the village, so that their mourning should not mar the brightness of the return of the tribe.

Brunilda, the wife of the chief, stood with her daughters a little apart from the crowd on a rising knoll of ground, and the chief, who was mounted upon a horse taken from the Romans at the Trebia, spurred forward towards them, while Malchus hung behind to let the first greeting pass over before he joined the family circle. He had, however, been noticed, and Clotilde's cheeks were colouring hotly when her father rode up, from some laughing remark from her sisters. Brunilda received Malchus cordially, saying that she had often heard of him in the messages sent by her husband.

"He has come to stop the winter with us," Allobrigius said. "I promised him a warm welcome, and he needs rest and quiet, as do we all, for it has been hard work even to seasoned men like us. What with snow and rain I have scarcely been dry since I left you."

"That would not, matter to the young Carthaginian lord," the eldest girl said with a smile; "we know that he rather likes getting wet, don't we, Clotilde?" she said, turning to her sister, who was, contrary to her usual custom, standing shyly behind her.

"I am afraid I shall never hear the last of that," Malchus laughed; "I can only say that I meant well."

"Of course you did," Allobrigius said; "you could not know that our Gaulish maidens could swim and march, and, if necessary, fight as stoutly as the men. The Romans before now have learned that, in the absence of the men from the camp, the women of Gaul can fight desperately for country, and home, and honour. Do not let yourself be troubled by what these wild girls say, my lord Malchus; you know our Gaulish women are free of tongue, and hold not their men in such awe and deference as is the custom among other nations."

"I am accustomed to be laughed at," Malchus said smiling; "I have two sisters at home, and, whatever respect women may pay to their lords in Carthage, I suppose that neither there nor anywhere else have girls respect for their brothers."

The music at this moment struck up, the harpers began a song which they had composed in honour of the occasion, the tribesmen fell into their ranks again, and Allobrigius placed himself at their head. Malchus dismounted, and, leading his horse, walked by the side of Brunilda, who, with the rest of the women, walked on the flanks of the column on its way back to the village.

The next three months passed very pleasantly to Malchus. In the day he hunted the boar, the bear, and the wolf among the mountains with Allobrigius; of an evening he sat by the fire and listened to the songs of the harpers or to the tales of the wars and wanderings of the Gaulish tribes, or himself told the story of Carthage and Tyre and the wars of the former with the Romans, described the life and manners of the great city, or the hunting of the lion in the Libyan deserts.

While his listeners wondered at the complex life and strange arts and magnificence of Carthage, Malchus was struck with the simple existence, the warm family ties, the honest sincerity, and the deep love of freedom of the Gauls. When Brunilda and her daughter sighed with envy at the thought of the luxuries and pleasures of the great city, he told them that they would soon weary of so artificial an existence, and that Carthage, with its corruption, its ever-present dread of the rising of one class against another, its constant fear of revolt from the people it had enslaved, its secret tribunals, its oppression and tyranny, had little which need be envied by the free tribes of Gaul.

"I grant," he said, "that you would gain greater comfort by adopting something of our civilization. You might improve your dwellings, hangings round your walls would keep out the bitter winds, well-made doors are in winter very preferable to the skins which hang at your entrance, and I do think that a Carthaginian cook might, with advantage, give lessons to the tribes as to preparations of food; but beyond that I think that you have the best of it."

"The well-built houses you speak of," Allobrigius said, "have their advantages, but they have their drawbacks. A people who once settle down into permanent abodes have taken the first step towards losing their freedom. Look at all the large towns in the plains; until lately each of them held a Roman garrison. In the first place, they offer an incentive to the attack of a covetous foe; in the second, they bind their owners to them. The inhabitants of a town cling to their houses and possessions, and, if conquered, become mere slaves to their captors; we who live in dwellings which cost but a few weeks of work, whose worldly goods are the work of our own hands, or the products of the chase, should never be conquered; we may be beaten, but if so, we can retire before our enemies and live in freedom in the forest or mountains, or travel beyond the reach of our foes.

"Had not your army come and freed us from Rome I was already meditating moving with my tribe across the great mountains to the north and settling among Brunilda's people in the German forests, far beyond the reach of Rome. What though, as she tells me, the winters are long and severe, the people ignorant of many of the comforts which we have adopted from our neighbours; at least we should be free, and of all blessings none is to compare with that."

"I agree with you," Malchus said, thinking of the plots and conspiracies, the secret denunciations, the tyranny and corruption of Carthage, "it is good to be great, but it is better to be free. However," he added more cheerfully, "I trust that we are going to free you from all future fear of Rome, and that you will be able to enjoy your liberty here without having to remove to the dark forests and long winter of the country north of the Alps."

So passed the winter. Early in the spring a messenger arrived from Hannibal bidding Malchus rejoin him, and calling upon Allobrigius to prepare to take the field against the Romans. Similar messages had been sent to all the Gaulish tribes friendly to Carthage, and early in March Hannibal prepared to cross the Apennines and to advance against Rome.

The position occupied by the two Roman armies barred the only two roads by which it was believed that Hannibal could march upon Rome, but as soon as the spring commenced Hannibal started by a path, hitherto untrodden by troops, across the Apennines. In the march the troops suffered even greater hardships than those which they had undergone in the passage of the Alps, for during four days and three nights they marched knee-deep in water, unable for a single moment to lie down.

While ever moving backwards and forwards among his men to encourage them with his presence and words, even the iron frame of Hannibal gave way under the terrible hardships. The long-continued strain, the want of sleep, and the obnoxious miasma from the marshes, brought on a fever and cost him the sight of one of his eyes. Of all the elephants but one survived the march, and it was with an army as worn out and exhausted as that which had issued from the Alps that he descended into the fertile plains of Tuscany, near Fiesole.

The army of Flaminius, 30,000 strong, was still lying at Arezzo, on his direct road south, and it was with this only that Hannibal had now to deal, the force of Servilius being still far away at Rimini. His own army was some 35,000 strong, and crossing the Upper Arno near Florence, Hannibal marched towards Arezzo. Flaminius, as soon as he had heard that Hannibal was ascending the slopes of the Apennines, had sent to Servilius to join him, but the latter, alleging that he feared an invasion by the Gaulish tribes on the north, refused to move, but sent four thousand cavalry to Flaminius. This brought the armies to nearly equal strength, but, although Hannibal marched his troops within sight of Arezzo, Flaminius would not issue from his camp to attack him.

He knew that Hannibal had defeated a force of tried troops, much exceeding his own in numbers, in the north, and that he would therefore probably be successful against one which scarcely equalled his own. He hoped, too, that Hannibal would attack him in his intrenched position. This the Carthaginian general had no intention of doing, but, leaving the camp behind him, marched on, plundering and ravaging the country towards Rome. Flaminius at once broke up his camp and followed on his track, preparing to take any opportunity which might occur to fall upon the Carthaginians, and knowing that the senate would at once call up the army of Servilius to assist him.

Hannibal, by means of scouts left in his rear, found that Flaminius was marching on with his troops in solid column, taking no precaution against surprise, secure in the belief that Hannibal's object was to march on Rome without a stop. The Carthaginian general prepared at once to take advantage of his enemy's carelessness. He halted his troops at Cortona. The road by which he had passed wound along the shore of Lake Trasimene, at the foot of a range of steep hills, which approached closely to the water.

Half-way along these hills a stream runs down a valley into the lake, and in the valley, completely hidden from the sight of an enemy approaching, Hannibal placed the Numidian cavalry and the Gaulish infantry. Among some woods clothing the lower slope of the hills facing the lake he placed his light troops, while the Spanish and African infantry and the Gaulish cavalry were similarly hidden on the outer slopes of the hill in readiness to close in on the rear of the Romans when they had entered on the road between the hills and the lake.

No better position could have been chosen for a surprise. When once the Romans had entered the path between the hills and the lake there was no escape for them. They were shut up between the wood-clad hills swarming with the Carthaginian light troops and the lake, while the heavy infantry and cavalry of Hannibal were ready to fall on them front and rear.

THE BATTLE OF LAKE TRASIMENE

When Flaminius arrived at Cortona late at night he heard of the ravages and executions committed by the Carthaginians, as they had passed through early in the morning, and resolved to press forward at daybreak in hopes of finding some opportunity for falling upon and punishing them. When day broke it seemed favourable to his design, for a thick mist was rising from the lake and marshes. This, he thought, would conceal his advance from the Carthaginians, while, as the high ground ahead rose above the mist, he would be enabled to see their position. He pushed forward then rapidly, thinking that he should be able to overtake the rear of the Carthaginian army as it moved slowly along encumbered with its plunder.

As he neared the entrance to the pass he caught sight of the heavy-armed Carthaginians on the distant hill above the level of the mist, and believing that his own movements were hidden from the enemy, pushed forward as fast as the infantry could march. But the moment the rear of his column had entered the narrow flat between the foot of the hills and the lake, the Numidians quietly moved down and closed the pass behind them, while Hannibal with his heavy infantry descended from the farther hill to confront him. When all was ready he gave the signal, and at once in front, of their right flank, and on their rear the Carthaginians fell upon them.

The light troops heralded their attack by rolling a vast quantity of rocks down the hill on the long column, and then, pressing down through the woods, poured their arrows and javelins into the struggling mass.

Taken wholly by surprise, unable to advance or retreat, desperate at finding themselves thus caught in a trap, the Romans fought bravely but in vain. An earthquake shook the ground on which the terrible fight was going on; but not for a moment did it interrupt the struggle. For three hours the Romans, although suffering terribly, still fought on; then Flaminius was killed, and from that time they thought only of escape. But this was next to impossible. Six thousand only cut their way out; fifteen thousand fell, and nine thousand were taken prisoners.

As soon as the battle was over Hannibal despatched Maharbal with his division of the army in pursuit of the six thousand who had escaped, and, overtaking them next morning at Perugia, Maharbal forced them to surrender. At the same time he detached a strong force against the four thousand horsemen, whom Servilius had despatched from Rimini to aid his colleague, and the whole of these were surrounded and taken prisoners. Thus of the Roman army, thirty-six thousand strong, not a single man escaped.

In all history there is no record of so great and successful a surprise. Hannibal retained as prisoners the Roman citizens and Latins, but released the rest of the captives, telling them that, far from being their enemy, he had invaded Italy for the purpose of liberating its helpless people from the tyranny of the Roman domination. The loss to the Carthaginians in the battle of Lake Trasimene was only fifteen hundred men.

Hannibal has been blamed for not advancing against Rome after the battle of Lake Trasimene; but he knew that he could not hope to subdue that city so long as she was surrounded by faithful allies. His army was numerically insufficient to undertake such a siege, and was destitute of the machines for battering the walls. Rome was still defended by the city legions, besides which every man capable of bearing arms was a soldier. The bitter hostility of the Latins would have rendered it difficult in the extreme for the army to have obtained provisions while carrying on the siege, while in its rear, waiting for an opportunity to attack, would have lain the army of Servilius, thirty thousand strong, and growing daily more numerous as the friends and allies of Rome flocked to its banners.

Hannibal saw that to undertake such an enterprise at present would be ruin. His course was clear. He had to beat the armies which Rome could put into the field; to shake the confidence of the Italian tribes in the power of Rome; to subsist his army upon their territories, and so gradually to detach them from their alliance with Rome. He hoped that, by the time this work was finished, Carthage would send another great army to his assistance provided with siege materials, and he would then be able to undertake with confidence the great task of striking a vital blow at Rome herself.

"Malchus," Hannibal said one day, "I wish you to ride north. The tribes at the foot of the hills promised to aid us, but have so far done nothing. If they would pour down to the plains now they would occupy the tribes friendly to the Romans, and would prevent them from sending men and stores to them. They sent me a message a month ago, saying that they were still willing to help us, and I then replied that I had been long waiting to hear that they had risen, and urged them to do so without loss of time. I have not heard since, and fear that the Roman agents have, by promises of money and privileges, prevailed upon them to keep quiet. It is a service of danger; for if they have been bought over they may seize you and send you in token of their good-will as a prisoner to Rome; but I know that will not deter you."

"I am ready to go," Malchus said, "and will start to-day. What force shall I take with me, and which of the chiefs shall I first see?"

"You had best go first to Ostragarth. He is the most powerful of the chiefs on this side of the Apennines. You can select from the treasury such presents as you may choose for him and the others. You can promise them large grants of the land of the tribes aiding the Romans, together with a share in the plunder of the cities. I leave you quite free. In those respects you will be guided by what you see they want; but any promises you may make I will ratify. As to men I should not take a large escort. Force will, of course, be of no avail, and the appearance of a large number of troops might alarm them at once. Twenty men will be sufficient for dignity, and as a protection against any small bodies of the hostile tribesmen you may meet on your way; but have no frays if you can avoid it. The mission is an important one, and its success should not be risked merely to defeat a body of tribesmen. Go in your handsomest armour, and make as brave a show as you can, as my ambassador and kinsman. Take twenty of the Carthaginian horse; they will impose more upon the barbarians than would the Libyans or Numidians. Take your friend Trebon as their commander and a companion for yourself."

In two hours Malchus and his escort were ready to start. As their journey would be rapid they carried no stores with them, save three days' provisions, which each man carried at his saddle-bow, and a bag containing a few feeds of corn for the horse.

They took with them, however, two baggage horses laden with arms, armour, garments, and other presents for the chiefs.

They passed rapidly across the country, meeting with no hostile parties, for the raids of Hannibal's light-armed horse had so terrified the people that the villages were for the most part deserted, the inhabitants having sought refuge in the fortified towns. After two days' brisk riding they arrived at the foot of the hills, and their progress was now slower. The village of Ostragarth lay far up among them, and, being ignorant of the direction, Malchus broke the troop up into parties of four, and sent them up different valleys with orders to capture the first native they came across, and oblige him either by threats or promises to act as a guide to the stronghold of the chief.

"I sincerely trust that this barbarian is friendly, Malchus, for the country looks wild and difficult in the extreme, and the forests which clothe these hills are thick and tangled. On the plain we can laugh at the natives, however numerous, and with twenty men I would charge a thousand of them; but among these hills it is different, one cannot find a level spot for a charge, and, if it comes to running, the mountaineers are as fleet as a horse on the broken ground of their hills."

"I agree with you, Trebon, that it would go hard with us, and that the utmost we could hope for would be a visit to Rome as captives. Still, these chiefs all offered alliance to Hannibal as he went south, and the success which has attended us should surely bind them to our interests. They are ever willing to join the winning side, and so far fortune has been wholly with us."

"That is so, Malchus, but then they see that the tribes of the plains still hold aloof from us and pin their faith on Rome. They must know that we are receiving no reinforcements to fill the gaps made in battle, and may well fear to provoke the anger of Rome by taking part with us before our success is, as they consider, absolutely secure."

"On the same grounds then, Trebon, they will be equally unwilling to offend us by any hostility until the scale is decidedly weighed down against us. Hannibal's anger might be as terrible as that of the Romans."

"There is something in that, Malchus, but not so much as

you think. If Rome wins, Rome will have ample time and ample power, with the aid of all her native allies, to punish any who may have declared against her. On the other hand, should Carthage triumph, they may consider it probable that we should sack and burn Rome and then retire, or that if we remain there will be so much to arrange, so many tribes in the plains to subjugate and pacify, that we shall be little likely to undertake expeditions in the mountains. Therefore, you see, prudent men would decide for Rome. Could we have marched straight on after the victory at Lake Trasimene and have captured Rome, all these mountain tribes would have taken the opportunity to pour down into the plains to plunder and slay under the pretence of being our allies."

It was not until nightfall that the five parties returned to the spot where they had left their leaders. Three of them had been entirely unsuccessful, but the other two had each brought in a native. These men looked sullen and obstinate, and it was not until Malchus had ordered a halter to be placed round their necks and threatened them with instant death that they consented to act as guides.

A vigilant watch was kept over them all night, and at daybreak next morning the party started. For some miles they rode along at the foot of the mountains, and then entered a valley up which a little-used track ran. The men upon being questioned intimated that it was several hours' journey to the village of the chief of whom they were in search.

This, indeed, proved to be the case, for it was not till the afternoon, after many hours' weary journey up gorges and through mountain valleys, that they arrived within sight of the village of Ostragarth. It was situated on one side of the valley, and consisted of huts surrounded by a rough stone wall of such height that only the tops of the circular roofs were visible above it. A loud shrill cry was heard as they came in sight, a cow-horn was blown in the village, and instantly men could be seen running in. Others, engaged in tending flocks of goats high up on the mountain side, left their charges and began to hurry down.

CHAPTER XV: A MOUNTAIN TRIBE

I T is a petty place for a chief of any power," Trebon said.
"Yes," Malchus agreed, "but I fancy these hill tribes are
broken up into a very large number of small villages in
isolated valleys, only uniting when the order of the chief
calls upon them to defend the mountains against an invader,
or to make a simultaneous raid upon the plains."

As they neared the village several persons were seen to
issue out from the gate, and among these was a small and elderly
man, evidently the chief of the party. His white hair descended to
his waist; a boy standing behind him carried his bow and several
javelins. The rest of the men appeared to be unarmed.

"He is a crafty-looking old fellow," Malchus said as he
alighted and advanced towards the chief, "but I suppose he has
made up his mind to receive us as friends, at any rate for the
present.

"I come, chief, as an ambassador from the Carthaginian
general. When we passed south he received messengers from
you, saying that you were ready to enter into an alliance with
him. To this he agreed, and sent presents. Since then you have
done nothing, although he has sent to you urging you to aid him
by making an attack on the tribes allied to Rome. In every battle
which he has fought with the Romans he has defeated them with
great slaughter; but, owing to the aid which they have received
from the tribes in alliance with them, they are enabled continually
to put fresh armies in the field. Therefore it is that he has sent me
to you and to the other chiefs of the tribes inhabiting the mountains,
to urge you to descend with your forces into the plains, and so

oblige the tribes there to turn their attention to their own defence rather than to the sending of assistance to Rome. He has sent by my hands many valuable presents, and has authorized me to promise you, in his name, such lands as you may wish to obtain beyond the foot of the hills. He promises you, also, a share in the booty taken at the sack of the Italian cities."

"Will you please to enter," the chief said, speaking a patois of Latin which Malchus found it difficult to understand. "We will then discuss the matters concerning which you speak."

So saying he led the way through the gates to a hut somewhat larger than the rest.

"Do you enter with me, Trebon, but let your men remain in their saddle, and hold our horses in readiness for us to mount speedily if there be need. I doubt the friendliness of this old fellow and his people."

Upon entering the hut Malchus observed at once that the walls were covered with hangings which were new and fresh, and he detected some costly armour half-hidden in a corner.

"The Romans have been here before us," he muttered to his companion; "the question is, how high have they bid for his support."

The chief took his seat on a roughly carved chair, and seats were brought in for his visitors. He began by asking an account of the state of affairs in the plains. Malchus answered him truthfully, except that he exaggerated a little the effects that the Carthaginian victories had produced among the natives. The chief asked many questions, and was evidently by some means well informed on the subject. He then expressed a desire to see the presents which they had brought him. Trebon went out and returned with two soldiers bearing them.

"I don't like the look of things," he said in a low voice. "The number of men in the village has trebled since we arrived, and they still keep coming in. None of them show arms at present, but no doubt they are hidden close at hand. I believe the chief is only keeping us in conversation till he considers that a sufficient force has arrived to make sure of us."

"We can't break it off now," Malchus said, "and must take our chance. It would not do to ensure a failure by showing suspicion."

The chief examined the presents with great care and announced his satisfaction at them. Then he entered upon the question of the land which he was to receive, inquired whether the towns were to be captured by the Carthaginians and handed over to him, or were to be captured by his forces. When these points had been arranged, as it seemed, satisfactorily, he entered upon questions in dispute between himself and other chiefs of the mountain tribes. Malchus said he had no instructions as to these points, which were new to him, but that in all questions between the chief and tribes hostile to Carthage, full satisfaction would be given him. As to those between himself and other chiefs, who might also join against the Romans, if they elected to submit them to Hannibal for decision he would arbitrate between them.

At this moment a horn was blown outside. A din of voices instantly arose, which was followed immediately afterwards by the clashing of weapons. Malchus and his companion leaped to their feet and rushed from the hut. They found that their men were attacked by a crowd of mountaineers. In an instant they leaped on their horses, and drawing their swords joined in the fray. The number of their foes was large, a great many men having come in since Trebon had last issued out. The attack was a determined one. Those next to the horsemen hewed at them with axes, those further back hurled darts and javelins, while others crept in among the horses and stabbed them from beneath with their long knives.

"We must get out of this or we are lost," Trebon exclaimed, and, encouraging the men with his shouts, he strove to hew away through the crowd to the gate, while Malchus faced some of the men round and covered the rear. Several of the Carthaginians were already dismounted, owing to their horses being slain, and some of them were despatched before they could gain their feet. Malchus shouted to the others to leap up behind their comrades.

By dint of desperate efforts Trebon and the soldiers with him cleared the way to the gate, but those behind were so hampered by the enemy that they were unable to follow. The natives clung to their legs and strove to pull them off their horses, while a storm of blows was hurled upon them. Trebon, seeing the danger of those behind, had turned, and in vain tried to cut his way back to them; but the number of the natives was too great. Malchus seeing this shouted at the top of his voice:

"Fly, Trebon, you cannot help us, save those you can."

Seeing that he could render his friend no assistance, Trebon turned round and galloped off with nine of the soldiers who had made their way with him to the gate. Five had already fallen, and Malchus shouted to the other six to throw down their arms and yield themselves as prisoners. This they did, but two of them were killed before the villagers perceived they had surrendered.

Malchus and the others were dragged from their horses, bound hand and foot, and thrown into one of the huts. The natives shouted in triumph, and yells of delight arose as the packages borne by the baggage animals were examined, and the variety of rich presents, intended for the various chiefs, divided among them.

Most of the captives were more or less severely wounded, and some of the natives presently came into the hut and examined and bound up the wounds.

"Keep up your spirits," Malchus said cheerfully, "it is evident they don't intend to kill us. No doubt they are going to send us prisoners to the Romans, and in that case we shall be exchanged sooner or later. At anyrate the Romans would not dare ill-treat us, for Hannibal holds more than a hundred prisoners in his hands to every one they have taken."

Three days passed, food was brought to the captives regularly, and their bonds were sufficiently relaxed for them to feed themselves. At the end of that time they were ordered to rise and leave the hut. Outside the chief with some forty of his followers were waiting them. All were armed, and the prisoners being placed in their midst, the party started.

They proceeded by the same road by which Malchus had ridden to the village, and some miles were passed without incident, when, as they were passing through a narrow valley, a great number of rocks came bounding down the hillside, and at

The success of Trebon's stratagem

different points along it several Carthaginians appeared. In these Malchus recognized at once the soldiers of his escort. One of these shouted out:

"Surrender, or you are all dead men. A strong force surrounds you on both sides, and my officers, whom you see, will give orders to their men, who will loose such an avalanche of rocks that you will all be swept away."

"It is only the men who escaped us," the chief cried; "push forward at once."

But the instant the movement began the Carthaginians all shouted orders, and a great number of rocks came bounding down, proving that they were, obeyed by an invisible army. Several of the mountaineers were crushed by the stones, and the old chief, struck by a great rock in the chest, fell dead. A Carthaginian standing next to Malchus was also slain.

The tribesmen gave a cry of terror. Hand to hand they were ready to fight valiantly, but this destruction by an unseen foe terrified them. The Carthaginian leader raised his hand, and the descent of the stones ceased.

"Now," he said, "you see the truth of my words. Hesitate any longer and all will be lost; but if you throw down your arms, and, leaving your captives behind, retire by the way you came, you are free to do so. Hannibal has no desire for the blood of the Italian people. He has come to free them from the yoke of Rome, and your treacherous chief, who, after our making an alliance with him, sold you to the Romans, has been slain, therefore I have no further ill-will against you."

The tribesmen, dismayed by the loss of their chief, and uncertain as to the strength of the foes who surrounded them, at once threw down their arms, and, glad to escape with their lives, fled at all speed up the pass towards their village, leaving their captives behind them.

The Carthaginians then descended, Trebon among them.

"I did not show myself, Malchus," the latter said as he joined his friend, "for the chief knew me by sight, and I wished him to be uncertain whether we were not a fresh party who had arrived."

"But who are your army?" Malchus asked; "you have astonished me as much as the barbarians."

"There they are," Trebon said, laughing, as some fifty or sixty women and a dozen old men and boys began to make their way down the hill. "Fortunately the tribesmen were too much occupied with their plunder and you to pursue us, and I got down safely with my men. I was, of course, determined to try to rescue you somehow, but did not see how it was to be done. Then a happy thought struck me, and the next morning we rode down to the plain till we came to a walled village. I at once summoned it to surrender, using threats of bringing up a strong body to destroy the place if they refused. They opened the gates sooner than I had expected, and I found the village inhabited only by women, old men, and children, the whole of the fighting men having been called away to join the Romans. They were, as you may imagine, in a terrible fright, and expected every one of them to be killed. However, I told them that we would not only spare their lives, but also their property, if they would obey my orders.

"They agreed willingly enough, and I ordered all those who were strong enough to be of any good to take each sufficient provisions for a week and to accompany me. Astonished as they were at the order, there was nothing for them to do but to obey, and they accordingly set out. I found by questioning them that the road we had travelled was the regular one up to the village, and that you would be sure to be brought down by it if the chief intended to send you to Rome.

"By nightfall we reached this valley. The next morning we set to work and cut a number of strong levers, then we went up on the hillside to where you saw us, and I posted them all behind the rocks. We spent all the day loosing stones and placing them in readiness to roll down, and were then prepared for your coming. At nightfall I assembled them all, and put a guard over them. We posted them again at daybreak yesterday, but watched all day in vain, and here we should have remained for a month if necessary, as I should have sent down some of the boys for more provisions when those they brought were gone. However, I was right glad when I saw you coming to-day, for it was dull work. I would have killed the whole of these treacherous savages if I had not been afraid of injuring you and the men. As it was I was in terrible fright when the stones went rushing down at you. One of our men has been killed, I see; but there was no help for it."

The whole party then proceeded down the valley. On emerging from the hills Trebon told his improvised army that they could return to their village, as he had no further need of their services, and, delighted at having escaped without damage or injury, they at once proceeded on their way.

"We had best halt here for the night," Trebon said, "and in the morning I will start off with the mounted men and get some horses from one of the villages for the rest of you. No doubt they are all pretty well stripped of fighting men."

The next day the horses were obtained, and Malchus, seeing that, now he had lost all the presents intended for the chiefs, it would be useless to pursue his mission further, especially as he had learned that the Roman agents had already been at work among the tribes, returned with his party to Hannibal's camp.

"I am sorry, Malchus," the Carthaginian general said, when he related his failure to carry out the mission, "that you have not succeeded, but it is clear that your failure is due to no want of tact on your part. The attack upon you was evidently determined upon the instant you appeared in sight of the village, for men must have been sent out at once to summon the tribe. Your friend Trebon behaved with great intelligence in the matter of your rescue, and I shall at once promote him a step in rank."

"I am ready to set out again and try whether I can succeed better with some of the other chiefs if you like," Malchus said.

"No, Malchus, we will leave them alone for the present. The Romans have been beforehand with us, and as this man was one of their principal chiefs, it is probable that, as he has forsaken his alliance with us, the others have done the same. Moreover, the news of his death, deserved as it was, at the hands of a party of Carthaginians, will not improve their feelings towards us. Nothing short of a general movement among the hill tribes would be of any great advantage to us, and it is clear that no general movement can be looked for now. Besides, now that we see the spirit which animates these savages, I do not care to risk your loss by sending you among them."

THE YOUNG CARTHAGINIAN

The news of the disaster of Lake Trasimene was met by Rome in a spirit worthy of her. No one so much as breathed the thought of negotiations with the enemy, not even a soldier was recalled from the army of Spain. Quintus Fabius Maximus was chosen dictator, and he with two newly raised legions marched to Ariminum and assumed the command of the army there, raised by the reinforcements he brought with him to fifty thousand men.

Stringent orders were issued to the inhabitants of the districts through which Hannibal would march on his way to Rome to destroy their crops, drive off their cattle, and take refuge in the fortified towns. Servilius was appointed to the command of the Roman fleet, and ordered to oppose the Carthaginians at sea. The army of Fabius was now greatly superior to that of Hannibal, but was inferior in cavalry. He had, moreover, the advantage of being in a friendly country, and of being provisioned by the people through whose country he moved, while Hannibal was obliged to scatter his army greatly to obtain provisions.

Fabius moved his army until within six miles of that of Hannibal, and then took up his position upon the hills, contenting himself with watching from a distance the movements of the Carthaginians. Hannibal marched unmolested through some of the richest provinces of Italy till he descended into the plain of Campania. He obtained large quantities of rich booty, but the inhabitants in all cases held aloof from him, their belief in the star of Rome being still unshaken in spite of the reverses which had befallen her.

Fabius followed at a safe distance, avoiding every attempt of Hannibal to bring on a battle.

The Roman soldiers fretted with rage and indignation at seeing the enemy, so inferior in strength to themselves, wasting and plundering the country at their will. Minucius, the master of horse and second in command, a fiery officer, sympathized to the full with the anger of the soldiers, and continually urged upon Fabius to march the army to the assault, but Fabius was immovable. The terrible defeats which Hannibal had inflicted upon two Roman armies showed him how vast would be the danger of engaging such an opponent unless at some great advantage.

Such advantage he thought he saw when Hannibal descended into the plain of Campania. This plain was inclosed on the south by the river Vulturnus, which could be passed only at the bridge at Casilinum, defended by the Roman garrison at that town, while on its other sides it was surrounded by an unbroken barrier of steep and wooded hills, the passes of which were strongly guarded by the Romans.

After seeing that every road over the hills was strongly held by his troops, Fabius sat down with his army on the mountains, whence he could watch the doings of Hannibal's force on the plains. He himself was amply supplied with provisions from the country in his rear, and he awaited patiently the time when Hannibal, having exhausted all the resources of the Campania, would be forced by starvation to attack the Romans in their almost impregnable position in the passes.

Hannibal was perfectly aware of the difficulties of his position. Had he been free and unencumbered by baggage he might have led his army directly across the wooded mountains, avoiding the passes guarded by the Romans, but with his enormous trail of baggage this was impossible unless he abandoned all the rich plunder which the army had collected. Of the two outlets from the plain, by the Appian and Latin roads which led to Rome, neither could be safely attempted, for the Roman army would have followed in his rear, and attacked him while endeavouring to force the passages in the mountains.

The same objection applied to his crossing the Vulturnus. The only bridge was strongly held by the Romans, and the river was far too deep and rapid for a passage to be attempted elsewhere with the great Roman army close at hand. The mountain range between the Vulturnus and Cades was difficult in the extreme, as the passes were few and very strongly guarded, but it was here that Hannibal resolved to make the attempt to lead his army from the difficult position in which it was placed. He waited quietly in the plain until the supplies of food were beginning to run low, and then prepared for his enterprise.

An immense number of cattle were among the plunder. Two thousand of the stoutest of these were selected, torches were fastened to their horns, and shortly before midnight the light troops drove the oxen to the hills, avoiding the position of the passes guarded by the enemy. The torches were then lighted, and the light troops drove the oxen straight up the hill. The animals, maddened by fear, rushed tumultuously forward, scattering in all directions on the hillside, but, continually urged by the troops behind them, mounting towards the summits of the hills.

The Roman defenders of the passes, seeing this great number of lights moving upwards, supposed that Hannibal had abandoned all his baggage, and was leading his army straight across the hills. This idea was confirmed by the light troops, on gaining the crest of the hills, commencing an attack upon the Romans posted below them in the pass through which Hannibal intended to move. The Roman troops thereupon quitted the pass, and scaled the heights to interrupt or harass the retreating foe.

As soon as Hannibal saw the lights moving on the top of the hills he commenced his march. The African infantry led the way; they were followed by the cavalry; then came the baggage and booty, and the rear was covered by the Spaniards and Gauls. The defile was found deserted by its defenders, and the army marched through unopposed. Meanwhile Fabius with his main army had remained inactive. The Roman general had seen with astonishment the numerous lights making their way up the mountain side, but he feared that this was some device on the part of Hannibal to entrap him into an ambush, as he had entrapped Flaminius on Lake Trasimene. He therefore held his army in readiness for whatever might occur until morning broke.

Then he saw that he had been outwitted. The rear of the Carthaginian army was just entering the defile, and in a short time Fabius saw the Gauls and Spaniards scaling the heights to the assistance of their comrades, who were maintaining an unequal fight with the Romans. The latter were soon driven with slaughter into the plain, and the Carthaginian troops descended into the defile and followed their retreating army. Hannibal now came down into the fertile country of Apulia, and determined to winter there. He took by storm the town of Geronium, where he stored his supplies and placed his sick in shelter, while his army occupied an intrenched camp which he formed outside the town.

THE YOUNG CARTHAGINIAN

CHAPTER XVI: IN THE DUNGEONS OF CARTHAGE

FABIUS after the escape of Hannibal from the trap in which he believed he had caught him, followed him into Apulia, and encamped on high ground in his neighbourhood intending to continue the same waiting tactics. He was, however, soon afterwards recalled to Rome to consult with the senate on matters connected with the army. He left Minucius in command, with strict orders that he should on no account suffer himself to be enticed into a battle. Minucius moved forward to within five miles of Geronium, and then encamped upon a spur of the hills. Hannibal, aware that Fabius had left, hoped to be able to tempt the impatient Minucius to an action. He accordingly drew nearer to the Romans and encamped upon a hill three miles from their position.

Another hill lay about half-way between the two armies. Hannibal occupied this during the night with two thousand of his light troops, but next day Minucius attacked the position, drove off its defenders, and encamped there with his whole army. For some days Hannibal kept his force united in his intrenchments, feeling sure that Minucius would attack him. The latter, however, strictly obeyed the orders of Fabius and remained inactive.

It was all-important to the Carthaginians to collect an ample supply of food before winter set in, and Hannibal, finding that the Romans would not attack him, was compelled to resume foraging expeditions. Two-thirds of the army were despatched in various directions in strong bodies, while the rest remained to guard the intrenchment.

IN THE DUNGEONS OF CARTHAGE

This was the opportunity for which Minucius had been waiting. He at once despatched the whole of his cavalry to attack the foraging parties, and with his infantry he advanced to the attack of the weakly-defended Carthaginian camp. For a time Hannibal had the greatest difficulty in resisting the assault of the Romans; but at last a body of four thousand of the foragers, who had beaten off the Roman cavalry and made their way into Geronium, came out to his support, and the Romans retired.

Hannibal, seeing the energy which Minucius had displayed, fell back to his old camp near Geronium, and Minucius at once occupied the position which he had vacated. The partial success of Minucius enabled the party in Rome who had long been discontented with the waiting tactics of Fabius to make a fresh attack upon his policy, and Minucius was now raised to an equal rank with Fabius.

Minucius, elated with his elevation, proposed to Fabius either that they should command the whole army on alternate days, or each should permanently command one-half. Fabius chose the latter alternative, for he felt certain that the impetuosity of his colleague would sooner or later get him into trouble with such an adversary as Hannibal, and that it was better to risk the destruction of half the army than of the whole.

Minucius withdrew the troops allotted to him, and encamped in the plains at a distance of a mile and a half from Fabius. Hannibal resolved at once to take advantage of the change, and to tempt the Romans to attack him by occupying a hill which lay about half-way between the camp of Minucius and Geronium.

The plain which surrounded the hill was level and destitute of wood, but Hannibal on a careful examination found that there were several hollows in which troops could be concealed, and in these during the night he posted five thousand infantry and five hundred cavalry. The position occupied by them was such that they would be able to take the Romans in flank and rear should they advance against the hill. Having made these dispositions he sent forward a body of light troops in the morning to occupy the hill. Minucius immediately despatched his light troops, supported by cavalry, to drive them from it. Hannibal reinforced his

Carthaginians by small bodies of troops, and the fight was obstinately maintained until Minucius, whose blood was now up, marched towards the hill with his legions in order of battle.

Hannibal on his side advanced with the remains of his troops, and the battle became fierce and general, until Hannibal gave the signal to his troops in ambush, who rushed out and charged the Romans in rear and flank. Their destruction would have been as complete and terrible as that which had befallen the army of Sempronius at the Trebia, had not Fabius moved forward with his troops to save the broken legions of Minucius.

Fabius now offered battle, but Hannibal, well content with the heavy blow which he had struck, and the great loss which he had inflicted upon the command of Minucius, fell back to his camp. Minucius acknowledged that Fabius had saved his army from total destruction, and at once resigned his command into his hands, and reverted to his former position under him. Both armies then went into winter quarters.

Malchus had not been present at the fighting near Geronium. Two days after Hannibal broke through the Roman positions round the plains of Campania he intrusted Malchus with an important commission. Commanding the body-guard of the general, and being closely related to him, Malchus was greatly in Hannibal's confidence, and was indeed on the same footing with Mago, Hannibal's brother, and two or three other of his most trusted generals. Gathered in the general's tent on the previous evening, these had agreed with their leader that final success could not be looked for in their enterprise unless reinforcements were received from Carthage.

It was now a year since they had emerged from the Alps on to the plains of Northern Italy. They had annihilated two Roman armies, had marched almost unopposed through some of the richest provinces of Italy, and yet they were no nearer the great object of their enterprise than they were when they crossed the Alps.

Some of the Cisalpine Gauls had joined them, but even in the plains north of the Apennines the majority of the tribes had remained firm to their alliance with the Romans, while south of that range of mountains the inhabitants had in every case shown themselves bitterly hostile. Everywhere on the approach of the Carthaginians they had retired to their walled towns, which Hannibal had neither the time nor the necessary machines to besiege.

Although Rome had lost two armies she had already equipped and placed in the field a third force superior in number to that of the Carthaginians; her army in Spain had not been drawn upon; her legion north of the Apennines was operating against the revolted tribes; other legions were in course of being raised and equipped, and Rome would take the field in the spring with an army greatly superior in strength to that of Carthage. Victorious as Hannibal had been in battle, the army which had struggled through the Alps had in the year which had elapsed, greatly diminished in numbers. Trebia and Trasimene had both lessened their strength, but their losses had been much heavier in the terrible march across the Apennines in the spring, and by fevers subsequently contracted from the pestiferous malaria of the marshes in the summer. In point of numbers the gaps had been filled up by the contingents furnished by their Gaulish allies. But the loss of all the elephants, of a great number of the cavalry, and of the Carthaginian troops, who formed the backbone of the army, was not to be replaced.

"Malchus," Hannibal said, "you know what we were speaking of yesterday evening. It is absolutely necessary that we should receive reinforcements. If Carthage aids me I regard victory as certain. Two or three campaigns like the last would alike break down the strength of Rome, and will detach her allies from her.

"The Latins and the other Italian tribes, when they find that Rome is powerless to protect them, that their flocks and herds, their crops and possessions are at our mercy, will at length become weary of supporting her cause, and will cast in their lot with us; but if the strife is to be continued, Carthage must make an effort—must rouse herself from the lethargy in which she appears to be sunk. It is impossible for me to leave the army, nor can I well spare Mago. The cavalry are devoted to him, and losing him would be like losing my right hand; yet it is clear that someone must go to Carthage who can speak in my name, and can represent the true situation here.

"Will you undertake the mission? It is one of great danger. In the first place you will have to make your way by sea to Greece, and thence take ship for Carthage. When you arrive there you will be bitterly opposed by Hanno and his faction, who are now all-powerful, and it may be that your mission may cost you your life; for not only do these men hate me and all connected with me, but, like most demagogues, they place their own selfish aims and ends, the advantage of their own faction, and the furtherance of their own schemes far above the general welfare of the state, the loss of all the colonies of Carthage, and the destruction of her imperial power. The loss of national prestige and honour are to these men as nothing in comparison with the question whether they can retain their places and emoluments as rulers of Carthage.

"Rome is divided as we are, her patricians and plebeians are ever bitterly opposed to each other; but at present patriotism rises above party, and both sink their disputes when the national cause is at stake. The time will doubtless come—that is, unless we cut her course short—that as Rome increases in wealth and in luxury she will suffer from the like evils that are destroying Carthage. Partly exigences will rise above patriotic considerations, and Rome will fall to pieces unless she finds some man strong and vigourous enough to grasp the whole power of the state, to silence the chattering of the politicians, and to rule her with a rod of iron. But I am wandering from my subject. Will you undertake this mission?"

"I will," Malchus replied firmly, "if you think me worthy of it. I have no eloquence as a speaker, and know nothing of the arts of the politician."

"There will be plenty of our friends there who will be able to harangue the multitude," Hannibal replied. "It is your presence there as the representative of the army, as my kinsman, and as the son of the general who did such good service to the state that will profit our cause.

IN THE DUNGEONS OF CARTHAGE

"It is your mission to tell Carthage that now is her time or never; that Rome already totters from the blows I have struck her, and that another blow only is requisite to stretch her in the dust. A mighty effort is needed to overthrow once for all our great rival.

"Sacrifices will be needed, and great ones, to obtain the object, but Rome once fallen the future of Carthage is secure. What is needed is that Carthage should obtain and keep the command of the sea for two years, that at least twenty-five thousand men should be sent over in the spring, and as many in the spring following. With such reinforcements I will undertake to destroy absolutely the power of Rome. To-morrow I will furnish you with letters to our friends at home, giving full details as to the course they should pursue and particulars of our needs.

"A party of horse shall accompany you to the coast, with a score of men used to navigation. There you will seize a ship and sail for Corinth, whence you will have no difficulty in obtaining passage to Carthage."

After nightfall the next day Malchus started, taking Nessus with him as his attendant and companion. The party travelled all night, and in the morning the long line of the sea was visible from the summits of the hills they were crossing. They waited for some hours to rest and refresh their horses, and then, continuing their journey, came down in the afternoon upon a little port at the mouth of the river Biferno. So unexpected was their approach that the inhabitants had not time to shut their gates, and the troops entered the town without resistance, the people all flying to their houses.

Malchus at once proclaimed that the Carthaginians came as friends, and would, if, unmolested, injure no one; but if any armed attempt was made against them they would sack and destroy the town. Two or three vessels were lying in the port; Malchus took possession of the largest, and, putting his party of seamen on board her, ordered the crew to sail for Corinth. The horsemen were to remain in the town until the vessel returned, when, with the party on board her, they would at once rejoin Hannibal.

THE YOUNG CARTHAGINIAN

The wind was favourable, and the next morning the mountains of Greece were in sight, and in the afternoon they entered the port of Corinth. The anchor was dropped at a short distance from the shore, the small boat was lowered, and Malchus, accompanied by Nessus, was rowed ashore by two of his own men. These then returned on board the ship, which at once weighed anchor and set sail on her return.

Corinth was a large and busy port, and the arrival and departure of the little vessel from Italy passed altogether unnoticed, and without attracting any particular attention Malchus and his companion made their way along the wharves. The trade of Corinth was large and flourishing, and the scene reminded Malchus of that with which he was so familiar in Carthage. Ships of many nationalities were ranged along the quays. Galleys from Tyre and Cyprus, from Syria and Egypt, from Carthage and Italy, were all assembled in this neutral port.

Corinth was, like Carthage, essentially a trading community; and while the power and glory of the rival cities of the Peloponnesus were rapidly failing Corinth was rising in rank, and was now the first city of Greece. Malchus had no difficulty in finding a Carthaginian trading ship. He was amply supplied with money, and soon struck a bargain that the captain should, without waiting to take in further cargo, at once sail for Carthage.

The captain was much surprised at the appearance in Corinth of a young Carthaginian evidently of high rank, but he was too well satisfied at the bargain he had made to ask any questions. An hour later the mooring ropes were cast off, and the vessel, spreading her sails, started on her voyage. The weather was warm and pleasant, and Malchus, stretched on a couch spread on the poop, greatly enjoyed the rest and quiet, after the long months which had been spent in almost incessant activity. Upon the following day Nessus approached him.

"My lord Malchus," he said, "there are some on board the ship who know you. I have overheard the men talking together, and it seems that one of them recognized you as having been in the habit of going out with a fisherman who lived next door to him at Carthage."

IN THE DUNGEONS OF CARTHAGE

"It matters not," Malchus said indifferently; "I have no particular motive in concealing my name, though it would have been as well that I should be able to meet my friends in Carthage and consult with them before my arrival there was generally known. However, before I leave the ship I can distribute some money among the crew, and tell them that for certain reasons of state I do not wish them to mention on shore that I have been a passenger."

Had Malchus been aware that the ship in which he had taken passage was one of the great fleet of traders owned by Hanno, he would have regarded the discovery of his personality by the sailors in a more serious light; as it was, he thought no more of the matter. No change in the manner of the captain showed that he was aware of the name and rank of his passenger, and Malchus, as he watched the wide expanse of sea, broken only by a few distant sails, was too intent upon the mission with which he was charged to give the matter another moment's thought.

The wind fell light and it was not until the evening of the eighth day after leaving Corinth that Carthage, with the citadel of Byrsa rising above it, could be distinguished. The ship was moving but slowly through the water, and the captain said that unless a change took place they would not make port until late the next morning. Malchus retired to his couch feeling sorry that the period of rest and tranquillity was at an end, and that he was now about to embark in a difficult struggle, which, though he felt its importance, was altogether alien to his taste and disposition.

He had not even the satisfaction that he should see his mother and sister, for news had come a short time before he sailed that their position was so uncomfortable at Carthage that they had left for Spain, to take up their abode there with Adherbal and Anna. His mother was, he heard, completely broken down in health by grief for the loss of his father.

He was wakened in the night by the splash of the anchor and the running out of he cable through the hawse-hole, and supposed that the breeze must have sprung up a little, and that they had anchored at the entrance to the harbour. He soon went

221

off to sleep again, but was presently aroused by what seemed to him the sound of a short struggle followed by another splash; he dreamingly wondered what it could be and then went off to sleep again. When he awoke it was daylight. Somewhat surprised at the non-appearance of Nessus, who usually came into his cabin the first thing in the morning to call him, he soon attired himself.

On going to the door of his cabin he was surprised to find it fastened without. He knocked loudly against it to attract attention, but almost immediately found himself in darkness. Going to the port-hole to discover the cause of this sudden change, he found that a sack had been stuffed into it, and immediately afterwards the sound of hammering told him that a plank was being nailed over this outside to keep it in its place.

The truth washed across him—he was a prisoner. Drawing his sword he flung himself with all his force against the door, but this had been so securely fastened without that it did not yield in the slightest to his efforts. After several vain efforts he abandoned the attempt, and sitting down endeavoured to realize the position. He soon arrived at something like the truth: the trading interests of Carthage were wholly at the disposal of Hanno and his party, and he doubted not that, having been recognized, the captain had determined to detain him as a prisoner until he communicated to Hanno the fact of his arrival, and received instructions from him as to whether Malchus was to be allowed to land.

Malchus recalled the sounds he had heard in the night, and uttered an exclamation of grief and anger as he concluded that his faithful follower had been attacked and doubtless killed and thrown overboard. At present he was powerless to do anything, and with his sword grasped in his hand he lay on the couch in readiness to start up and fight his way out, as soon as he heard those without undoing the fastenings of the door.

The day passed slowly. He could hear voices without and footsteps on the deck of the poop overhead, but no one came near him; and after a time his watchfulness relaxed, as he made up his mind that his captors, whatever their intentions might be, would not attempt to carry them out until after nightfall. At last he heard a moving of the heavy articles which had been piled against the door; he sprang to his feet, the door opened two or three inches, and a voice said:

"In the name of the republic I declare you to be my prisoner."

"I warn you I shall resist," Malchus exclaimed. "I am Malchus, the son of Hamilcar, late a general of the republic, and I come to Carthage on a mission from Hannibal. Whatever complaint the state may have against me I am ready to answer at the proper time, and shall not fail to appear when called upon; but at present I have Hannibal's mission to discharge, and those who interfere with me are traitors to the republic, whomsoever they may be, and I will defend myself until the last."

"Open the door and seize him," a voice exclaimed.

As the door was opened Malchus sprang forward, but the lights of several lanterns showed a dozen men with levelled spears standing in front of the cabin.

"I surrender," he said, seeing that against such a force as this resistance would be vain, "but in the name of Hannibal I protest against this interference with the messenger whom he has sent to explain, in his name, to the senate the situation in Italy."

So saying Malchus laid down his shield and sword, took off his helmet, and walked quietly from the cabin. At an order from their superior four of the men laid down their weapons and seized him. In a minute he was bound hand and foot, a gag was forced into his mouth, a cloak thrown over his head, and he was roughly thrown into a large boat alongside the ship.

Short as was the time which he had at liberty, Malchus had thrown a glance over the bulwarks of each side of the ship, and perceived that any resistance would have been useless, for far away lay the lights of Carthage; and it was evident that the vessel had made little progress since he had retired to rest on the previous evening. Had she been inside the harbour he had intended to spring overboard at once and to trust to escape by swimming,

The person in command of the party which had seized Malchus took his place at the helm of the boat, and his twelve agents seated themselves at the oars and rowed away towards Carthage. The town was nearly eight miles away, and they were two hours before they arrived there. The place where they landed was at some distance from the busy part of the port. Two men were waiting for them there with a stretcher. Upon this Malchus was laid, four men lifted it on their shoulders, the others fell in round it as a guard, and the party then proceeded through quiet streets towards the citadel.

The hour was late and but few people were about. Any who paused for a moment to look at the little procession, shrank away hastily on hearing the dreaded words, "In the name of the republic," uttered by the leader of the party. The citizens of Carthage were too well accustomed to mid-night arrests to give the matter further thought, save a momentary wonder as to who was the last victim of the tyrants of the city, and to indulge, perhaps, in a secret malediction upon them. Malchus had from the first no doubt as to his destination, and when he felt a sudden change in the angle at which the stretcher was carried, knew that he was being taken up the steep ascent to Byrsa.

He heard presently the challenge of a sentry, then there was a pause as the gates were opened, then he was carried forward for awhile, there was another stop, and the litter was lowered to the ground, his cords were unfastened, and he was commanded to rise. It needed but a glance upwards to tell him where he was. Above him towered the dark mass of the temple of Moloch, facing him was a small door known to every citizen of Carthage as leading to the dungeons under the temple.

Brave as he was, Malchus could not resist a shudder as he entered the portal, accompanied by four of his guards and preceded by a jailer. No questions were asked by the latter, and doubtless the coming of the prisoner had been expected and prepared for. The way lay down a long flight of steps and through several passages, all hewn in the solid rock. They passed many closed doors, until at last they turned into one which stood open. The gag was then removed from Malchus' mouth, the door was closed behind him, he heard the bolts fastened, and then remained alone in perfect darkness.

IN THE DUNGEONS OF CARTHAGE

Malchus felt round the walls of his cell and found that it was about six feet square. In one corner was a bundle of straw, and, spreading this out, he threw himself upon it and bitterly meditated over the position into which he had fallen. His own situation was desperate enough. He was helpless in the hands of Hanno. The friends and partisans of Hannibal were ignorant of his coming, and he could hope for no help from them. He had little doubt as to what his fate would be; he would be put to death in some cruel way, and Hannibal, his relatives, and friends would never know what had become of him from the moment when he left the Italian vessel in the port of Corinth.

But hopeless as was his own situation, Malchus thought more of Hannibal and his brave companions in arms than of himself. The manner in which he had been kidnapped by the agents of Hanno, showed how determined was that demagogue to prevent the true state of things which prevailed in Italy from becoming known to the people of Carthage. In order to secure their own triumph, he and his party were willing to sacrifice Hannibal and his army, and to involve Carthage in the most terrible disasters.

At last Malchus slept. When he awoke a faint light was streaming down into his cell. In the centre of the room was an opening of about a foot square, above which a sort of chimney extended twenty feet up through the solid rock to the surface, where it was covered with an iron grating. Malchus knew where he was. Along each side of the great temple extended a row of these gratings level with the floor, and every citizen knew that it was through these apertures that light and air reached the prisoners in the cells below. Sometimes groans and cries were heard to rise, but those who were near would hurry from the spot, for they knew that the spies of the law were ever on the watch, and that to be suspected of entering into communication with the prisoners would be sufficient to ensure condemnation and death.

It was the sight of these gratings, and the thought of the dismal cells below, which had increased the aversion which Malchus had felt as a boy to enter the blood-stained temple, little as he had dreamed that the day would come when he himself would be lying a prisoner in one of them. He knew that it was useless for him to attempt by shouting to inform his friends in the city of his presence there. The narrowness of the air passage and the closeness of the grating above deadened and confused the voice, unless to a person standing immediately above the opening, and as the visitors to the temple carefully avoided the vicinity of the gratings, it would be but a waste of breath to attempt to call their attention.

As to escape it was out of the question. The cell was cut in the solid rock. The door was of enormous strength, and even could that have been overcome, there were many others which would have to be passed before he could arrive at the entrance to the dungeon.

In a short time a Nubian entered, bearing some bread and a pitcher of water. Malchus addressed him; but the negro opened his mouth, and Malchus saw that his tongue had been cut out, perhaps in childhood, perhaps as a punishment for a crime; but more probably the man was a slave captured in war, who had been mutilated to render him a safe and useful instrument of the officers of the law.

Three hours later the door again opened, and two men appeared. They ordered Malchus to follow them, and led him through a number of meandering passages, until at last, opening a door, they ushered him into a large chamber. This was lighted by torches. At a table in the centre of the room were seated seven figures. In the one seated in a chair very slightly above the others Malchus at once recognized Hanno. His companions were all leading men of his faction.

"Malchus, son of Hamilcar," Hanno said, "what have you to say why you thus secretly come to Carthage?"

"I come not secretly," Malchus replied, "I come hither as the messenger of Hannibal to the senate. I am charged by him to lay before them the exact situation in Italy, to tell them how much he has already accomplished, and what yet remains to be done, and to explain to them the need there is that reinforcements should be despatched to him to carry out his great designs for the annihilation of the power of Rome. I come not in secret. I

226

passed in a ship from Italy to Corinth, and there at once hired a vessel to convey me hither."

"As we are members of the senate," Hanno said, "you can deliver your message to us."

"I fear that it will go no further," Malchus replied. "The fact that I have been thus secretly seized and carried here, shows how far it is your wish that the people of Carthage should know my message. Still, as even in your breasts all patriotism may not yet be dead, and as my words may move you yet to do something to enable Hannibal to save the republic, I will give you the message he sent me to deliver to the senate."

A murmur of angry surprise arose from the seven men at the bold words and the defiant bearing of their prisoner.

"How dare you thus address your judges?" Hanno exclaimed.

"Judges!" Malchus repeated scornfully, "executioners, you should say. Think you that I know not that my death is resolved on? Even if you would you dare not free a noble of Carthage, a son of a general who has lost his life in her service, a cousin of the great Hannibal, after you have thus treacherously seized and thrown him into a dungeon. Cowed as the people of Carthage are by your tyranny, corrupted as they are by your gold, this lawless act of oppression would rouse them to resistance. No, Hanno, it is because I know that my doom is sealed I thus fearlessly defy you and your creatures."

Malchus then proceeded to deliver the message of Hannibal to the senate. He showed the exact situation of affairs in Italy, urged that if the reinforcements asked for were sent, the success of the arms of Carthage and the final defeat and humiliation of Rome were assured; while, on the other hand, if Hannibal were left unaided, his army must in time dwindle away until too feeble to resist the assaults of the Romans and their allies. He warned his hearers that if this catastrophe should come about, Rome, flushed with victory, smarting under the defeats and humiliation which Hannibal had inflicted upon them, would in turn become the aggressor, and would inflict upon Carthage a blow similar to that with which Rome had been menaced by Hannibal.

Hanno and his companions listened in silence. Malchus for a time forgot his own position and the character of the men he addressed, and pleaded with an earnestness and passion such as he would have used had he been addressing the whole senate. When he had finished, Hanno without a word motioned to the jailers, and these, placing themselves one on each side of Malchus, led him back to his cell.

THE YOUNG CARTHAGINIAN

CHAPTER XVII: THE ESCAPE

FOR the next two days Malchus was visited only by the Nubian who brought his food. The third night, as he was lying on his straw, wondering how long Hanno would be before he decided his fate, he started to his feet as he heard, apparently close at hand, his name whispered. It was repeated, and he now perceived that it came from above.

"Yes," he said in a low tone, looking upwards, "I am Malchus. Who speaks to me?"

"It is I, Nessus," the voice replied. "Thanks to the gods, I have found my lord."

"How did you get here, Nessus? I feared that you were drowned."

"I swam to shore," the Arab said, "and then watched outside the gate here. I saw several prisoners brought in, and doubted not that you were among them. I was at the port when the ship came in, and found that she brought no passenger. Then I came up here again, soon found friends among the Arab regiment in the garrison; these obtained me employment in the stables of the elephants. Each night, when all has been still, I have crept here, and have whispered your name down each of the gratings. To-night you have heard me. Now that I know where you are, I will set to work to contrive your escape. Is the passage from your cell here wide enough to admit your being drawn up?"

"Yes," Malchus replied; "it would be a close fit, but with a rope you could get me up through it."

"I will set to work to loosen these bars at once," Nessus said; "but the difficulty is not to get you out from here, but to get you beyond the gates of the citadel. The watch is extremely strict, and the gates are not opened until nine o'clock. Before that your escape would be discovered, and it will be impossible for you to pass out undetected. I must find a hiding-place where you can lie concealed until the search is over, and the vigilance of the sentries is relaxed; but it will be no easy matter. And now let us speak no more; it is dangerous to breathe, much less to speak here."

Not another word was spoken for hours. Malchus could hear a low continuous scraping noise as Nessus with his dagger worked away upon the stone into which the grating fitted. At last Nessus spoke again. "I have nearly finished, my lord, the greater part of the grating is loose, and in half an hour I can complete the work. Daylight will soon be breaking and I must go. To-morrow night I will return with a rope. I hope to-day to find some place where you may be concealed."

Malchus with renewed hope threw himself upon the straw, and lay there until about noon when he was again summoned to the presence of his judges. They were the same whom he had seen previously.

"Malchus, son of Hamilcar," Hanno said, "you are now brought before us to hear the crime with which you are charged. We have here before us the written list of the names of the members of the conspiracy, headed by Giscon, which had for its aim the murder of many of the senate of Carthage and the overthrow of her constitution. We have also here the confession of several of the conspirators confirming this list, and saying that you were one of the party."

"I do not deny," Malchus said firmly, "that I did once visit the place in which those you speak of met, and that my name was then entered on the roll; but when I went there I was wholly ignorant of the purposes of the association, and as soon as I learned their aims and objects I withdrew from them, and did not again visit their place of meeting."

"You could not well do that," Hanno said, "since it is writ down that you sailed very shortly afterwards for Spain."

"I own that I did so," Malchus replied, "but I told Giscon on the very day that I accompanied him to the meeting that I would go there no more. Moreover, your commissioners with

Hannibal's army have already inquired into the circumstances, and they, in consideration of the fact that I was then little more than sixteen years old, that I was led ignorantly into the plot, and at once separated myself from it, absolved me from blame."

"The commissioners had no authority to do so," Hanno replied; "they were ordered to send you to Carthage, and failed to carry out their orders only because Hannibal then, as always, set himself above the authority of the republic. As you have confessed that you were a member of this conspiracy, no further trial is needed, and this court awards to you the same punishment which was meted to all the others concerned in the conspiracy–you will to-morrow be put to death by the usual punishment of the press."

Malchus abstained from all reply, for it struck him at once that were he to defy and anger his judges they might order him to be instantly executed. He therefore without a word turned and accompanied his jailer to his cell. He waited impatiently for night, and the hours seemed long indeed before he heard the whisper of Nessus above. Directly the Arab received the reply, assuring him that Malchus was still there, he again set to work.

In an hour the grating was removed and the rope lowered. Malchus fastened it under his arms, knotting it in front, and then whispered to Nessus that he was ready. The Arab drew him slowly and steadily up until his head was in the entrance of the narrow passage. Malchus had grasped the rope as high as possible above his head and hung by his hands, thereby drawing the shoulders upwards, and reducing their width as much as possible. He then managed to swing himself so that his body was diagonally across the opening, and when thus placed he found to his joy that the passage was large enough for him to pass through without much difficulty.

Slowly and steadily Nessus drew him up until his shoulders were above the level of the ground, when Malchus, placing his hands on the pavement, sprang noiselessly out. The grating was replaced, and without a word being spoken they glided from the temple. Not a word was said until they had gone some little distance.

"You have saved my life again, Nessus," Malchus said, laying his hand upon his shoulder. "Another twelve hours and it would have been too late. I was to have been put to death in the morning."

Nessus gave a fierce exclamation and placed his hand on his knife.

"Had they slain my lord," he said, "I would have avenged you. I would have dogged your enemies night and day till, one by one, my knife should have found its way to their hearts!"

"Have you found a hiding-place, Nessus?"

"There is but one place of safety, my lord, that I can think of. I have talked it over with two or three faithful friends, and they agree that so rigid will be the search that it will be well-nigh impossible for anyone within the walls of the citadel to escape detection. The spies of Hanno are everywhere, and men fear within these walls even to whisper what they think. At anyrate, no more secure hiding-place could be found than that which we have decided upon."

"And where is that, Nessus?"

"It is in the reservoirs. With four water-skins and some planks we have prepared a raft. My two friends are waiting for us at one of the entrances. They will have fitted the raft together, and all will be in readiness. They are not likely to search for you there."

"The idea is excellent, Nessus."

The reservoirs of Carthage were of enormous extent, and some of these remain to this day and are the wonder and admiration of travellers. They were subterranean, and were cut from the solid rock, the stone extracted from them being used for the walls of the buildings of the city. Pillars were left at intervals to support the roof; and it was calculated that these underground lakes—for they were no less—contained sufficient water to supply the wants of the great city for at least six months. These vast storing-places for water were an absolute necessity in a climate like that of Northern Africa, where the rain falls but seldom. Without them, indeed, Carthage would have been at the mercy of the first army which laid siege to it.

The greatest pains were devoted to the maintenance of the water supply. The rainfall from the roofs of the temples and houses was conducted to the reservoirs, and these stores were never drawn upon on ordinary occasions, the town being supplied with water brought by aqueducts from long distances among the hills. Here and there openings were cut in the rock which formed the roof of the reservoirs, for the admission of air, and at a few points steps from the surface led down to the water. Iron gates guarded the entrance to these.

Nessus and his friends had the evening before unfastened one of these gates. The lock was old and little used, as the gate was placed rather to prevent children and others going down to the water than for any other purpose, and the Arabs had found little difficulty in picking the rough lock.

Malchus followed Nessus down the steps until he reached the edge of the water, some fifty feet below the surface. Here stood two Arabs bearing torches. At the foot of the steps floated the raft, formed, as Nessus had said, of four inflated sheepskins connected by a framework of planks. Across these a bullock's hide had been stretched, forming a platform. On this were some rugs, a skin of wine, and a pile of flat cakes and fruit, together with half a dozen torches.

"Thanks, my friends!" Malchus said to the Arabs. "Some day I may be able to prove that I am grateful to you."

"The friends of Nessus are our friends," one of the Arabs replied simply; "his lord is our master."

"Here is a paddle, my lord," Nessus said. "I propose that you should paddle straight away as far as you can see a torch burning here; then that you should fasten the raft to a pillar. Every other night I will come with provisions here and show a light. If you see the light burn steadily it is safe for you to approach, and I come only to bring food or news; if you see the torch wave to and fro, it is a warning that they intend to search the reservoirs. I do not think it likely they will do so; still it is best to be prepared, and in that case you must paddle far away in the recesses. They might search for a long time before they find you. I trust that your imprisonment here will not be long, but that we may hit upon some plan of getting you out of the citadel. I would gladly go with you to share your solitude, but I must remain outside to plan some way of escape."

The hiding-place in the reservoirs under Carthage

THE ESCAPE

With a short farewell to his faithful follower Malchus took his place on the raft, having lit a torch and fastened it upright upon it. Then he paddled slowly away, keeping between the lines of heavy columns. His rate of progress was slow, and for half an hour he kept the torch in sight. By this time he felt sure that he must be approaching the boundary of the reservoir. He therefore moored his raft against a pillar and waved his torch backwards and forwards. The signal was answered by a similar movement of the distant light, which then disappeared. Malchus now extinguished his own torch, placed the means of relighting it with which Nessus had furnished him close to his hand, and then, wrapping himself in a rug, lay down to sleep.

When he awoke it was day. The light was streaming down on to the water from an opening two or three hundred yards away, while far in the distance he could see a faint light which marked the place of the steps at which he had embarked. In the neighbourhood of the opening the columns stood up clear and gray against the dark background. A little further off their outlines were dim and misty; and wherever else he looked an inky darkness met his eye, save one or two faint bands of misty light, which marked the position of distant openings.

The stillness which reigned in this vast cavern, was almost oppressive. Sometimes a faint rustling whisper, the echo of some sound in the citadel above, passed among the columns; and the plaintive squeak of a bat was heard now and then, for numbers of these creatures were flitting noiselessly in the darkness, their forms visible for an instant as they passed and repassed between Malchus and the, light. He wondered vaguely what they could find to eat here, and then remembered that he had heard that at nightfall numbers of bats could be seen flying up from the openings to the reservoirs to seek food without, returning to their hiding-places when morning approached.

Malchus amused himself by thinking over the fury and astonishment of Hanno and his colleagues on hearing that their prisoner had disappeared, and he pictured to himself the hot search which was no doubt going on throughout the citadel. He thought it improbable in the extreme that any search would be made in the reservoir. Nessus would refasten the gate after passing through it again, and the idea, that he could be floating on the subterranean lake could hardly occur to them.

Then he turned over in his mind the various devices by which it might be possible to get beyond the walls of the citadel. The anxiety of Hanno and those acting with him to prevent the manner in which they had kidnapped and sentenced to death the messenger and kinsman of Hannibal from becoming known in the city, would be so great that extraordinary vigilance would be used to prevent any from leaving the citadel. The guards on the walls would be greatly increased; none would be allowed to pass the gate without the most rigourous examination; while every nook and corner of the citadel, the temples, the barracks, storehouses, and stables, would be searched again and again. Even should a search be made in the reservoir, Malchus had little fear of discovery; for even should a boat come towards the spot where he was lying, he would only have to pass the raft round to the opposite side of the great pillar, some twelve feet square, against which he was lying.

When the light faded out he again lay down to sleep. As before, he slept soundly; for, however great the heat above, the air in the subterranean chambers was always fresh and cool, and he could well bear the rugs which Nessus had provided. The next day passed more slowly, for he had less to think about. After the daylight had again faded he began to look forward expectantly for the signal, although he knew that many hours must still elapse before Nessus would be able to make his way to the place of meeting.

So slowly did the hours pass, indeed, that he began at last to fear that something must have happened–perhaps that Nessus had been in some way recognized, and was now in the dungeons below the temple of Moloch. At last, however, to his joy Malchus saw the distant light; it burned steadily, and he at once set out to paddle towards it. He did not light his torch—it would have taken time, and he knew that, quietly as he paddled, the sound would be borne along the surface of the water to Nessus. At last he arrived at the steps. Nessus was there alone; beside him was a basket of fresh provisions.

"Well, Nessus, what news?"

"All is well, my lord; but Hanno is moving heaven and earth to find you. The gates of the citadel were kept closed all day yesterday; and although to-day they have again been opened, the examination of those who pass out is so strict that no disguise would avail to deceive the scrutiny of the searchers. One or other of the men who attended you in the prison is always at the gate. The barracks have been searched from end to end, the troops occupying them being all turned out while the agents of the law searched them from top to bottom. The same has been done with the stables; and it is well that we did not attempt to hide you above ground, for assuredly if we had done so they would have found you, however cunningly we had stowed you away. Of course the name of the prisoner who has escaped is known to none, but the report that an important prisoner had escaped from the state prisons beneath the temple has created quite an excitement in the city, for it is said that such an event never took place before. At present I can hit on no plan whatever for getting you free."

"Then I must be content to wait for a while, Nessus. After a time their vigilance is sure to relax, as they will think that I must have got beyond the walls."

"Are there any to whom you would wish me to bear news that you are here?"

This was a question which Malchus had debated with himself over and over again. It appeared to him, however, that Hanno's power was so great that it would be dangerous for anyone to come forward and accuse him. No doubt every one of the leading men of the Barcine party was strictly watched; and did Hanno suspect that any of them were in communication with the escaped prisoner, he would take instant steps against them. He thought it better, therefore, that none should be acquainted with the secret until he was free. He therefore replied in the negative to the question of Nessus.

"I must wait till I am free. Any action now might bring down the vengeance of Hanno upon others. He would find no difficulty in inventing some excuse for dealing a blow at them. You think here is no possibility of escape at present?"

"I can think on no plan, my lord. So strict is the search that when the elephants went down to-day to the fountains for water every howdah was examined to see that no one was hidden within it."

"It will be necessary also, Nessus, if you do hit upon some plan for getting me out, to arrange a hiding-place in the city."

"That will be easy enough," Nessus replied. "My friends have many relations in the Arab quarter, and once free, you might be concealed there for any time. And now I will wait no longer, for last night visits were made in all the barracks and stables by the agents of the law, to see that every man was asleep in his place. Therefore I will return without delay. In two days I will be here again; but should anything occur which it is needful to tell you I will be here to-morrow night."

Malchus watched for the light on the following evening with but faint hope of seeing it, but at about the same hour as before he saw it suddenly appear again. Wondering what had brought Nessus before his time, he paddled to the stairs.

"Well, Nessus, what is your news?"

"We have hit upon a plan of escape, my lord. As I told you my friend and I are in the stable with the elephants, our duties being to carry in the forage for the great beasts, and to keep the stables in order. We have taken one of the Indian mahouts into our confidence, and he has promised his aid; the elephant of which he is in charge is a docile beast, and his driver has taught him many tricks. At his signal he will put up his trunk and scream and rush here and there as if in the state which is called *must*, when they are dangerous of approach. The mahout, who is a crafty fellow, taught him to act thus, because when in such a state of temper the elephants cannot be worked with the others, but remain in the stables, and their drivers have an easy time of it.

"On the promise of a handsome reward the mahout has agreed that to-morrow morning, before the elephants are taken out, you shall be concealed in the bottom of the howdah. He will manage that the elephant is the first in the procession. When we get out into the court-yard he will slyly prick the beast, and give him the signal to simulate rage; he will then so direct him that, after charging several times about the court, he shall make a rush at the gate. You may be sure that the guards there will step aside quickly enough, for a furious elephant is not a creature to be hindered.

"When he is once down to the foot of the hill the driver will direct him to some quiet spot. That he will find easily enough, for at his approach there will be a general stampede. When he reaches some place where no one is in sight he will halt the elephant and you will at once drop off him. I shall be near at hand and will join you. The elephant will continue his course for some little distance, and the mahout, feigning to have at last recovered control over him, will direct him back to the citadel."

"The idea is a capital one," Malchus said, "and if carried out will surely succeed. You and I have often seen during our campaigns elephants in this state, and know how every one flies as they come along screaming loudly, with their trunks high, and their great ears out on each side of their heads. At anyrate it is worth trying, Nessus, and if by any chance we should fail in getting through the gate, the mahout would, of course, take his elephant back to the stable, and I might slip out there and conceal myself till night, and then make my way back here again."

"That's what we have arranged," Nessus said. "And now, my lord, I will leave you and go back to the stables, in case they should search them again to-night. If you will push off and lie a short distance away from the steps I will be here again half an hour before daybreak. I will bring you a garb like my own, and will take you direct to the stable where the animal is kept. There will be no one there save the mahout and my two friends, so that it will be easy for us to cover you in the howdah before the elephants go out. There is little chance of anyone coming into the stables before that, for they have been searched so frequently during the last two days that Hanno's agents must by this time be convinced that wherever you are hidden you are not there. Indeed, to-day the search has greatly relaxed, although the vigilance at the gate and on the walls is as great as ever; so I think that they despair of finding you, and believe that you must either have made your escape already, or that if not you will sooner or later issue from your hiding-place and fall into their hands."

Malchus slept little that night, and rejoiced when he again saw Nessus descending the steps. A few strokes of his paddle sent the raft alongside. Nessus fastened a cord to it to prevent it from drifting away.

"We may need it again," he said briefly. Malchus placed his own clothes upon it and threw over his shoulders the bernous which Nessus had brought. He then mounted the steps with him, the gate was closed and the bolt shot, and they then made their way across to the stables. It was still perfectly dark, though a very faint light, low in the eastern sky, showed that ere long the day would break.

Five minutes' walking and they arrived at the stables of the elephants. These, like those of the horses and the oxen which drew the cumbrous war-machines, were formed in the vast thickness of the walls, and were what are known in modern times as casemates. As Nessus had said, the Indian mahout and the other two Arabs were the only human occupants of the casemate. The elephant at once showed that he perceived the new-comer to be a stranger by an uneasy movement, but the mahout quieted him.

While they were waiting for morning, Nessus described, more fully than he had hitherto had an opportunity of doing, the attack made upon him on board the ship.

"I was," he said, "as my lord knows, uneasy when I found that they had recognized you, and when we were within a day's sail of Carthage I resolved to keep a look-out; therefore, although I wrapped myself in my cloak and lay down, I did not go to sleep. After awhile I thought I heard the sound of oars, and, standing up, went to the bulwark to listen. Suddenly some of the sailors, who must have been watching me, sprang upon me from behind, a cloak was thrown over my head, a rope was twisted round my arms, and in a moment I was lifted and flung overboard.

"I did not cry out, because I had already made up my mind that it was better not to arouse you from sleep whatever happened, as, had you run out, you might have been killed, and I thought it likely that their object would be, if you offered no resistance, to take you a prisoner, in which case I trusted that I might later on hope to free you. As my lord knows, I am a good swimmer. I let myself sink, and when well below the surface soon got rid of the rope which bound me, and which was, indeed, but hastily twisted round my arms. I came up to the surface as noiselessly as possible, and after taking a long breath dived and swam under water as far as I could. When I came up the ship was so far away that there was little fear of their seeing me; however, I dived again and again until in perfect safety.

"I heard a boat rowed by many oars approach the vessel. I listened for a time and found that all was quiet, and then laid myself out for the long swim to shore, which I reached without difficulty. All day I kept my eye on the vessel, which remained at anchor. As I could not tell to which landing-place you might be brought I went up in the evening and took my post on the road leading up here, and when towards morning a party entered, carrying one with them on a stretcher, I had little doubt that it was you.

"I was sure to find friends among the Arabs either belonging to the regiment stationed in Byrsa or those employed in the storehouses or stables; so the next morning I entered the citadel and soon met these men, who belonged to my tribe and village. After that my way was plain; my only fear was that they might kill you before I could discover the place in which you were confined, and my heart sank the first night when I found that, though I whispered down every one of the gratings, I could obtain no reply.

"I had many answers, indeed, but not from you. There might be many cells besides those with openings into the temple, and were you placed in one of these I might never hear of you again. I had resolved that if the next night passed without my being able to find you, I would inform some of those known to be friends of Hannibal that you were a prisoner, and leave it in their hands to act as they liked, while I still continued my efforts to communicate with you. You may imagine with what joy I heard your reply on the following night."

"I must have been asleep the first night," Malchus said, "and did not hear your voice."

"I feared to speak above a whisper, my lord; there are priests all night in the sanctuary behind the great image."

241

Day had by this time broken, and a stir and bustle commenced in front of the long line of casemates; the elephants were brought out from their stables and stood rocking themselves from side to side while their keepers rubbed their hides with pumice-stone. Nessus was one of those who was appointed to make the great flat cakes of coarse flour which formed the principal food of the elephants. The other Arabs busied themselves in bringing in fresh straw, which Malchus scattered evenly over the stall; heaps of freshly cut forage were placed before each elephant.

In a short time one of the Arabs took the place of Nessus in preparing the cakes, while Nessus moved away and presently went down into the town to await the coming of Malchus. By this arrangement if the superintendent of the stables came round he would find the proper number of men at work, and was not likely to notice the substitution of Malchus for Nessus, with whose face he could not yet have become familiar. By this time numbers of the townsmen were as usual coming up to the citadel to worship in the temple or to visit friends dwelling there. Malchus learned that since his escape had been known each person on entrance received a slip of brass with a stamp on it which he had to give up on leaving.

All employed in the citadel received a similar voucher, without which none could pass the gate. The time was now come when the elephants were accustomed to be taken down to the fountains in the town below, and the critical moment was at hand. The mahout had already begun to prepare his elephant for the part he was to play. It had been trumpeting loudly and showing signs of impatience and anger. The animal was now made to kneel by the door of its stable, where Malchus had already lain down at the bottom of the howdah, a piece of sacking being thrown over him by the Arabs. The two Arabs and the mahout carried the howdah out, placed it on the elephant, and securely fastened it in its position.

These howdahs were of rough construction, being in fact little more than large open crates, for the elephants after being watered went to the forage-yard, where the crates were filled with freshly cut grass or young boughs of trees, which they carried up for their own use to the citadel.

The mahout took his position on its neck, and the elephant then rose to its feet. The symptoms of bad temper which it had already given were now redoubled. It gave vent to a series of short vicious squeals, it trumpeted loudly and angrily, and, although the mahout appeared to be doing his best to pacify it, it became more and more demonstrative. The superintendent of the elephants rode up.

"You had better dismount and take that brute back to the stable," he said; "he is not safe to take out this morning." As he approached the elephant threw up his trunk, opened his mouth, and rushed suddenly at him. The officer fled hastily, shouting loudly to the other mahouts to bring their animals in a circle round the elephant; but the mahout gave him a sudden prod with his pricker and the elephant set off with great strides, his ears out, his trunk in the air, and with every sign of an access of fury, at the top of his speed. He rushed across the great court-yard, the people flying in all directions with shouts of terror; he made two or three turns up and down, each time getting somewhat nearer to the gate.

As he approached it for the third time the mahout guided him towards it, and, accustomed at this hour to sally out, the elephant made a sudden rush in that direction. The officer on guard shouted to his men to close the gate, but before they could attempt to carry out the order the elephant charged through, and at the top of his speed went down the road towards the town.

CHAPTER XVIII: CANNÆ

AS the elephant tore down the road to the town many were the narrow escapes that, as they thought, those coming up had of being crushed or thrown into the air by the angry beast. Some threw themselves on their faces, others got over the parapet and hung by their hands until he had passed, while some squeezed themselves against the wall; but the elephant passed on without doing harm to any.

On reaching the foot of the descent the mahout guided the animal to the left, and, avoiding the busy streets of the town, directed its course towards the more quiet roads of the opulent quarter of Megara. The cries of the people at the approach of the elephant preceded its course, and all took refuge in gardens or houses. The latter became less and less frequent, until, at a distance of two miles from the foot of the citadel, the mahout, on looking round, perceived no one in sight. He brought the elephant suddenly to a standstill.

"Quick, my lord," he exclaimed, "now is the time."

Malchus threw off the sack, climbed out of the howdah, and slipped down by the elephant's tail, the usual plan for dismounting when an elephant is on its feet. Then he sprang across the road, leaped into a garden, and hid himself among some bushes. The mahout now turned the elephant, and, as if he had succeeded at last in subduing it, slowly retraced his steps towards the citadel.

A minute or two later Malchus issued out and quietly followed it. He had gone some distance when he saw an Arab approaching him, and soon recognized Nessus. They turned off together from the main road and made their way by by-streets until they reached the lower city. At a spot near the port they found one of the Arabs from above awaiting them, and he at once led the way to the house inhabited by his family. The scheme had been entirely successful. Malchus had escaped from the citadel without the possibility of a suspicion arising that he had issued from its gates, and in his Arab garb he could now traverse the streets unsuspected.

Nessus was overjoyed at the success of the stratagem, and Malchus himself could hardly believe that he had escaped from the terrible danger which threatened him. Nessus and the Arab at once returned to the citadel. It was agreed that the former had better continue his work as usual until the evening, and then ask for his discharge on the plea that he had received a message requiring his presence in his native village, for it was thought that suspicion might be excited were he to leave suddenly without drawing his pay, and possibly a search might be instituted in the city to discover his whereabouts.

At nightfall he returned, and then went to the house of one of the leaders of the Barcine party with a message from Malchus to tell him where he was, and the events which had occurred since his landing at Carthage, and asking him to receive him privately in two hours' time, in order that he might consult him as to the best plan to be followed.

Nessus returned saying that Manon was at home and was awaiting him, and the two at once set out for his house. Manon, who was a distant relation of Malchus, received him most warmly, and listened in astonishment to his story of what had befallen him. Malchus then explained the mission with which Hannibal had charged him, and asked his advice as to the best course to be adopted. Manon was silent for a time.

"Hanno's faction is all-powerful at present," he said, "and were Hannibal himself here I doubt whether his voice could stir the senate into taking action such as is needed. The times have been hard, and Hanno and his party have lavished money so freely among the lower classes that there is no hope of stirring the populace up to declare against him. I think it would be in the highest degree dangerous were we, as you propose, to introduce you suddenly to the senate as Hannibal's ambassador to them, and leave you to plead his cause. You would obtain no hearing. Hanno would rise in his place and denounce you as one already condemned by the tribunals as an enemy to the republic, and would demand your instant execution, and, as he has a great majority of votes in the senate, his demand would be complied with. You would, I am convinced, throw away your life for no good purpose, while your presence and your mysterious escape from prison would be made the pretense for a fresh series of persecutions of our partisans. I understand as well as you do the urgency for reinforcements being sent to Italy; but in order to do this the navy, now rotting in our harbours, must be repaired, the command of the sea must be regained, and fresh levies of troops made.

"To ask Carthage to make these sacrifices in her present mood is hopeless; we must await an opportunity. I and my friends will prepare the way, will set our agents to work among the people, and when the news of another victory arrives and the people's hopes are aroused and excited, we will strike while the iron is hot, and call upon them to make one great effort to bring the struggle to a conclusion and to finish with Rome forever.

"Such is, in my opinion, the only possible mode of proceeding. To move now would be to ensure a rejection of our demands, to bring fresh persecutions upon us, and so to weaken us that we should be powerless to turn to good account the opportunity which the news of another great victory would afford. I will write at once to Hannibal and explain all the circumstances of the situation, and will tell him why I have counselled you to avoid carrying out his instructions, seeing that to do so now would be to ensure your own destruction and greatly damage our cause.

"In the meantime you must, for a short time, remain in concealment, while I arrange for a ship to carry you back to Italy."

"The sooner the better," Malchus said bitterly, "for Carthage with its hideous tyranny, its foul corruption, its forgetfulness of its glory, its honour, and even its safety, is utterly hateful to me. I trust that never again shall I set foot within its walls. Better a thousand times to die in a battle-field than to live in this accursed city."

"It is natural that you should be indignant," Manon said, "for the young blood runs hotly in your veins, and your rage at seeing the fate which is too certainly impending over Carthage, and which you are powerless to prevent, is in no way to be blamed. We old men bow more resignedly to the decrees of the gods. You know the saying, 'Those whom the gods would destroy they first strike with madness.' Carthage is such. She sees unmoved the heroic efforts which Hannibal and his army are making to save her, and she will not stretch out a hand to aid him. She lives contentedly under the constant tyranny of Hanno's rule, satisfied to be wealthy, luxurious, and slothful, to carry on her trade, to keep her riches, caring nothing for the manly virtues, indifferent to valour, preparing herself slowly and surely to fall an easy prey to Rome.

"The end probably will not come in my time, it may come in yours, but come it certainly and surely will. A nation which can place a mere handful of its own citizens in the line of battle voluntarily dooms herself to destruction."

"Whether it comes in my time or not," Malchus said, "I will be no sharer in the fate of Carthage. I have done with her; and if I do not fall in the battle-field I will, when the war is over, seek a refuge among the Gauls, where, if the life is rough, it is at least free and independent, where courage and manliness and honour count for much, and where the enervating influence of wealth is as yet unknown. Such is my firm resolution."

"I say nothing to dissuade you, Malchus," the old man replied, "such are the natural sentiments of your age; and methinks, were my own time to come over again, I too would choose such a life in preference to an existence in the polluted atmosphere of ungrateful Carthage. And now, will you stop here with me, or will you return to the place where you are staying? I need not say how gladly I would have you here, but I cannot answer certainly for your safety. Every movement of those belonging to our party is watched by Hanno, and I doubt not that he has his spies among my slaves and servants.

"Therefore deem me not inhospitable if I say that it were better for you to remain in hiding where you are. Let your follower come nightly to me for instructions; let him enter the gate and remain in the garden near it. I will come down and see him; his visits, were they known, would excite suspicion. Bid him on his return watch closely to see that he is not followed, and tell him to go by devious windings and to mix in the thickest crowds in order to throw any one who may be following off his track before he rejoins you. I trust to be able to arrange for a ship in the course of three or four days. Come again and see me before you leave. Here is a bag of gold; you will need it to reward those who have assisted in your escape."

Malchus at once agreed that it would be better for him to return to his abode among the Arabs, and thanking Manon for his kindness he returned with Nessus, who had been waiting without.

As they walked along Malchus briefly related to his follower the substance of his interview with Manon. Suddenly Nessus stopped and listened, and then resumed his walk.

"I think we are followed, my lord," he said, "one of Hanno's spies in Manon's household is no doubt seeking to discover who are the Arabs who have paid his master a visit. I have thought once before that I heard a footfall, now I am sure of it. When we get to the next turning do you walk on and I will turn down the road. If the man behind us be honest he will go straight on; if he be a spy, he will hesitate and stop at the corner to decide which of us he shall follow; then I shall know what to do."

Accordingly at the next crossroad they came to Nessus turned down and concealed himself a few paces away, while Malchus, without pausing, walked straight on. A minute later Nessus saw a dark figure come stealthily along. He stopped at the junction of the roads and stood for a few seconds in hesitation, then he followed Malchus.

Nessus issued from his hiding-place, and, with steps as silent and stealthy as those of a tiger tracking his prey, followed the man. When within a few paces of him he gave a sudden spring and flung himself upon him, burying his knife between his shoulders. Without a sound the man fell forward on his face. Nessus coolly wiped his knife upon the garments of the spy, and then proceeded at a rapid pace until he overtook Malchus.

"It was a spy," he said, "but he will carry no more tales to Hanno."

Two days later, Nessus, on his return from his visit to Manon, brought news that the latter had arranged with the captain of a ship owned by a friend to carry them across to Corinth, whence they would have no difficulty in taking a passage to Italy. They were to go on board late the following night, and the ship would set sail at day-break.

The next evening Malchus accompanied by Nessus paid a farewell visit to Manon, and repeated to him all the instructions of Hannibal, and Manon handed him his letter for the general, and again assured him that he would, with his friends, at once set to work to pave the way for an appeal to the populace at the first favourable opportunity.

After bidding farewell to the old noble, Malchus returned to the house of the Arab and prepared for his departure. He had already handsomely rewarded the two men and the mahout for the services they had rendered him. In the course of the day he had provided himself with the garments of a trader, the character which he was now about to assume.

At midnight, when all was quiet, he and Nessus set out and made their way down to the port, where, at a little-frequented landing-stage, a boat was awaiting them, and they were at once rowed to the ship, which was lying at anchor half a mile from the shore in readiness for an early start in the morning.

Although it seemed next to impossible that they could have been traced, Malchus walked the deck restlessly until the morning, listening to every sound, and it was not until the anchor was weighed, the sails hoisted, and the vessel began to draw away from Carthage that he went into his cabin. On the sixth day after leaving Carthage the ship entered the port of Corinth.

There were several vessels there from Italian ports, but before proceeding to arrange for a passage Malchus went to a shop and bought, for himself and Nessus, such clothing and arms as would enable them to pass without difficulty as fighting men belonging to one of the Latin tribes. Then he made inquiries on the quay, and, finding that a small Italian craft was to start that afternoon for Brundusium, he went on board and accosted the captain.

"We want to cross to Italy," he said, "but we have our reasons for not wishing to land at Brundusium, and would fain be put ashore at some distance from the town. We are ready, of course, to pay extra for the trouble."

The request did not seem strange to the captain. Malchus had spoken in Greek, the language with which all who traded on the Mediterranean were familiar. He supposed that they had in some way embroiled themselves with the authorities at Brundusium, and had fled for awhile until the matter blew over, and that they were now anxious to return to their homes without passing through the town. He asked rather a high price for putting them ashore in a boat as they wished, and Malchus haggled over the sum for a considerable time, as a readiness to pay an exorbitant price might have given rise to doubts in the captain's mind as to the quality of his passengers. Once or twice he made as if he would go ashore, and the captain at last abated his demands to a reasonable sum.

When this was settled Malchus went no more ashore, but remained on board until the vessel sailed, as he feared that he might again be recognized by some of the sailors of the Carthaginian vessels in port. The weather was fair and the wind light, and on the second day after sailing the vessel lay to in a bay a few miles from Brundusium. The boat was lowered, and Malchus and his companions set on shore.

They had before embarking laid in a store of provisions not only for a voyage, but for their journey across the country, as the slight knowledge which Malchus had of the Latin tongue would have betrayed him at once were he obliged to enter a town or village to purchase food. Carrying the provisions in bundles they made for the mountains, and after three days' journey reached without interruption or adventure the camp of Hannibal. He was still lying in his intrenched camp near Geronium. The Roman army was as before watching him at a short distance off.

Malchus at once sought the tent of the general, whose surprise at seeing him enter was great, for he had not expected that he would return until the spring. Malchus gave him an account of all that had taken place since he left him. Hannibal was indignant in the extreme at Hanno having ventured to arrest and condemn his ambassador. When he learned the result of the interview with Manon, and heard how completely the hostile faction were the masters of Carthage, he agreed that the counsels of the old nobleman were wise, and that Malchus could have done no good, whereas he would have exposed himself to almost certain death, by endeavouring further to carry out the mission with which he had been charged.

"Manon knows what is best, and, no doubt, a premature attempt to excite the populace to force Hanno into sending the reinforcements we so much need would have not only failed, but would have injured our cause. He and his friends will doubtless work quietly to prepare the public mind, and I trust that ere very long some decisive victory will give them the opportunity for exciting a great demonstration on our behalf."

The remainder of the winter passed quietly. Malchus resumed his post as the commander of Hannibal's body-guard, but his duties were very light. The greater part of his time was spent in accompanying Hannibal in his visits to the camps of the soldiers, where nothing was left undone which could add to the comfort and contentment of the troops. There is no stronger evidence of the popularity of Hannibal and of the influence which he exercised over his troops than the fact that the army under him, composed, as it was, of men of so many nationalities, for the most part originally compelled against their will to enter the service of Carthage, maintained their discipline unshaken, not only by the hardships and sacrifices of the campaigns, but through the long periods of enforced idleness in their winter quarters.

From first to last, through the long war, there was neither grumbling, nor discontent, nor insubordination among the troops. They served willingly and cheerfully. They had absolute confidence in their general, and were willing to undertake the most tremendous labours and to engage in the most arduous conflicts to please him, knowing that he, on his part, was unwearied in promoting their comfort and well-being at all other times.

As the spring advanced the great magazines which

Hannibal had brought with him became nearly exhausted, and no provisions could be obtained from the surrounding country, which had been completely ruined by the long presence of the two armies. It became, therefore, necessary to move from the position which he had occupied during the winter. The Romans possessed the great advantage over him of having magazines in their rear constantly replenished by their allies, and move where they might, they were sure of obtaining subsistence without difficulty. Thus, upon the march, they were unembarrassed by the necessity of taking a great baggage-train with them, and, when halted, their general could keep his army together in readiness to strike a blow whenever an opportunity offered; while Hannibal, on the other hand, was forced to scatter a considerable portion of the army in search of provisions.

The annual elections at Rome had just taken place, and Terentius Varro and Emilius Paulus had been chosen consuls. Emilius belonged to the aristocratic party, and had given proof of military ability three years before when he had commanded as consul in the Illyrian war. Varro belonged to the popular party, and is described by the historians of the period as a coarse and brutal demagogue, the son of a butcher, and having himself been a butcher. But he was unquestionably an able man, and possessed some great qualities. The prætor Marcellus, who had slain a Gaulish king with his own hand in the last Gaulish war, was at Ostia with a legion. He was destined to command the fleet and to guard the southern coasts of Italy, while another prætor, Lucius Postumius, with one legion, was in Cisalpine Gaul keeping down the tribes friendly to Carthage.

But before the new consuls arrived to take the command of the army Hannibal had moved from Geronium.

The great Roman magazine of Apulia was at Cannæ, a town near the river Aufidus. This important place was but fifty miles by the shortest route across the plain from Geronium; but the Romans were unable to follow directly across the plain, for at this time the Carthaginians greatly outnumbered them in cavalry, and they would, therefore, have to take the road round the foot of the mountains, which was nearly seventy miles long; and yet, by some unaccountable blunder, they neglected to place a sufficient guard over their great magazines at Cannæ to defend them for even a few days against a sudden attack.

Hannibal saw the opportunity, and when spring was passing into summer broke up his camp and marched straight to Cannæ, where the vast magazines of the Romans at once fell into his hands. He thus not only obtained possession of his enemy's supplies, but interposed between the Romans and the low-lying district of Southern Apulia, where alone, at, this early season of the year, the corn was fully ripe.

The Romans had now no choice but to advance and fight a battle for the recovery of their magazines, for, had they retired, the Apulians, who had already suffered terribly from the war, would, in sheer despair, have been forced to declare for Carthage, while it would have been extremely difficult to continue any longer the waiting tactics of Fabius, as they would now have been obliged to draw their provisions from a distance, while Hannibal could victual his army from the country behind him. The senate therefore, having largely reinforced the army, ordered the consuls to advance and give battle.

They had under them eight full legions, or eighty thousand infantry and seven thousand two hundred cavalry. To oppose these Hannibal had forty thousand infantry and ten thousand excellent cavalry, of whom two thousand were Numidians. On the second day after leaving the neighbourhood of Geronium the Romans encamped at a distance of six miles from the Carthaginians. Here the usual difference of opinion at once arose between the Roman consuls, who commanded the army on alternate days. Varro wished to march against the enemy without delay, while Emilius was adverse to risking an engagement in a country which, being level and open, was favourable to the action of Hannibal's superior cavalry.

On the following day Varro, whose turn it was to command, marched towards the hostile camp. Hannibal attacked the Roman advanced guard with his cavalry and light infantry, but Varro had supported his cavalry not only by his light troops, but by a strong body of his heavy armed infantry, and after an engagement, which lasted for several hours, he repulsed the Carthaginians with considerable loss.

That evening the Roman army encamped about three miles from Cannæ, on the right bank of the Aufidus. The next morning Emilius, who was in command, detached a third of his force across the river, and encamped them there for the purpose of supporting the Roman foraging parties on that side and of interrupting those of the Carthaginians.

The next day passed quietly, but on the following morning Hannibal quitted his camp and formed his army in order of battle to tempt the Romans to attack; but Emilius, sensible that the ground was against him, would not move, but contented himself with further strengthening his camps. Hannibal, seeing that the Romans would not fight, detached his Numidian cavalry across the river to cut off the Roman foraging parties and to surround and harass their smaller camp on that side of the river. On the following morning Hannibal, knowing that Varro would be in command, and feeling sure that, with his impetuous disposition, the consul would be burning to avenge the insult offered by the surrounding of his camp by the Numidians, moved his army across the river, and formed it in order of battle, leaving eight thousand of his men to guard his camp.

By thus doing he obtained a position which he could the better hold with his inferior forces, while the Romans, deeming that he intended to attack their camp on that side of the river, would be likely to move their whole army across and to give battle. This in fact Varro proceeded to do. Leaving ten thousand men in his own camp with orders to march out and attack that of Hannibal during the engagement, he led the rest of his troops over the river, and having united his force with that in the camp on the right bank, marched down the river until he faced the position which Hannibal had taken up.

This had been skilfully chosen. The river, whose general course was east and west, made a loop, and across this Hannibal had drawn up his army with both wings resting upon the river. Thus the Romans could not outflank him, and the effect of their vastly superior numbers in infantry would to some extent be neutralized. The following was the disposition of his troops.

The Spaniards and Gauls occupied the centre of the line

of infantry. The Africans formed the two wings. On his left flank between the Africans and the river he placed his heavy African and Gaulish horse, eight thousand strong, while the two thousand Numidians were posted between the infantry and the river on the right flank. Hannibal commanded the centre of the army in person, Hanno the right wing, Hasdrubal the left wing; Maharbal commanded the cavalry.

Varro placed his infantry in close and heavy order, so as to reduce their front to that of the Carthaginians. The Roman cavalry, numbering two thousand four hundred men, was on his right wing, and was thus opposed to Hannibal's heavy cavalry, eight thousand strong. The cavalry of the Italian allies, four thousand eight hundred strong, was on the left wing facing the Numidians.

Emilius commanded the Roman right, Varro the left. The Carthaginians faced north, so that the wind, which was blowing strongly from the south, swept clouds of dust over their heads full into the faces of the enemy. The battle was commenced by the light troops on both sides, who fought for some time obstinately and courageously, but without any advantage to either. While this contest was going on, Hannibal advanced his centre so as to form a salient angle projecting in front of his line. The whole of the Gauls and Spaniards took part in this movement, while the Africans remained stationary; at the same time he launched his heavy cavalry against the Roman horse.

The latter were instantly overthrown, and were, driven from the field with great slaughter. Emilius himself was wounded, but managed to join the infantry. While the Carthaginian heavy horse were thus defeating the Roman cavalry, the Numidians maneuvered near the greatly superior cavalry of the Italian allies, and kept them occupied until the heavy horse, after destroying the Roman cavalry, swept round behind their infantry and fell upon the rear of the Italian horse, while the Numidians charged them fiercely in front.

Thus caught in a trap the Italian horse were completely annihilated, and so, before the heavy infantry of the two armies met each other, not a Roman cavalry soldier remained alive and unwounded on the field.

THE YOUNG CARTHAGINIAN

The Roman infantry now advanced to the charge, and from the nature of Hannibal's formation their centre first came in contact with the head of the salient angle formed by the Gauls and Spaniards. These resisted with great obstinacy. The principes, who formed the second line of the Roman infantry, came forward and joined the spearmen, and even the triarii pressed forward and joined in the fight. Fighting with extreme obstinacy the Carthaginian centre was forced gradually back until they were again in a line with the Africans on their flanks.

The Romans had insensibly pressed in from both flanks upon the point where they had met with resistance, and now occupied a face scarcely more than half that with which they had begun the battle. Still further the Gauls and Spaniards were driven back until they now formed an angle in rear of the original line, and in this angle the whole of the Roman infantry in a confused mass pressed upon them. This was the moment for which Hannibal had waited. He wheeled round both his flanks, and the Africans, who had hitherto not struck a blow, now fell in perfect order upon the flanks of the Roman mass, while Hasdrubal with his victorious cavalry charged down like a torrent upon their rear. Then followed a slaughter unequalled in the records of history. Unable to open out, to fight, or to fly, with no quarter asked or given, the Romans and their Latin allies fell before the swords of their enemies, till, of the seventy thousand infantry which had advanced to the fight, forty thousand had fallen on the field. Three thousand were taken prisoners, seven thousand escaped to the small camp, and ten thousand made their way across the river to the large camp, where they joined the force which had been left there, and which had, in obedience to Varro's orders, attacked the Carthaginian camp, but had been repulsed with a loss of two thousand men. All the troops in both camps were forced to surrender on the following morning, and thus only fifteen thousand scattered fugitives escaped of the eighty-seven thousand two hundred infantry and cavalry under the command of the Roman consuls.

Hannibal's loss in the battle of Cannæ amounted to about six thousand men.

THE YOUNG CARTHAGINIAN

CHAPTER XIX: IN THE MINES

THE exultation of the Carthaginians at the total destruction of their enemies was immense, and Maharbal and some of the other leaders urged Hannibal at once to march upon Rome; but Hannibal knew the spirit of the Roman people, and felt that the capture of Rome, even after the annihilation of its army, would be a greater task than he could undertake. History has shown how desperate a defence may be made by a population willing to die rather than surrender, and the Romans, an essentially martial people, would defend their city until the last gasp. They had an abundance of arms, and there were the two city legions, which formed the regular garrison of the capital.

The instant the news of the defeat reached Rome, a levy of all males over seventeen years of age was ordered, and this produced another ten thousand men and a thousand cavalry. Eight thousand slaves who were willing to serve were enlisted and armed, and four thousand criminals and debtors were released from prison and pardoned, on the condition of their taking up arms. The prætor Marcellus was at Ostia with the ten thousand men with which he was about to embark for Sicily.

Thus Rome would be defended by forty-three thousand men, while Hannibal had but thirty-three thousand infantry, and his cavalry, the strongest arm of his force, would be useless. From Cannæ to Rome was twelve days' march with an army encumbered with booty. He could not, therefore, hope for a surprise. The walls of Rome were exceedingly strong, and he had with him none of the great machines which would have been necessary for a siege. He must have carried with him the supplies he had accumulated for the subsistence of his force, and when these were consumed he would be destitute. Fresh Roman levies would gather on his rear, and before long his whole army would be besieged.

In such an undertaking he would have wasted time, and lost the prestige which be had acquired by his astonishing victory. Varro, who had escaped from the battle, had rallied ten thousand of the fugitives at the strong place of Canusium, and these would be a nucleus round which the rest of those who had escaped would rally, and would be joined by fresh levies of the Italian allies of Rome.

The Romans showed their confidence in their power to resist a siege by at once despatching Marcellus with his ten thousand men to Canusium. Thus, with a strongly defended city in front, an army of twenty thousand Roman soldiers, which would speedily increase to double that number, in his rear, Hannibal perceived that were he to undertake the siege of Rome he would risk all the advantages he had gained. He determined, therefore, to continue the policy which he had laid down for himself, namely, to move his army to and fro among the provinces of Italy until the allies of Rome one by one fell away from her, and joined him, or until such reinforcements arrived from Carthage as would justify him in undertaking the siege of Rome.

Rome herself was never grander than in this hour of defeat; not for a moment was the courage and confidence of her citizens shaken. The promptness with which she prepared for defence, and still more the confidence which she showed by despatching Marcellus with his legion to Canusium instead of retaining him for the defence of the city, show a national spirit and manliness worthy of the highest admiration. Varro was ordered to hand over his command to Marcellus, and to return to Rome to answer before the senate for his conduct.

Varro doubted not that his sentence would be death, for the Romans, like the Carthaginians, had but little mercy for a defeated general. His colleague and his army had undoubtedly been sacrificed by his rashness. Moreover, the senate was composed of his bitter political enemies, and he could not hope that a lenient view would be taken of his conduct. Nevertheless Varro returned to Rome and appeared before the senate. That body nobly responded to the confidence manifested in it; party feeling was suspended, the political adversary, the defeated general, were alike forgotten, it was only remembered how Varro had rallied his troops, how he had allayed the panic which prevailed among them, and had at once restored order and discipline. His courage, too, in thus appearing, after so great a disaster, to submit himself to the judgment of the country, counted in his favour. His faults were condoned, and the senate publicly thanked him, because he had not despaired of the commonwealth.

Hannibal, in pursuance of his policy to detach the allies of Italy from Rome, dismissed all the Italian prisoners without ransom. The Roman prisoners he offered to admit to ransom, and a deputation of them accompanied an ambassador to offer terms of peace. The senate, however, not only refused to discuss any terms of peace, but absolutely forbade the families and friends of the prisoners to ransom them, thinking it politic neither to enrich their adversary nor to show indulgence to soldiers who had surrendered to the enemy.

The victory of Cannæ and Hannibal's clemency began to bear the effects which he hoped for. Apulia declared for him at once, and the towns of Arpi and Celapia opened their gates to him; Bruttium, Lucania, and Samnium were ready to follow. Mago with one division of the army was sent into Bruttium to take possession of such towns as might submit. Hanno was sent with another division to do the same in Lucania. Hannibal himself marched into Samnium, and making an alliance with the tribes, there stored his plunder, and proceeded into Campania, and entered Capua, the second city of Italy, which concluded an alliance with him. Mago embarked at one of the ports of Bruttium to carry the news of Hannibal's success to Carthage, and to demand reinforcements.

Neither Rome nor Carthage had the complete mastery of the sea, and as the disaster which had befallen Rome by land would greatly lessen her power to maintain a large fleet, Carthage could now have poured reinforcements in by the ports of Bruttium without difficulty. But unfortunately Hannibal's bitterest enemies were to be found not in Italy but in the senate of Carthage, where, in spite of the appeals of Mago and the efforts of the patriotic party, the intrigues of Hanno and his faction and the demands made by the war in Spain, prevented the reinforcements from being forwarded which would have enabled him to terminate the struggle by the conquest of Rome.

Hannibal, after receiving the submission of several other towns and capturing Casilinum, went into winter quarters at Capua. During the winter Rome made gigantic efforts to place her army upon a war footing, and with such success that, excluding the army of Scipio in Spain, she had, when the spring began, twelve legions or a hundred and twenty thousand men again under arms; and as no reinforcements, save some elephants and a small body of cavalry, ever reached Hannibal from Carthage, he was, during the remaining thirteen years of the war, reduced to stand wholly, on the defensive, protecting his allies, harassing his enemy, and feeding his own army at their expense; and yet so great was the dread which his genius had excited that, in spite of their superior numbers, the Romans after Cannæ never ventured again to engage him in a pitched battle.

Soon after the winter set in Hannibal ordered Malchus to take a number of officers and a hundred picked men, and to cross from Capua to Sardinia, where the inhabitants had revolted against Rome, and were harassing the prætor, Quintus Mucius, who commanded the legion which formed the garrison of the island. Malchus and the officers under him were charged with the duty of organizing the wild peasantry of the island, and of drilling them in regular tactics; for unless acting as bodies of regular troops, however much they might harass the Roman legion, they could not hope to expel them from their country. Nessus of course accompanied Malchus.

The party embarked in two of the Capuan galleys. They had not been many hours at sea when the weather, which had when they started been fine, changed suddenly, and ere long one of the fierce gales which are so frequent in the Mediterranean burst upon them. The wind was behind them, and there was nothing to do but to let the galleys run before it. The sea got up with great rapidity, and nothing but the high poops at their stern prevented the two galleys being sunk by the great waves which followed them. The oars were laid in, for it was impossible to use them in such a sea.

As night came on the gale increased rather than diminished. The Carthaginian officers and soldiers remained calm and quiet in the storm, but the Capuan sailors gave themselves up to despair, and the men at the helm were only kept at their post by Malchus threatening to have them thrown overboard instantly if they abandoned it. After nightfall he assembled the officers in the cabin in the poop.

"The prospects are bad," he said. "The pilot tells me that unless the gale abates or the wind changes we shall, before morning, be thrown upon the coast of Sardinia, and that will be total destruction; for upon the side facing Italy the cliffs, for the most part, rise straight up from the water, the only port on that side being that at which the Romans have their chief castle and garrison. He tells me there is nothing to be done, and I see nought myself. Were we to try to bring the galley round to the wind she would be swamped in a moment, while even if we could carry out the operation, it would be impossible to row in the teeth of this sea. Therefore, my friends, there is nothing for us to do save to keep up the courage of the men, and to bid them hold themselves in readiness to seize upon any chance of getting to shore should the vessel strike."

All night the galley swept on before the storm. The light on the other boat had disappeared soon after darkness had set in. Half the soldiers and crew by turns were kept at work baling out the water which found its way over the sides, and several times so heavily did the seas break into her that all thought that she was lost. However, when morning broke she was still afloat. The wind had hardly shifted a point since it had begun to blow, and the pilot told Malchus that they must be very near to the coast of Sardinia. As the light brightened every eye was fixed ahead over the waste of angry foaming water. Presently the pilot, who was standing next to Malchus, grasped his arm.

"There is the land," he cried, "dead before us."

Not until a few minutes later could Malchus make out the

faint outline through the driving mist. It was a lofty pile of rock standing by itself.

"It is an island!" he exclaimed.

"It is Caralis," the pilot replied; "I know its outline well; we are already in the bay. Look to the right, you can make out the outline of the cliffs at its mouth, we have passed it already. You do not see the shore ahead because the rock on which Caralis stands rises from a level plain, and to the left a lagoon extends for a long way in; it is there that the Roman galleys ride. The gods have brought us to the only spot along the coast where we could approach it with a hope of safety."

"There is not much to rejoice at," Malchus said; "we may escape the sea, but only to be made prisoners by the Romans."

"Nay, Malchus, the alternative is not so bad," a young officer who was standing next to him said. "Hannibal has thousands of Roman prisoners in his hands, and we may well hope to be exchanged. After the last twelve hours any place on shore, even a Roman prison, is an elysium compared to the sea."

The outline of the coast was now clearly visible. The great rock of Caralis, now known as Cagliari, rose dark and threatening, the low shores of the bay on either side were marked by a band of white foam, while to the left of the rock was the broad lagoon, dotted with the black hulls of a number of ships and galleys rolling and tossing heavily, for as the wind blew straight into the bay the lagoon was covered with short, angry waves.

The pilot now ordered the oars to be got out. The entrance to the lagoon was wide, but it was only in the middle that the channel was deep, and on either side of this long breakwaters of stone were run out from the shore, to afford a shelter to the shipping within. The sea was so rough that it was found impossible to use the oars, and they were again laid in and a small sail was hoisted. This enabled the head to be laid towards the entrance of the lagoon. For a time it was doubtful whether the galley could make it, but she succeeded in doing so, and then ran straight on towards the upper end of the harbour.

"That is far enough," the pilot said presently; "the water shoals fast beyond. We must anchor here."

The sail was lowered, the oars got out on one side, and the

head of the galley brought to the wind. The anchor was then dropped. As the storm-beaten galley ran right up the lagoon she had been viewed with curiosity and interest by those who were on board the ships at anchor. That she was an Italian galley was clear, and also that she was crowded with men, but no suspicion was entertained that these were Carthaginians.

The anchor once cast Malchus held a council with the other officers. They were in the midst of foes, and escape seemed altogether impossible. Long before the gale abated sufficiently to permit them to put to sea again, they would be visited by boats from the other vessels to ask who they were and whence they came. As to fighting their way out it was out of the question, for there were a score of triremes in the bay, any one of which could crush the Capuan galley, and whose far greater speed rendered the idea of flight as hopeless as that of resistance. The council therefore agreed unanimously that the only thing to be done was to surrender without resistance.

The storm continued for another twenty-four hours, then the wind died out almost as suddenly as it began.

As soon as the sea began to abate two galleys were seen putting out from the town, and these rowed directly towards the ship. The fact that she had shown no flag had no doubt excited suspicion in the minds of the garrison. Each galley contained fifty soldiers. As they rowed alongside a Roman officer on the poop of one of the galleys hailed the ship, and demanded whence it came.

"We are from Capua," the pilot answered. "The gale has blown us across thence. I have on board fifty Carthaginian officers and soldiers, who now surrender to you."

As in those days, when vessels could with difficulty keep the sea in a storm, and in the event of a gale springing up were forced to run before it, it was by no means unusual for galleys to be blown into hostile ports, the announcement excited no great surprise.

"Who commands the party?" the Roman officer asked.

"I do," Malchus replied. "I am Malchus, the son of Hamilcar, who was killed at the Trebia, a cousin of Hannibal and captain of his guard. I surrender with my followers, seeing that resistance is hopeless."

"It is hopeless," the Roman replied, "and you are right not to throw away the lives of your men when there is no possibility of resistance."

As he spoke he stepped on board, ordered the anchor to be weighed, and the galley, accompanied by the two Roman boats, was rowed to the landing-place. A messenger was at once sent up to Mucius to tell him what had happened, and the prætor himself soon appeared upon the spot. The officer acquainted him with the name and rank of the leader of the Carthaginian party, and said that there were with him two officers of noble families of the Carthaginians.

"That is well," the prætor said, "it is a piece of good fortune. The Carthaginians have so many of our officers in their hands, that it is well to have some whom we may exchange for them. Let them be landed."

As they left the ship the Carthaginians laid down their arms and armour. By this time a large number of the Roman garrison, among whom the news had rapidly spread, were assembled at the port. Many of the young soldiers had never yet seen a Carthaginian, and they looked with curiosity and interest at the men who had inflicted such terrible defeats upon the armies of the Romans. They were fine specimens of Hannibal's force, for the general had allowed Malchus to choose his own officers and men, and, knowing that strength, agility, and endurance would be needed for a campaign in so mountainous a country as Sardinia, he had picked both officers and men with great care.

His second in command was his friend Trebon, who had long since obtained a separate command, but who, on hearing from Malchus of the expedition on which he was bound, had volunteered to accompany him. The men were all Africans accustomed to desert fighting and trained in warfare in Spain. The Romans, good judges of physical strength, could not repress a murmur of admiration at the sight of these sinewy figures. Less heavy than themselves, there was about them a spring and an elasticity resembling that of the tiger. Long use had hardened their muscles until they stood up like cords through their tawny skin, most of them bore numerous scars of wounds received in battle, and the Romans, as they viewed them, acknowledged to themselves what formidable opponents these men would be.

A strong guard formed up on either side of the captives, and they were marched through the town to the citadel on the upper part of the rock. Here a large chamber, opening on to the court-yard, was assigned to the officers, while the men, who were viewed in the light of slaves, were at once set to work to carry stores up to the citadel from a ship which had arrived just as the storm broke.

A fortnight later a vessel arrived from Rome with a message from the senate that they would not exchange prisoners, and that the Carthaginians were at once to be employed as slaves in the mines. The governor acquainted Malchus with the decision.

"I am sorry," he said, "indeed, that it is so; but the senate are determined that they will exchange no prisoners. Of course their view of the matter is, that when a Roman lays down his arms he disgraces himself, and the refusal to ransom him or allow him to be exchanged is intended to act as a deterrent to others. This may be fair enough in cases where large numbers surrender to a few, or where they lay down their arms when with courage and determination they might have cut their way through the enemy; but in cases where further resistance would be hopeless, in my mind men are justified in surrendering. However, I can only obey the orders I have received, and to-morrow must send you and your men to the mines."

As Malchus had seen the Iberian captives sent to labour as slaves in the mines in Spain, the fate thus announced to him did not appear surprising or barbarous. In those days captives taken in war were always made slaves when they were not put to death in cold blood, and although Hannibal had treated with marked humanity and leniency the Roman and Italian captives who had fallen into his hands, this had been the result of policy, and was by no means in accordance with the spirit in which war was then conducted.

Accordingly, the next day the Carthaginians were, under a strong guard, marched away to the mines, which lay on the other side of the island, some forty miles due west of the port, and three miles from the western sea-coast of the island. The road lay for some distance across a dead flat. The country was well cultivated and thickly studded with villages, for Rome drew a heavy tribute in corn annually from the island.

After twenty miles' march they halted for the night, pursuing their way on the following morning. They had now entered a wide and fertile valley with lofty hills on either side. In some places there were stagnant marshes, and the officer in charge of the guard informed Malchus that in the autumn a pestilential miasma rose from these, rendering a sojourn in the valley fatal to the inhabitants of the mainland. The native people were wild and primitive in appearance, being clad chiefly in sheep-skins. They lived in bee-hive shaped huts. The hills narrowed in towards the end of the day's march, and the valley terminated when the party arrived within half a mile of their destination. Here stood a small town named Metalla, with a strong Roman garrison, which supplied guards over the slaves employed in working the mines. This town is now called Iglesias.

The principal mine was situated in a narrow valley running west from the town down to the sea-coast. The officer in command of the escort handed over Malchus and his companions to the charge of the officer at the head mining establishment.

Malchus was surprised at the large number of people gathered at the spot. They lived for the most part in low huts constructed of boughs or sods, and ranged in lines at the bottom of the valley or along the lower slopes of the hill. A cordon of Roman sentries was placed along the crest of the hill at either side, and a strong guard was posted in a little camp in the centre of the valley, in readiness to put down any tumult which might arise.

The great majority of the slaves gathered there were Sards, men belonging to tribes which had risen in insurrection against the Romans. There were with them others of their countrymen who were not like them slaves, though their condition was but little better except that they received a nominal rate of payment. These were called free labourers, but their labour was as much forced as was that of the slaves—each district in the island being compelled to furnish a certain amount of labourers for this or the mines further to the north. The men so conscripted were changed once in six months. With the Sards were mingled people of many nations. Here were Sicilians and members of many Italian tribes conquered by the Romans, together with Gauls from the northern plains and from Marseilles.

There were many mines worked in different parts of the island, but Metalla was the principal. The labour, in days when gunpowder had not become the servant of man, was extremely hard. The rocks had to be pierced with hand labour, the passages and galleries were of the smallest possible dimensions, the atmosphere was stifling; consequently the mortality was great, and it was necessary to keep up a constant importation of labour.

"If these people did but possess a particle of courage," Trebon said, "they would rise, overpower the guard, and make for the forests. The whole island is, as the officer who brought us here told us, covered with mountains with the exception of the two broad plains running through it; as we could see the hills are covered with woods, and the whole Roman army could not find them if they once escaped."

"That is true enough," Malchus said, "but there must be at least five or six thousand slaves here. How could these find food among the mountains? They might exist for a time upon berries and grain, but they would in the end be forced to go into the valleys for food, and would then be slaughtered by the Romans. Nevertheless a small body of men could no doubt subsist among the hills, and the strength of the guard you see on the heights shows that attempts to escape are not rare. Should we find our existence intolerable here, we will at anyrate try to escape. There are fifty of us, and if we agreed in common action we could certainly break through the guards and take to the hills. As you may see by their faces, the spirit of these slaves is broken. See how bent most of them are by their labour, and how their shoulders are wealed by the lashes of their taskmasters!"

The officer in charge of the mines told Malchus that he should not put him and the other two officers to labour, but would appoint them as overseers over gangs of the men, informing them that he had a brother who was at present a captive in the hands of Hannibal; and he trusted that Malchus, should he have an opportunity, would use his kind offices on his behalf.

One of the lines of huts near the Roman camp was assigned to the Carthaginians, and that evening they received rations of almost black bread similar to those served out to the others. The following morning they were set to work. Malchus and his two friends found their tasks by no means labourious, as they were appointed to look after a number of Sards employed in breaking up and sorting the lead ore as it was brought up from the mine. The men, however, returned in the evening worn out with toil. All had been at work in the mines. Some had had to crawl long distances through passages little more than three feet high and one foot wide, until they reached the broad lode of lead ore.

Here some of the party had been set to work, others had been employed in pushing on the little galleries, and there had sat for hours working in a cramped position, with pick, hammer, and wedge. Others had been lowered by ropes down shafts so narrow that when they got to the bottom it was only with extreme difficulty that they were able to stoop to work at the rock beneath their feet. Many, indeed, of these old shafts have been found in the mines of Montepone, so extremely narrow that it is supposed that they must have been bored by slaves lowered by ropes, headforemost, it appearing absolutely impossible for a man to stoop to work if lowered in the ordinary way.

The Carthaginians, altogether unaccustomed to work of this nature, returned to their huts at night utterly exhausted, cramped, and aching in every limb. Many had been cruelly beaten for not performing the tasks assigned to them. All were filled with a dull despairing rage. In the evening a ration of boiled beans, with a little native wine, was served out to each, the quantity of the food being ample, it being necessary to feed the slaves well to enable them to support their fatigues.

After three days of this work five or six of the captive were so exhausted that they were unable to take their places with the gang when ordered for work in the morning. They were, however, compelled by blows to rise and take their places with the rest. Two of them died during the course of the day in their stifling working-places; another succumbed during the night; several, too, were attacked by the fever of the country. Malchus and his friends were full of grief and rage at the sufferings of their men.

"Anything were better than this," Malchus said. "A thousand times better to fall beneath the swords of the Romans than to die like dogs in the holes beneath that hill!"

"I quite agree with you, Malchus," Halco, the other officer with the party, said, "and am ready to join you in any plan of escape, however desperate."

"The difficulty is about arms," Trebon observed. "We are so closely watched that it is out of the question to hope that we should succeed in getting possession of any. The tools are all left in the mines; and as the men work naked, there is no possibility of their secreting any. The stores here are always guarded by a sentry; and although we might overpower him, the guard would arrive long before we could break through the solid doors. Of course if we could get the other slaves to join us, we might crush the guard even with stones."

"That is out of the question," Malchus said. "In the first place, they speak a strange language, quite different to the Italians. Then, were we seen trying to converse with any of them, suspicions might be roused; and even could we get the majority to join us, there would be many who would be only too glad to purchase their own freedom by betraying the plot to the Romans. No, whatever we do must be done by ourselves alone; and for arms we must rely upon stones, and upon the stoutest stakes we can draw out from our huts. The only time that we have free to ourselves is the hour after work is over, when we are allowed to go down to the stream to wash and to stroll about as we will until the trumpet sounds to order us to retire to our huts for the night.

"It is true that at that time the guards are particularly vigilant, and that we are not allowed to gather into knots; and an Italian slave I spoke to yesterday told me that he dared not speak to me, for the place swarms with spies, and that any conversation between us would be sure to be reported, and those engaged in it put to the hardest and cruelest work. I propose, therefore, that to-morrow—

for if it is to be done, the sooner the better, before the men lose all their strength—the men shall on their return from work at once eat their rations; then each man, hiding a short stick under his garment and wrapping a few heavy stones in the corner of his robe, shall make his way up towards the top of the hill above the mine.

"No two men must go together—all must wander as if aimlessly among the huts. When they reach the upper line on that side and see me, let all rapidly close up, and we will make a sudden rush at the sentries above. They cannot get more than five or six together in time to oppose us, and we shall be able to beat them down with our stones. Once through them, the heavy armed men will never be able to overtake us till we reach the forest, which begins, I believe, about half a mile beyond the top."

The other two officers at once agreed to the plan; and when the camp was still Malchus crept cautiously from hut to hut, telling his men of the plan that had been formed and giving orders for the carrying of it out.

All assented cheerfully; for although the stronger were now becoming accustomed to their work, and felt less exhausted than they had done the first two days, there was not one but felt that he would rather suffer death than endure this terrible fate. Malchus impressed upon them strongly that it was of the utmost consequence to possess themselves of the arms of any Roman soldiers they might overthrow, as they would to a great extent be compelled to rely upon these to obtain food among the mountains.

Even the men who were most exhausted, and those stricken with fever, seemed to gain strength at once at the prospect of a struggle for liberty, and when the gang turned out in the morning for work none lagged behind.

THE YOUNG CARTHAGINIAN

CHAPTER XX: THE SARDINIAN FORESTS

THE Carthaginians returned in the evening in groups from the various scenes of their labour and without delay consumed the provisions provided for them. Then one by one they sauntered away down towards the stream. Malchus was the last to leave, and having seen that all his followers had preceded him, he, too, crossed the stream, paused a moment at a heap of débris from the mine, and picking up three or four pieces of rock about the size of his fist, rolled them in the corner of his garment, and holding this in one hand moved up the hill.

Here and there he paused a moment as if interested in watching the groups of slaves eating their evening meal, until at last he reached the upper line of little huts. Between these and the hill-top upon which the sentries stood was a distance of about fifty yards, which was kept scrupulously clear to enable them to watch the movements of any man going beyond the huts. The sentries were some thirty paces apart, so that, as Malchus calculated, not more than four or five of them could assemble before he reached them, if they did not previously perceive anything suspicious which might put them on the alert.

Looking round him Malchus saw his followers scattered about among the slaves at a short distance. Standing behind the shelter of the hut he raised his hand, and all began to move towards him. As there was nothing in their attire, which consisted of one long cloth wound round them, to distinguish them from the other slaves, the movement attracted no attention from the sentries, who were, from their position, able to overlook the low huts.

271

THE YOUNG CARTHAGINIAN

When he saw that all were close, Malchus gave a shout and dashed up the hill, followed by his comrades.

The nearest sentry, seeing a body of fifty men suddenly rushing towards him, raised a shout, and his comrades from either side ran towards him; but so quickly was the movement performed that but five had gathered when the Carthaginians reached them, although many others were running towards the spot. The Carthaginians, when they came close to their levelled spears, poured upon them a shower of heavy stones, which knocked two of them down and so bruised and battered the others that they went down at once when the Carthaginians burst upon them.

The nearest Romans halted to await the arrival of their comrades coming up behind them, and the Carthaginians, seizing the swords, spears, and shields of their fallen foes, dashed on at full speed. The Romans soon followed, but with the weight of their weapons, armour, and helmets they were speedily distanced, and the fugitives reached the edge of the forest in safety and dashed into its recesses.

After running for some distance they halted, knowing that the Romans would not think of pursuing except with a large force. The forests which covered the mountains of Sardinia were for the most part composed of evergreen oak, with, in some places, a thick undergrowth of shrubs and young trees. Through this the Carthaginians made their way with some difficulty, until, just as it became dark, they reached the bottom of a valley comparatively free of trees and through which ran a clear stream.

"Here we will halt for the night," Malchus said; "there is no fear of the Romans pursuing at once, if indeed they do so at all, for their chance of finding us in these mountains, covered with hundreds of square miles of forests, is slight indeed; however, we will at once provide ourselves with weapons."

The five Roman swords were put into requisition, and some straight young saplings were felled, and their points being sharpened they were converted into efficient spears, each some fourteen feet long.

"It is well we have supped," Malchus said; "our breakfast will depend on ourselves. To-morrow we must keep a sharp

The Carthaginian prisoners escape from the Roman guard

look-out for smoke rising through the trees; there are sure to be numbers of charcoal burners in the forest, for upon them the Romans depend for their fuel. One of the first things to do is to obtain a couple of lighted brands. A fire is essential for warmth among these hills, even putting aside its uses for cooking."

"That is when we have anything to cook," Halco said laughingly.

"That is certainly essential," Malchus agreed; "but there is sure to be plenty of wild-boar and deer among these forests. We have only to find a valley with a narrow entrance, and post ourselves there and send all the men to form a circle on the hills around it and drive them down to us; besides, most likely we shall come across herds of goats and pigs, which the villagers in the lower valleys will send up to feed on the acorns. I have no fear but we shall be able to obtain plenty of flesh; as to corn, we have only to make a raid down into the plain, and when we have found out something about the general lay of the country, the hills and the extent of the forest, we will choose some spot near its centre and erect huts there. If it were not for the peasants we might live here for years, for all the Roman forces in Sardinia would be insufficient to rout us out of these mountains; but unfortunately, as we shall have to rob the peasants, they will act as guides to the Romans, and we shall be obliged to keep a sharp look-out against surprise. If it gets too hot for us we must make a night march across the plain to the mountains on the eastern side. I heard at Caralis that the wild part there is very much larger than it is on this side of the island, and it extends without a break from the port right up to the north of the island."

Safe as he felt from pursuit Malchus posted four men as sentries, and the rest of the band lay down to sleep, rejoicing in the thought that on the morrow they should not be wakened to take their share in the labours in the mine.

At daybreak all were on the move, and a deep spot having been found in the stream, they indulged in the luxury of a bath. That done they started on the march further into the heart of the forest. The hills were of great height, with bare crags often beetling up among the trees hundreds of feet, with deep valleys and rugged precipices. In crossing one of these valleys Nessus suddenly lifted his hand.

"What is it?" Malchus asked.

"I heard a pig grunt," Nessus replied, "on our right there."

Malchus at once divided the band in two and told them to proceed as quietly as possible along the lower slopes of the hill, leaving a man at every fifteen paces.

When all had been posted, the ends of the line were to descend until they met in the middle of the valley, thus forming a circle. A shout was to tell the rest that this was done, and then all were to move down until they met in the centre. One officer went with each party, Malchus remained at the spot where he was standing. In ten minutes the signal was heard, and then all moved forward, shouting as they went, and keeping a sharp look-out between the trees to see that nothing passed them. As the narrowing circle issued into the open ground at the bottom of the valley there was a general shout of delight, for, huddled down by a stream, grunting and screaming with fright, was a herd of forty or fifty pigs, with a peasant, who appeared stupefied with alarm at the sudden uproar.

On seeing the men burst out with their levelled spears from the wood, the Sard gave a scream of terror and threw himself upon his face. When the Carthaginians came up to him Malchus stirred him with his foot, but he refused to move; he then pricked him with the Roman spear he held, and the man leaped to his feet with a shout. Malchus told him in Italian that he was free to go, but that the swine must be confiscated for the use of his followers. The man did not understand his words, but, seeing by his gestures that he was free to go, set off at the top of his speed, hardly believing that he could have escaped with his life, and in no way concerned at the loss of the herd. This was, indeed, the property of various individuals in one of the villages at the foot of the hills—it being then, as now, the custom for several men owning swine to send them together under the charge of a herdsman into the mountains, where for months together they live in a half-wild state on acorns and roots, a villager going up occasionally with supplies of food for the swineherd.

No sooner had the peasant disappeared than a shout from one of the men some fifty yards away called the attention of Malchus.

"Here is the man's fire, my lord."

A joyous exclamation rose from the soldiers, for, the thought of all this meat and no means of cooking it was tantalizing every one. Malchus hurried to the spot, where, indeed, was a heap of still glowing embers. Some of the men at once set to work to collect dried sticks, and in a few minutes a great fire was blazing. One of the pigs was slaughtered and cut up into rations, and in a short time each man was cooking his portion stuck on a stick over the fire.

A smaller fire was lit for the use of the officers a short distance away, and here Nessus prepared their share of the food for Malchus and his two companions. After the meal the spears were improved by the points being hardened in the fire. When they were in readiness to march two of the men were told off as fire-keepers, and each of these took two blazing brands from the fire, which, as they walked, they kept crossed before them, the burning points keeping each other alight. Even with one man there would be little chance of losing the fire, but with two such a misfortune could scarcely befall them.

A party of ten men took charge of the herd of swine, and the whole then started for the point they intended to make to in the heart of the mountains. Before the end of the day a suitable camping-place was selected in a watered valley. The men then set to work to cut down boughs and erect arbours. Fires were lighted and another pig being killed those who preferred it roasted his flesh over the fire, while others boiled their portions, the Roman shields being utilized as pans.

"What do you think of doing, Malchus?" Halco asked as they stretched themselves out on a grassy bank by the stream when they had finished their meal. "We are safe here, and in these forests could defy the Romans to find us for months. Food we can get from the villages at the foot of the hills, and there must be many swine in the forest beside this herd which we have captured. The life will not be an unpleasant one, but—" and he stopped.

"But you don't wish to end your days here," Malchus put in for him, "nor do I. It is pleasant enough, but every day we spend here is a waste of our lives, and with Hannibal and our comrades combating the might of Rome we cannot be content to live like members of the savage tribes here. I have no doubt that we shall excite such annoyance and alarm by our raids among the villages in the plains that the Romans will ere long make a great effort to capture us, and doubtless they will enlist the natives in their search. Still, we may hope to escape them, and there are abundant points among these mountains where we may make a stand and inflict such heavy loss upon them that they will be glad to come to terms. All I would ask is that they shall swear by their gods to treat us well and to convey us as prisoners of war to Rome, there to remain until exchanged. In Rome we could await the course of events patiently. Hannibal may capture the city. The senate, urged by the relatives of the many prisoners we have taken, may agree to make an exchange, and we may see chances of our making our escape. At anyrate we shall be in the world and shall know what is going on."

"But could we not hold out and make them agree to give us our freedom?"

"I do not think so," Malchus said. "It would be too much for Roman pride to allow a handful of escaped prisoners to defy them in that way, and even if the prefect of this island were to agree to the terms, I do not believe that the senate would ratify them. We had better not ask too much. For myself I own to a longing to see Rome. As Carthage holds back and will send no aid to Hannibal, I have very little hope of ever entering it as a conqueror, and rather than not see it at all I would not mind entering it as a prisoner. There are no mines to work there, and the Romans, with so vast a number of their own people in the hands of Hannibal, would not dare to treat us with any cruelty or severity.

"Here it is different. No rumour of our fate will ever reach Hannibal, and had every one of us died in those stifling mines he would never have been the wiser."

The two officers both agreed with Malchus; as for the soldiers, they were all too well pleased with their present liberty and their escape from the bondage to give a thought to the morrow.

The next day Malchus and his companions explored the hills of the neighbourhood, and chose several points commanding the valleys by which their camp could be approached, as look-out places. Trees were cleared away, vistas cut, and wood piled in readiness for making bonfires, and two sentries were placed at each of these posts, their orders being to keep a vigilant look-out all over the country, to light a fire instantly the approach of any enemy was perceived, and then to descend to the camp to give particulars as to his number and the direction of his march.

A few days later, leaving ten men at the camp with full instructions as to what to do in case of an alarm by the enemy, Malchus set out with the rest of the party across the mountains. The sun was their only guide as to the direction of their course, and it was late in the afternoon before they reached the crest of the easternmost hills and looked down over the wide plain which divides the island into two portions. Here they rested until the next morning, and then, starting before daybreak, descended the slopes. They made their way to a village of some size at the mouth of a valley, and were unnoticed until they entered it. Most of the men were away in the fields; a few resisted, but were speedily beaten down by the short heavy sticks which the Carthaginians carried in addition to their spears.

Malchus had given strict orders that the latter weapons were not to be used, that no life was to be taken, and that no one was to be hurt or ill-used unless in the act of offering resistance. For a few minutes the confusion was great, women and children running about screaming in wild alarm. They were, however, pacified when they found that no harm was intended.

On searching the village large stores of grain were discovered and abundance of sacks were also found, and each soldier filled one of these with as much grain as he could conveniently carry. A number of other articles which would be useful to them were also taken—cooking pots, wooden platters, knives, and such arms as could be found. Laden with these the

Carthaginians set out on their return to camp. Loaded as they were it was a long and toilsome journey, and they would have had great difficulty in finding their way back had not Malchus taken the precaution of leaving four or five men at different points with instructions to keep fires of damp wood burning so that the smoke should act as a guide. It was, however, late on the second day after their leaving the village before they arrived in camp. Here the men set to work to crush the grain between flat stones, and soon a supply of rough cakes were baking in the embers.

A month passed away. Similar raids to the first were made when the supplies became exhausted, and as at the second village they visited they captured six donkeys, which helped to carry up the burdens, the journeys were less fatiguing than on the first occasion. One morning as the troop were taking their breakfast a column of bright smoke rose from one of the hill-tops. The men simultaneously leaped to their feet.

"Finish your breakfast," Malchus said, "there will be plenty of time. Slay two more hogs and cut them up. Let each man take three or four pounds of flesh and a supply of meal."

Just as the preparations were concluded the two men from the look-out arrived and reported that a large force was winding along one of the valleys. There were now but six of the herd of swine left; these were driven into the forest. The grain and other stores were also carried away and carefully hidden, and the band, who were now all well armed with weapons taken in the different raids on the villages, marched away from their camp.

Malchus had already with his two comrades explored all the valleys in the neighbourhood of the camp, and had fixed upon various points for defence. One of these was on the line by which the enemy were approaching. The valley narrowed in until it was almost closed by perpendicular rocks on either side. On the summit of these the Carthaginians took their post. They could now clearly make out the enemy; there were upwards of a thousand Roman troops, and they were accompanied by fully five hundred natives.

When the head of the column approached the narrow path of the valley the soldiers halted and the natives went on ahead to reconnoitre. They reported that all seemed clear, and the column then moved forward. When it reached the gorge a shout was heard above and a shower of rocks fell from the crags, crushing many of the Romans. Their commander at once recalled the soldiers, and these then began to climb the hillside, wherever the ground permitted their doing so. After much labour they reached the crag from which they had been assailed, but found it deserted.

All day the Romans searched the woods, but without success. The natives were sent forward in strong parties. Most of these returned unsuccessful, but two of them were suddenly attacked by the Carthaginians, and many were slaughtered.

For four days the Romans pursued their search in the forest, but never once did they obtain a glimpse of the Carthaginians save when, on several occasions, the latter appeared suddenly in places inaccessible from below and hurled down rocks and stones upon them. The Sards had been attacked several times, and were so disheartened by the losses inflicted upon them that they now refused to stir into the woods unless accompanied by the Romans.

At the end of the fourth day, feeling it hopeless any longer to pursue the fugitive band over these forest-covered mountains, the Roman commander ordered the column to move back towards its starting-place. He had lost between forty and fifty of his men and upwards of a hundred of the Sards had been killed. Just as be reached the edge of the forest he was overtaken by one of the natives.

"I have been a prisoner in the hands of the Carthaginians," the man said, "and their leader released me upon my taking an oath to deliver a message to the general." The man was at once brought before the officer.

"The leader of the escaped slaves bids me tell you," he said, "that had you ten times as many men with you it would be vain for you to attempt to capture them. You searched, in these four days, but a few square miles of the forest, and, although he was never half a mile away from you, you did not succeed in capturing him. There are hundreds of square miles, and, did he choose to elude you, twenty thousand men might search in vain. He bids me say that he could hold out for years and harry all the villages of the plains; but he and his men do not care for living the life of a mountain tribe, and he is ready to discuss terms of surrender with you, and will meet you outside the forest here with two men with him if you on your part will be here with the same number at noon to-morrow. He took before me a solemn oath that he will keep the truce inviolate, and requires you to do the same. I have promised to take back your answer."

The Roman commander was greatly vexed at his non-success, and at the long-continued trouble which he saw would arise from the presence of this determined band in the mountains. They would probably be joined by some of the recently subdued tribes, and would be a thorn in the side of the Roman force holding the island. He was, therefore, much relieved by this unexpected proposal.

"Return to him who sent you," he said, "and tell him that I, Publius Manlius, commander of that portion of the 10th Legion here, do hereby swear before the gods that I will hold the truce inviolate, and that I will meet him here with two officers, as he proposes, at noon to-morrow."

At the appointed hour Malchus, with the two officers, standing just inside the edge of the forest, saw the Roman general advancing with two companions; they at once went forward to meet them.

"I am come," Malchus said, "to offer to surrender to you on certain terms. I gave you my reasons in the message I yesterday sent you. With my band here I could defy your attempts to capture me for years, but I do not care to lead the life of a mountain robber. Hannibal treats his captives mercifully, and the treatment which was bestowed upon me and my companions, who were not even taken in fair fight, but were blown by a tempest into your port, was a disgrace to Rome. My demand is this, that we shall be treated with the respect due to brave men, that we be allowed to march without guard or escort down to the port, where we will go straight on board a vessel there prepared for us. We will then lay down our arms and surrender as prisoners of war, under the solemn agreement taken and signed by you and the governor of the island, and approved and ratified by the senate of

Rome, that, in the first place, the garments and armour of which we were deprived when captured, shall be restored to us, and that we shall then be conveyed in the ship to Rome, there to remain as prisoners of war until exchanged, being sent nowhere else, and suffering no pains or penalties whatever for what has taken place on this island."

The Roman general was surprised and pleased with the moderation of the demand. He had feared that Malchus would have insisted upon being restored with his companions to the Carthaginian army in Italy. Such a proposition he would have been unwilling to forward to Rome, for it would have been a confession that all the Roman force in the island was incapable of overcoming this handful of desperate men, and he did not think that the demand if made would have been agreed to by the senate. The present proposition was vastly more acceptable. He could report without humiliation that the Carthaginian slaves had broken loose and taken to the mountains, where there would be great difficulty in pursuing them, and they would serve as a nucleus round which would assemble all the disaffected in the island; and could recommend that, as they only demanded to be sent to Rome as prisoners of war, instead of being kept in the island, the terms should be agreed to. After a moment's delay, therefore, he replied:

"I agree to your terms, sir, as far as I am concerned, and own they appear to me as moderate and reasonable. I will draw out a document, setting them forth and my acceptance of them, and will send it at once to the prefect, praying him to sign it, and to forward it to Rome for the approval of the senate. Pending an answer I trust that you will abstain from any further attacks upon the villages."

"It may be a fortnight before the answer returns," Malchus replied; "but if you will send up to this point a supply of cattle and flour sufficient for our wants till the answer comes, I will promise to abstain from all further action."

To this the Roman readily agreed, and for a fortnight Malchus and his friends amused themselves by hunting deer and wild-boar among the mountains. After a week had passed a man had been sent each day to the spot agreed upon to see if any answer had been received from Rome. It was nearly three weeks before he brought a message to Malchus that the terms had been accepted, and that the Roman commander would meet him there on the following day with the document. The interview took place as arranged, and the Roman handed to Malchus the document agreeing to the terms proposed, signed by himself and the prefect, and ratified by the senate. He said that if Malchus with his party would descend into the road on the following morning three miles below Metalla they would send an escort of Roman soldiers awaiting them, and that a vessel would be ready at the port for them to embark upon their arrival.

Next day, accordingly, Malchus with his companions left the forest, and marched down to the valley in military order. At the appointed spot they found twenty Roman soldiers under an officer. The latter saluted Malchus, and informed him that his orders were to escort them to the port, and to see that they suffered no molestation or interference at the hands of the natives on their march. Two days' journey took them to Caralis, and in good order and with proud bearing they marched through the Roman soldiers, who assembled in the streets to view so strange a spectacle. Arrived at the port they embarked on board the ship prepared for them, and there piled their arms on deck. A Roman officer received them, and handed over, in accordance with the terms of the agreement, the whole of the clothing and armour of which they had been deprived. A guard of soldiers then marched on board, and an hour later sails were hoisted and the vessel started for her destination.

Anxiously Malchus and his companions gazed round the horizon in hopes that some galleys of Capua or Carthage might appear in sight, although indeed they had but small hopes of seeing them, for no Carthaginian ship would be likely to be found so near the coast of Italy, except indeed if bound with arms for the use of the insurgents in the northern mountains of Sardinia. However, no sail appeared in sight until the ship entered the mouth of the Tiber. As they ascended the river, and the walls and towers of Rome were seen in the distance, the prisoners forgot their own position in the interest excited by the appearance of the great rival of Carthage.

At that time Rome possessed but little of the magnificence which distinguished her buildings in the days of the emperors. Everything was massive and plain, with but slight attempt at architectural adornment. The temples of the gods rose in stately majesty above the mass of buildings, but even these were far inferior in size and beauty to those of Carthage, while the size of the city was small indeed in comparison to the wide-spreading extent of its African rival.

The vessel anchored in the stream until the officer in command landed to report his arrival with the prisoners and to receive instructions. An hour later he returned, the prisoners were landed and received by a strong guard of spearmen at the water-gate. The news had spread rapidly through the city. A crowd of people thronged the streets, while at the windows and on the roofs were gathered numbers of ladies of the upper classes. A party of soldiers led the way, pushing back the crowd as they advanced. A line of spearmen marched on either side of the captives, and a strong guard brought up the rear to prevent the crowd from pressing in there. Malchus walked at the head of the prisoners, followed by his officers, after whom came the soldiers walking two and two.

There was no air of dejection in the bearing of the captives, and they faced the regards of the hostile crowd with the air rather of conquerors than of prisoners. They remembered that it was but by accident that they had fallen into the hands of the Romans, that in the battle-field they had proved themselves over and over again more than a match for the soldiers of Rome, and that it was the walls of the city alone which had prevented their marching through her streets as triumphant conquerors.

It was no novel sight in Rome for Carthaginian prisoners to march through the streets, for in the previous campaigns large numbers of Carthaginians had been captured; but since Hannibal crossed the Alps and carried his victorious army through Italy, scarce a prisoner had been brought to Rome, while tens of thousands of Romans had fallen into the hands of Hannibal. The lower class of the population of Rome were at all times rough and brutal, and the captives were assailed with shouts of exultation, with groans and menaces, and with bitter curses by those whose friends and relatives had fallen in the wars.

The better classes at the windows and from the house-tops abstained from any demonstration, but watched the captives as they passed with a critical eye, and with expressions of admiration at their fearless bearing and haughty mien.

"Truly, that youth who marches at their head might pose for a Carthaginian Apollo, Sempronius," a Roman matron said as she sat at the balcony of a large mansion at the entrance to the Forum. "I have seldom seen a finer face. See what strength his limbs show, although he walks as lightly as a girl. I have a fancy to have him as a slave; he would look well to walk behind me and carry my mantle when I go abroad. See to it, Sempronius; as your father is the military prætor, you can manage this for me without trouble."

"I will do my best, Lady Flavia," the young Roman said; "but there may be difficulties."

"What difficulties?" Flavia demanded imperiously. "I suppose the Carthaginians will as usual be handed over as slaves; and who should have a better right to choose one among them than I, whose husband, Tiberius Gracchus, is Consul of Rome?"

"None assuredly," Sempronius replied. "It was only because, as I hear, that youth is a cousin of Hannibal himself, and, young as he is, the captain of his body-guard, and I thought that my father might intend to confine him in the prison for better security."

Flavia waved her hand imperiously.

"When did you ever hear of a slave escaping from Rome, Sempronius? Are not the walls high and strong, and the sentries numerous? And even did they pass these, would not the badge of slavery betray them at once to the first who met them without, and they would be captured and brought back? No, I have set my mind upon having him as a slave. He will go well with that Gaulish maiden whom Postumius sent me from the banks of the Po last autumn. I like my slaves to be as handsome as my other

other surroundings, and I see no reason why I should be baulked of my fancy."

"I will do my best to carry out your wishes, Lady Flavia," Sempronius replied deferentially, for the wife of the consul was an important personage in Rome. Her family was one of the most noble and powerful in the city, and she herself—wealthy, luxurious, and strong-willed–was regarded as a leader of society at Rome.

Sempronius deemed it essential for his future advancement to keep on good terms with her. At the same time he was ill-pleased at this last fancy of hers. In the first place, he was a suitor for the hand of her daughter Julia. In the second, he greatly admired the northern beauty of the Gaulish slave girl whom she had spoken of, and had fully intended that when Flavia became tired of her—and her fancies seldom lasted long—he would get his mother to offer to exchange a horse, or a hawk, or something else upon which Flavia might set her mind, for the slave girl. In which case she would, of course, be in his power. He did not, therefore, approve of Flavia's intention of introducing this handsome young Carthaginian as a slave into her household. It was true that he was but a slave at present, but he was a Carthaginian noble of rank as high as that of Flavia.

That he was brave was certain, or he would not be the captain of Hannibal's body-guard. Julia was fully as capricious as her mother, and might take as warm a fancy for Malchus as Flavia had done, while, now the idea of setting this Gaulish girl and the Carthaginian together had seized Flavia, it would render more distant the time when the Roman lady might be reasonably expected to tire of the girl. However, he felt that Flavia's wishes must be carried out; whatever the danger might be, it was less serious than the certainty of losing that lady's favour unless he humoured her whims.

His family was far less distinguished than hers, and her approval of his suit with Julia was an unexpected piece of good fortune which he owed, as he knew, principally to the fact that Gracchus wished to marry his daughter to Julius Marcius, who had deeply offended Flavia by an outspoken expression of opinion, that the Roman ladies mingled too much in public affairs, and that they ought to be content to stay at home and rule their households and slaves.

He knew that he would have no difficulty with his father. The prætor was most anxious that his son should make an alliance with the house of Gracchus, and it was the custom that such prisoners taken in war, as were not sacrificed to the gods, should be given as slaves to the nobles. As yet the great contests in the arena, which cost the lives of such vast numbers of prisoners taken in war, were not instituted. Occasional combats, indeed, took place, but these were on a small scale, and were regarded rather as a sacrifice to Mars than as an amusement for the people.

Sempronius accordingly took his way moodily home. The prætor had just returned, having seen Malchus and the officers lodged in prison, while the men were set to work on the fortifications. Sempronius stated Flavia's request. The prætor looked doubtful.

"I had intended," he said, "to have kept the officers in prison until the senate decided what should be done with them; but, of course, if Flavia has set her mind on it I must strain a point. After all there is no special reason why the prisoners should be treated differently to others. Of course I cannot send the leader of the party to Flavia and let the others remain in prison. As there are two of them I will send them as presents to two of the principal families in Rome, so that if any question arises upon the subject I shall at once have powerful defenders; at anyrate, it will not do to offend Flavia."

Malchus, as he was led through the streets of Rome, had been making comparisons by no means to the favour of Carthage. The greater simplicity of dress, the absence of the luxury which was so unbridled at Carthage, the plainness of the architecture of the houses, the free and manly bearing of the citizens, all impressed him. Rough as was the crowd who jeered and hooted him and his companions, there was a power and a vigour among them which was altogether lacking at home. Under the influence of excitement the populace there was capable of rising and asserting themselves, but their general demeanour was that of subservience to the wealthy and powerful.

THE YOUNG CARTHAGINIAN

The tyranny of the senate weighed on the people, the numerous secret denunciations and arrests inspired each man with a mistrust of his neighbour, for none could say that he was safe from the action of secret enemies. The Romans, on the other hand, were no respecters of persons. Every free citizen deemed himself the equal of the best; the plebeians held their own against the patricians, and could always return one of the consuls, generally selecting the man who had most distinguished himself by his hostility to the patricians.

The tribunes, whose power in Rome was nearly equal to that of the consuls, were almost always the representatives and champions of the plebeians, and their power balanced that of the senate, which was entirely in the interests of the aristocracy. Malchus was reflecting over these things in the prison, when the door of his cell opened and Sempronius, accompanied by two soldiers, entered. The former addressed him in Greek.

"Follow me," he said. "You have been appointed by my father, the prætor Caius, to be the domestic slave of the lady Flavia Gracchus, until such time as the senate may determine upon your fate."

As Carthage also enslaved prisoners taken in war Malchus showed no surprise, although he would have preferred labouring upon the fortifications with his men to domestic slavery, however light the latter might be. Without a comment, then, he rose and accompanied Sempronius from his prison.

Domestic slavery in Rome was not as a whole a severe fate. The masters, indeed, had the power of life and death over their slaves, they could flog and ill-use them as they chose; but as a rule they treated them well and kindly.

The Romans were essentially a domestic people, kind to their wives, and affectionate, although sometimes strict, with their children. The slaves were treated as the other servants; and, indeed, with scarce an exception, all servants were slaves. The rule was easy and the labour by no means hard. Favourite slaves were raised to positions of trust and confidence, they frequently amassed considerable sums of money, and were often granted their freedom after faithful services.

THE YOUNG CARTHAGINIAN

CHAPTER XXI: THE GAULISH SLAVE

O N arriving at the mansion of Gracchus, Sempronius led Malchus to the apartment occupied by Flavia. Her face lighted with satisfaction.

"You have done well, my Sempronius," she said; "I shall not forget your ready gratification of my wish. So this is the young Carthaginian? My friends will all envy me at having so handsome a youth to attend upon me. Do you speak our tongue?" she asked graciously.

"A few words only," Malchus answered. "I speak Greek."

"It is tiresome," Flavia said, addressing Sempronius, "that I do not know that language; but Julia has been taught it. Tell him, Sempronius, that his duties will be easy. He will accompany me when I walk abroad, and will stand behind me at table, and will have charge of my pets. The young lion cub that Tiberius procured for me is getting troublesome and needs a firm hand over him; he nearly killed one of the slaves yesterday."

Sempronius translated Flavia's speech to Malchus.

"I shall dress him," Flavia said, "in white and gold; he will look charming in it."

"It is hardly the dress for a slave," Sempronius ventured to object.

"I suppose I can dress him as I please. Lesbia, the wife of Emilius, dresses her household slaves in blue and silver, and I suppose I have as much right as she has to indulge my fancies."

"Certainly, Lady Flavia," Sempronius said reverentially. "I only thought that such favours shown to the Carthaginian might make the other slaves jealous."

Flavia made no answer, but waved her fan to Sempronius in token of dismissal. The young Roman, inwardly cursing her haughty airs, took his leave at once, and Flavia handed Malchus over to the charge of the chief of the household, with strict directions as to the dress which was to be obtained for him, and with orders to give the animals into his charge.

Malchus followed the man, congratulating himself that if he must serve as a slave, at least he could hardly have found an easier situation. The pets consisted of some bright birds from the East, a Persian greyhound, several cats, a young bear, and a half-grown lion. Of these the lion alone was fastened up, in consequence of his attack upon the slave on the previous day.

Malchus was fond of animals, and at once advanced boldly to the lion. The animal crouched as if for a spring, but the steady gaze of Malchus speedily changed its intention, and, advancing to the full length of its chain, it rubbed itself against him like a great cat. Malchus stroked its side, and then, going to a fountain, filled a flat vessel with water and placed it before it. The lion lapped the water eagerly. Since its assault upon the slave who usually attended to it, none of the others had ventured to approach it. They had, indeed, thrown it food, but had neglected to supply it with water.

"We shall get on well together, old fellow," Malchus said. "We are both African captives, and ought to be friends."

Finding from the other slaves that until the previous day the animal had been accustomed to run about the house freely and to lie in Flavia's room, Malchus at once unfastened the chain and for some time played with the lion, which appeared gentle and good-tempered. As the master of the household soon informed the others of the orders he had receiving respecting Malchus, the slaves saw that the newcomer was likely, for a time at least, to stand very high in the favour of their capricious mistress, and therefore strove in every way to gain his good-will.

Presently Malchus was sent for again, and found Julia sitting on the couch by the side of her mother, and he at once acknowledged to himself that he had seldom seen a fairer woman. She was tall, and her figure was full and well proportioned. Her glossy hair was wound in a coil at the back of her head, her neck and arms were bare, and she wore a garment of light green silk, and embroidered with gold stripes along the bottom, reaching down to her knees, while beneath it a petticoat of Tyrian purple reached nearly to the ground.

"Is he not good-looking, Julia?" Flavia asked. "There is not a slave in Rome like him. Lesbia and Fulvia will be green with envy."

Julia made no reply, but sat examining the face of Malchus with as much composure as if he had been a statue. He had bowed on entering, as he would have done in the presence of Carthaginian ladies, and now stood composedly awaiting Flavia's orders.

"Ask him, Julia, if it is true that he is a cousin of Hannibal and the captain of his guard. Such a youth as he is, I can hardly believe it; and yet how strong and sinewy are his limbs, and he has an air of command in his face. He interests me, this slave."

Julia asked in Greek the questions that her mother had dictated.

"Ask him now, Julia," Flavia said, when her daughter had translated the answer, "how he came to be captured."

Malchus recounted the story of his being blown by a gale into the Roman ports; then, on her own account, Julia inquired whether he had been present at the various battles of the campaign. After an hour's conversation Malchus was dismissed. In passing through the hall beyond he came suddenly upon a female who issued from one of the female apartments. They gave a simultaneous cry of astonishment.

"Clotilde!" Malchus exclaimed, "you here, and a captive?"

"Alas ! yes," the girl replied. "I was brought here three months since."

"I have heard nothing of you all," Malchus said, "since your father returned with his contingent after the battle of Trasimene. We knew that Postumius with his legion was harrying Cisalpine Gaul, but no particular has reached us."

"My father is slain," the girl said. "He and the tribe were defeated. The next day the Romans attacked the village. We, the women and the old men, defended it till the last. My two sisters were killed. I was taken prisoner and sent hither as a present to

Flavia by Postumius. I have been wishing to die, but now, since you are here, I shall be content to live even as a Roman slave."

While they were speaking they had been standing with their hands clasped. Malchus, looking down into her face, over which the tears were now streaming as she recalled the sad events at home, wondered at the change which eighteen months had wrought in it. Then she was a girl, now she was a beautiful woman—the fairest he had ever seen, Malchus thought, with her light brown hair with a gleam of gold, her deep gray eyes, and tender, sensitive mouth.

"And your mother?" he asked.

"She was with my father in the battle, and was left for dead on the field; but I heard from a captive, taken a month after I was, that she had survived, and was with the remnant of the tribe in the well-nigh inaccessible fastnesses at the head of the Orcus."

"We had best meet as strangers," Malchus said. "It were well that none suspect we have met before. I shall not stay here long if I am not exchanged. I shall try to escape whatever be the risks, and if you will accompany me I will not go alone."

"You know I will, Malchus," Clotilde answered frankly. "Whenever you give the word I am ready, whatever the risk is. It should break my heart were I left here alone again."

A footstep was heard approaching, and Clotilde, dropping Malchus' hands, fled away into the inner apartments, while Malchus walked quietly on to the part of the house appropriated to the slaves. The next day, having assumed his new garments, and having had a light gold ring, as a badge of servitude, fastened round his neck, Malchus accompanied Flavia and her daughter on a series of visits to their friends.

The meeting with Clotilde had delighted as much as it had surprised Malchus. The figure of the Gaulish maiden had been often before his eyes during his long night watches. When he was with her last he had resolved that when he next journeyed north he would ask her hand of the chief, and since his journey to Carthage his thoughts had still more often reverted to her. The loathing which he now felt for Carthage had converted what was, when he was staying with Allobrigius, little more than an idea, into a fixed determination that he would cut himself loose altogether from corrupt and degenerate Carthage, and settle among the Gauls. That he should find Clotilde captive in Rome had never entered his wildest imagination, and he now blessed, as a piece of the greatest good fortune, the chance, which had thrown him into the hands of the Romans, and brought him into the very house where Clotilde was a slave. Had it not been for that he would never again have heard of her. When he returned to her ruined home he would have found that she had been carried away by the Roman conquerors, but of her after fate no word could ever have reached him.

Some weeks passed, but no mode of escape presented itself to his mind. Occasionally for a few moments he saw Clotilde alone, and they were often together in Flavia's apartment, for the Roman lady was proud of showing off to her friends her two slaves, both models of their respective races.

Julia had at first been cold and hard to Malchus, but gradually her manner had changed, and she now spoke kindly and condescendingly to him, and would sometimes sit looking at him from under her dark eyebrows with an expression which Malchus altogether failed to interpret. Clotilde was more clear-sighted. One day meeting Malchus alone in the atrium she said to him: "Malchus, do you know that I fear Julia is learning to love you. I see it in her face, in the glance of her eye, in the softening of that full mouth of hers."

"You are dreaming, little Clotilde," Malchus said laughing.

"I am not," she said firmly; "I tell you she loves you."

"Impossible!" Malchus said incredulously. "The haughty Julia, the fairest of the Roman maidens, fall in love with a slave! You are dreaming, Clotilde."

"But you are not a common slave, Malchus, you are a Carthaginian noble and the cousin of Hannibal. You are her equal in all respects."

"Save for this gold collar," Malchus said, touching the badge of slavery lightly.

"Are you sure you do not love her in return, Malchus? She is very beautiful."

"Is she?" Malchus said carelessly. "Were she fifty times more beautiful it would make no difference to me, for, as you know as well as I do, I love some one else."

Clotilde flushed to the brow. "You have never said so," she said softly.

"What occasion to say so when you know it? You have always known it, ever since the day when we went over the bridge together."

"But I am no fit mate for you," she said. "Even when my father was alive and the tribe unbroken, what were we that I should wed a great Carthaginian noble? Now the tribe is broken, I am only a Roman slave."

"Have you anything else to observe?" Malchus said quietly.

"Yes, a great deal more," she went on urgently. "How could you present your wife, an ignorant Gaulish girl, to your relatives, the haughty dames of Carthage? They would look down upon me and despise me."

"Clotilde, you are betraying yourself," Malchus said smiling, "for you have evidently thought the matter over in every light. No," he said, detaining her, as, with an exclamation of shame, she would have fled away, "you must not go. You knew that I loved you, and for every time you have thought of me, be it ever so often, I have thought of you a score. You knew that I loved you and intended to ask your hand from your father. As for the dames of Carthage, I think not of carrying you there; but if you will wed me I will settle down for life among your people."

A footstep was heard approaching. Malchus pressed Clotilde for a moment against his breast, and then he was alone. The new-comer was Sempronius. He was still a frequent visitor, but he was conscious that he had lately lost rather than gained ground in the good graces of Julia. Averse as he had been from the first to the introduction of Malchus into the household, he was not long in discovering the reason for the change in Julia, and the dislike he had from the first felt of Malchus had deepened to a feeling of bitter hatred.

"Slave," he said haughtily, "tell your mistress that I am here."

"I am not your slave," Malchus said calmly, "and shall not obey your orders when addressed in such a tone."

THE GAULISH SLAVE

"Insolent hound," the young Roman exclaimed, "I will chastise you," and he struck Malchus with his stick. In an instant the latter sprang upon him, struck him to the ground, and wrenching the staff from his hand laid it heavily across him. At that moment Flavia, followed by her daughter, hurried in at the sound of the struggle. "Malchus," she exclaimed, "what means this?"

"It means," Sempronius said rising livid with passion, "that your slave has struck me—me, a Roman patrician. I will lodge a complaint against him, and the penalty, you know, is death."

"He struck me first, Lady Flavia," Malchus said quietly, "because I would not do his behests when he spoke to me as a dog."

"If you struck my slave, Sempronius," Flavia said coldly, "I blame him not that he returned the blow. Although a prisoner of war, he is, as you well know, of a rank in Carthage superior to your own, and I wonder not that, if you struck him, he struck you in return. You know that you had no right to touch my slave, and if you now take any steps against him I warn you that you will never enter this house again."

"Nor will I ever speak a word to you," Julia added.

"But he has struck me," Sempronius said furiously; "he has knocked me down and beaten me."

"Apparently you brought it upon yourself," Flavia said. "None but ourselves know what has happened; therefore, neither shame nor disgrace can arise from it. My advice to you is, go home now and remain there until those marks of the stick have died out; it will be easy for you to assign an excuse. If you follow the matter up, I will proclaim among my friends how I found you here grovelling on the ground while you were beaten. What will then be said of your manliness? Already the repeated excuses which have served you from abstaining to join the armies in the field have been a matter for much comment. You best know whether it would improve your position were it known that you had been beaten by a slave. Why, you would be a jest among young Romans."

Sempronius stood irresolute. His last hopes of winning Julia were annihilated by what had happened. The tone of contempt in which both mother and daughter had spoken sufficiently indicated their feelings, and for a moment he hesitated whether he would not take what revenge he could by denouncing Malchus. But the thought was speedily put aside. He had been wrong in striking the domestic slave of another; but the fact that Malchus had been first attacked, and the whole influence of the house of Gracchus, its relations, friends, and clients exerted in his behalf, would hardly suffice to save him. Still the revenge would be bought dearly in the future hostility of Flavia and her friends, and in the exposure of his own humiliating attitude. He, therefore, with a great effort subdued all signs of anger and said:

"Lady Flavia, your wish has always been law to me, and I would rather that anything should happen than that I should lose your favour and patronage, therefore, I am willing to forget what has happened, the more so as I own that I acted wrongly in striking your slave. I trust that after this apology you will continue to be the kindly friend I have always found you."

"Certainly, Sempronius," Flavia said graciously, "and I shall not forget your ready acquiescence in my wishes."

It was the more easy for Sempronius to yield, inasmuch as Malchus had, after stating that he had been first struck, quietly left the apartment. For some little time things went on as before. Malchus was now at home in Rome. As a slave of one of the most powerful families, as was indicated by the badge he wore on his dress, he was able, when his services were not required, to wander at will in the city. He made the circuit of the walls, marked the spots which were least frequented and where an escape would be most easily made; and, having selected a spot most remote from the busy quarter of the town, he purchased a long rope, and carrying it there concealed it under some stones close to one of the flights of steps by which access was obtained to the summit of the wall.

The difficulty was not how to escape from Rome, for that, now that he had so much freedom of movement, was easy, but how to proceed when he had once gained the open country. For himself he had little doubt that he should be able to make his way through the territories of the allies of Rome, but the difficulty of travelling with Clotilde would be much greater.

"Clotilde," he said one day, "set your wits to work and try and think of some disguise in which you might pass with me. I have already prepared for getting beyond the walls; but the pursuit after us will be hot, and until we reach the Carthaginian lines every man's hand will be against us."

"I have thought of it, Malchus; the only thing that I can see is for me to stain my skin and dye my hair and go as a peasant boy."

"That is what I, too, have thought of, Clotilde. The disguise would be a poor one, for the roundness of your arms and the colour of your eyes would betray you at once to any one who looked closely at you. However, as I can see no better way, I will get the garments and some for myself to match, and some stuff for staining the skin and hair."

The next day Malchus bought the clothes and dye and managed to bring them into the house unobserved, and to give to Clotilde those intended for her.

The lion, under the influence of the mingled firmness and kindness of Malchus, had now recovered his docility, and followed him about the house like a great dog, sleeping stretched out on a mat by the side of his couch.

Sempronius continued his visits. Malchus was seldom present when he was with Flavia, but Clotilde was generally in the room. It was now the height of summer, and her duty was to stand behind her mistress with a large fan, with which she kept up a gentle current of air over Flavia's head and drove off the troublesome flies. Sometimes she had to continue doing so for hours, while Flavia chatted with her friends.

Sempronius was biding his time. The two slaves were still high in Flavia's favour, but he was in hopes that something might occur which would render her willing to part with them. He watched Julia narrowly whenever Malchus entered the room, and became more and more convinced that she had taken a strong fancy for the Carthaginian slave, and the idea occurred to him that by exciting her jealousy he might succeed in obtaining his object. So careful were Malchus and Clotilde that he had no idea whatever that any understanding existed between them. This, however, mattered but little; nothing was more likely than that these two handsome slaves should fall in love with each other, and he determined to suggest the idea to Julia.

Accordingly one day when he was sitting beside her, while Flavia was talking with some other visitors, he remarked carelessly, "Your mother's two slaves, the Carthaginian and the Gaul, would make a handsome couple."

He saw a flush of anger in Julia's face. For a moment she did not reply, and then said in a tone of indifference:

"Yes, they are each well-favoured in their way."

"Methinks the idea has occurred to them," Sempronius said. "I have seen them glance at each other, and doubt not that when beyond your presence they do not confine themselves to looks."

Julia was silent, but Sempronius saw, in the tightly compressed lips and the lowering brow with which she looked from one to the other, that the shaft had told.

"I have wondered sometimes," he said, "in an idle moment, whether they ever met before. The Carthaginians were for some time among the Cisalpine Gauls, and the girl was, you have told me, the daughter of a chief there; they may well have met."

Julia made no reply, and Sempronius, feeling that he had said enough, began to talk on other subjects. Julia scarcely answered him, and at last impatiently waved him away. She sat silent and abstracted until the last of the visitors had left, then she rose from her seat and walked quietly up to her mother and said abruptly to Clotilde, who was standing behind her mistress: "Did you know the slave Malchus before you met here?"

The suddenness of the question sent the blood up into the cheeks of the Gaulish maiden, and Julia felt at once that the hints of Sempronius were fully justified.

"Yes," Clotilde answered quietly, "I met him when, with Hannibal, he came down from the Alps into our country."

"Why did you not say so before?" Julia asked passionately. "Mother, the slaves have been deceiving us."

"Julia," Flavia said in surprise, "why this heat? What matters it to us whether they have met before?"

Julia did not pay any attention, but stood with angry eyes waiting for Clotilde's answer.

"I did not know, Lady Julia," the girl said quietly, "that the affairs of your slaves were of any interest to you. We recognized each other when we first met. Long ago now, when we were both in a different position—"

"And when you loved each other?" Julia said in a tone of concentrated passion.

"And when we loved each other," Clotilde repeated, her head thrown back now, and her bearing as proud and haughty as that of Julia.

"You hear that, mother ? you hear this comedy that these slaves have been playing under your nose? Send them both to the whipping-post."

"My dear Julia," Flavia exclaimed, more and more surprised at her anger, "what harm has been done? You astonish me. Clotilde, you can retire. What means all this, Julia?" she went on more severely when they were alone; "why all this strange passion because two slaves, who by some chance have met each other before, are lovers? What is this Gaulish girl, what is this Carthaginian slave, to you?"

"I love him, mother!" Julia said passionately.

"You!" Flavia exclaimed in angry surprise; "you, Julia, of the house of Gracchus, love a slave! You are mad, girl, and shameless."

"I say so without shame," Julia replied, "and why should I not? He is a noble of Carthage, though now a prisoner of war. What if my father is a consul? Malchus is the cousin of Hannibal, who is a greater man than Rome has ever yet seen. Why should I not wed him?"

"In the first place, it seems, Julia," Flavia said gravely, "because he loves someone else. In the second place, because, as I hear, he is likely to be exchanged very shortly for a prætor taken prisoner at Cannæ, and will soon be fighting against us. In the third place, because all Rome would be scandalized were a Roman maiden of the patrician order, and of the house of Gracchus, to marry one of the invaders of her country. Go to,

Julia, I blush for you! So this is the reason why of late you have behaved so coldly to Sempronius. Shame on you, daughter! What would your father say, did he, on his return from the field, hear of your doings? Go to your chamber, and do not let me see you again till you can tell me that you have purged this madness from your veins."

Without a word Julia turned and left the room. Parental discipline was strong in Rome, and none dare disobey a parent's command, and although Julia had far more liberty and license than most unmarried Roman girls, she did not dare to answer her mother when she spoke in such a tone.

Flavia sat for some time in thought, then she sent for Malchus. He had already exchanged a few words with Clotilde, and was therefore prepared for her questions.

"Malchus, is it true that you love my Gaulish slave girl?"

"It is true," Malchus replied quietly. "When we met in Gaul, two years since, she was the daughter of a chief, I a noble of Carthage. I loved her; but we were both young, and with so great a war in hand it was not a time to speak of marriage."

"Would you marry her now?"

"Not as a slave," Malchus replied; "when I marry her it shall be before the face of all men—I as a noble of Carthage, she as a noble Gaulish maiden."

"Hannibal is treating for your exchange now," Flavia said. "There are difficulties in the way, for, as you know, the senate have refused to allow its citizens who surrender to be ransomed or exchanged; but the friends of the prætor Publius are powerful and are bringing all their influence to bear to obtain the exchange of their kinsman, whom Hannibal has offered for you. I will gladly use what influence I and my family possess to aid them. I knew when you came to me that, as a prisoner of war, it was likely that you might be exchanged."

"You have been very kind, my Lady Flavia," Malchus said, "and I esteem myself most fortunate in having fallen into such hands. Since you know now how it is with me and Clotilde, I can ask you at once to let me ransom her of you. Any sum that you like to name I will bind myself, on my return to the Carthaginian camp, to pay for her."

Flavia interrogates her slave Malchus

"I will think it over," Flavia said graciously. "Clotilde is useful to me, but I can dispense with her services, and will ask you no exorbitant amount for her. If the negotiations for your exchange come to aught, you may rely upon it that she shall go hence with you."

With an expression of deep gratitude Malchus retired. Flavia, in thus acceding to the wishes of Malchus, was influenced by several motives. She was sincerely shocked at Julia's conduct, and was most desirous of getting both Malchus and Clotilde away, for she knew that her daughter was headstrong as she was passionate, and the presence of Clotilde in the house would, even were Malchus absent, be a source of strife and bitterness between herself and her daughter.

In the second place, it would be a pretty story to tell her friends, and she should be able to take credit to herself for her magnanimity in parting with her favourite attendant. Lastly, in the present state of affairs it might possibly happen that it would be of no slight advantage to have a friend possessed of great power and influence in the Carthaginian camp. Her husband might be captured in fight—it was not beyond the bounds of possibility that Rome itself might fall into the hands of the Carthaginians. It was, therefore, well worth while making a friend of a man who was a near relation of Hannibal.

For some days Julia kept her own apartment. All the household knew that something had gone wrong, though none were aware of the cause. A general feeling of uneasiness existed, for Julia had from a child in her fits of temper been harsh with her slaves, venting her temper by cruelly beating and pinching them. Many a slave had been flogged by her orders at such a time, for her mother, although herself an easy mistress, seldom interfered with her caprices, and all that she did was good in the eyes of her father.

At the end of the week Flavia told Malchus that the negotiations for his release had been broken off, the Roman senate remaining inflexible in the resolve that Romans who surrendered to the enemy should not be exchanged. Malchus was much disappointed, as it had seemed that the time of his release was near; however, he had still his former plan of escape to fall back upon.

A day or two later Julia sent a slave with a message to Sempronius, and in the afternoon sallied out with a confidential attendant, who always accompanied her when she went abroad. In the Forum she met Sempronius, who saluted her.

"Sempronius," she said coming at once to the purpose, "will you do me a favour?"

"I would do anything to oblige you, Lady Julia, as you know."

"That is the language of courtesy," Julia said shortly; "I mean would you be ready to run some risk?"

"Certainly," Sempronius answered readily.

"You will do it the more readily, perhaps," Julia said, "inasmuch as it will gratify your revenge. You have reason to hate Malchus, the Carthaginian slave."

Sempronius nodded.

"Your suspicion was true, he loves the Gaulish slave; they have been questioned and have confessed it. I want them separated."

"But how?" Sempronius asked, rejoicing inwardly at finding that Julia's wishes agreed so nearly with his own.

"I want her carried off," Julia said shortly. "When once you have got her you can do with her as you will; make her your slave, kill her, do as you like with her, that is nothing to me—all I want is that she shall go. I suppose you have some place where you could take her?"

"Yes," Sempronius said, "I have a small estate among the Alban Hills where she would be safe enough from searchers; but how to get her there? She never goes out except with Lady Flavia."

"She must be taken from the house," Julia said shortly; "pretty slaves have been carried off before now, and no suspicion need light upon you. You might find some place in the city to hide her for a few days, and then boldly carry her through the gates in a litter. None will think of questioning you."

"The wrath of Lady Flavia would be terrible," Sempronius said doubtfully.

"My mother would be furious at first," Julia said coldly; "but get her a new plaything, a monkey or a Nubian slave boy, and she will soon forget all about the matter."

"But how do you propose it should be done?" Sempronius asked.

"My slave shall withdraw all the bolts of the back entrance to the house," Julia said; "do you be there at two in the morning, when all will be sound asleep; bring with you a couple of barefooted slaves. My woman will be at the door and will guide you to the chamber where the girl sleeps; you have only to gag her and carry her quietly off."

Sempronius stood for a moment in doubt. The enterprise was certainly feasible. Wild adventures of this kind were not uncommon among the dissolute young Romans, and Sempronius saw at once that were he detected Julia's influence would prevent her mother taking the matter up hotly. Julia guessed his thoughts.

"If you are found out," she said, "I will take the blame upon myself, and tell my mother that you were acting solely at my request."

"I will do it, Julia," he agreed; "to-night at two o'clock I will be at the back-door with two slaves whom I can trust. I will have a place prepared to which I can take the girl till it is safe to carry her from the city."

THE YOUNG CARTHAGINIAN

CHAPTER XXII: THE LION

MALCHUS was sleeping soundly that night when he was awakened by a low angry sound from the lion. He looked up, and saw by the faint light of a lamp which burned in the hall, from which the niche-like bed-chambers of the principal slaves opened, that the animal had risen to its feet. Knowing that, docile as it was with those it knew, the lion objected to strangers, the thought occurred to him that some midnight thief had entered the house for the purpose of robbery. Malchus took his staff and sallied out, the lion walking beside him.

He traversed the hall and went from room to room until he entered the portion of the house inhabited by Flavia and the female slaves. Here he would have hesitated, but the lion continued its way, crouching as it walked, with its tail beating its sides with short quick strokes.

There was no one in the principal apartment. He entered the corridor, from which as he knew issued the bed-chambers of the slaves. Here he stopped in sudden surprise at seeing a woman holding a light, while two men were issuing from one of the apartments bearing between them a body wrapped up in a cloak. Sempronius stood by the men directing their movements. The face of the person carried was invisible, but the light of the lamp fell upon a mass of golden brown hair, and Malchus knew at once that it was Clotilde who was being carried off.

Malchus sprang forward and with a blow of his staff levelled one of the slaves to the ground; Sempronius with a furious exclamation drew his sword and rushed at him, while the other slave, dropping his burden, closed with Malchus and threw his arms around him. For a moment Malchus felt powerless, but before Sempronius could strike there was a deep roar, a dark body sprang forward and hurled itself upon him, levelling him to the ground with a crushing blow of its paw, and then seized him by the shoulder and shook him violently. The slave who held Malchus loosed his hold and fled with a cry of affright, the female slave dropped the light and fled also. Clotilde had by this time gained her feet.

"Quick, love!" Malchus said; "seize your disguise and join me at the back gate. Sempronius is killed; I will join you as quickly as I can."

By this time the household was alarmed, the shout of Malchus and the roar of the lion had aroused everyone, and the slaves soon came hurrying with lights to the spot. Malchus checked them as they came running out.

"Fetch the net," he said. The net in question had been procured after the lion had before made an attack upon the slave, but had not since been required.

Malchus dared not approach the creature now, for though he was not afraid for himself, it was now furious, and might, if disturbed, rush among the others and do terrible destruction before it could be secured. The net was quickly brought, and Malchus, with three of the most resolute of the slaves, advanced and threw it over the lion, which was lying upon the prostrate body of Sempronius. It sprang to its feet, but the net was round it, and in its struggle to escape it fell on its side. Another twist of the net and it was helplessly inclosed; the four men lifted the ends and carried it away. Cutting a portion of the net Malchus placed the massive iron collar attached to the chain round its neck and then left it, saying to the others:

"We can cut the rest of the net off it afterwards."

He then hurried back to the scene of the struggle. Flavia was already there.

"What is all this, Malchus," she asked. "Here I find Sempronius dead and one of his slaves senseless beside him; they tell me when he first arrived you were here."

"I know nothing of it, lady," Malchus replied, "save that the lion aroused me by growling, and thinking that robbers might have entered the house, I arose and searched it and came upon three men. One I levelled to the ground with my staff; doubtless he is only stunned and will be able to tell you more when he recovers. I grappled with another, and while engaged in a struggle with him the third attacked me with a sword, and would have slain me had not the lion sprang upon him and felled him. The other man then fled—this is all I know about it."

"What can it all mean?" Flavia said. "What could Sempronius with two slaves be doing in my house after midnight? It is a grave outrage, and there will be a terrible scandal in Rome to-morrow—the son of a prætor and a friend of the house!"

She then ordered the slaves to raise the body of Sempronius and carry it to a couch, and to send at once for a leech. She also bade them throw water on the slave and bring him to consciousness, and then to bring him before her to be questioned.

"Where is my daughter?" she said suddenly; "has she not been roused by all this stir?" One of the female slaves stole into Julia's apartment, and returned saying that her mistress was sound asleep on her couch.

An expression of doubt crossed Flavia's face, but she only said, "Do not disturb her," and then thoughtfully returned to her room. It was not until an hour later that the prisoner was sufficiently recovered to be brought before Flavia. He had already heard that his master was killed, and, knowing that concealment would be useless, he threw himself on the ground before Flavia, and owned that he and another slave had been brought by Sempronius to carry off a slave girl.

Acting on his instructions they had thrust a kerchief into her mouth, and wrapped a cloak round her, and were carrying her off when a man rushed at him, and he supposed struck him, for he remembered nothing more. He then with many tears implored mercy, on the ground that he was acting but on his master's orders. At this moment the prætor himself arrived, Flavia having sent for him immediately she had ascertained that Sempronius was dead. He was confused and bewildered at the suddenness of his loss.

"I thought at first," Flavia said, "that he must have been

engaged in some wild scheme to carry off Julia, though why he should do so I could not imagine, seeing that he had my approval of his wooing; but Julia is asleep, not having been a wakened by the noise of the scuffle. It must have been one of the slave girls."

"Ah!" she exclaimed suddenly. "I did not see Clotilde." She struck a bell, and her attendant entered.

"Go," she said, "and summon Clotilde here."

In a few minutes the slave returned, saying that Clotilde was not to be found.

"She may have been carried off by the other slave," Flavia said, "but Malchus was there, and would have pursued. Fetch him here."

But Malchus too was found to be missing.

"They must have fled together," Flavia said. "There was an understanding between them. Doubtless Malchus feared that this affair with your son might cause him to be taken away from here. Perhaps it is best so, and I trust that they may get away, though I fear there is little chance, since no slaves are allowed to leave the city without a pass, and even did they succeed in gaining the open country they would be arrested and brought back by the first person who met them. But that is not the question for the present."

"What think you, my friend, what are we to do in this terrible business?"

"I know not," the prætor said with a groan.

"The honour of both our families is concerned," Flavia said calmly. "Your son has been found in my house at night and slain by my lion. All the world knows that he was a suitor for Julia's hand. There's but one thing to be done; the matter must be kept secret. It would not do to try and remove Sempronius to-night, for the litter might be stopped by the watch; it must be taken boldly away in daylight. Send four slaves whom you can trust, and order them to be silent on pain of death. I will tell my household that if a word is breathed of what has taken place to-night, I will hand whoever disobeys me over to the executioners. When you have got your son's body home you can spread a rumour that he is sick of the fever. There will be no difficulty in bribing the leech. Then in a few days you will give out that he is dead, and none will be any the wiser."

The prætor agreed that this was the best plan that could be adopted, and it was carried out in due course, and so well was the secret kept that no one in Rome ever doubted that Sempronius had fallen a victim to fever.

Julia's anger in the morning, when she heard that the Gaulish slave girl and the Carthaginian were missing, was great, and she hurried to her mother's room to demand that a hue and cry should be at once made for them, and a reward offered for their apprehension. She had, when informed of the scenes which had taken place in the night, and of the death of Sempronius, expressed great astonishment and horror, and indeed the news that her accomplice had been killed had really shocked her. The sentiment, however, had faded to insignificance in the anger which she felt when, as the narrative continued, she heard of the escape of the two slaves.

A stormy scene took place between her and her mother, Julia boldly avowing that she was the author of the scheme which had had so fatal a termination. Flavia, in her indignation at her daughter's conduct, sent her away at once to a small summer retreat belonging to her in the hills, and there she was kept for some months in strict seclusion under the watchful guardianship of some old and trusted slaves.

Malchus, having seen the lion fastened up, had seized the bundle containing his disguise, and hurried away to the gate where Clotilde was awaiting him.

"How long you have been!" she said with a gasp of relief.

"I could not get away until the lion was secured," he said, "for I should have been instantly missed. Now we will be off at once." Both had thrown large dark cloaks over their garments, and they now hurried along through the deserted streets, occasionally drawing aside into by-lanes as they heard the tramp of the city watch.

At last, after half an hour's walking, they reached the wall. Malchus knew the exact spot where he had hidden the rope, and had no difficulty in finding it. They mounted the steps and stood on the battlements. The sentries were far apart, for no enemy was in the neighbourhood of Rome. Malchus fastened the rope round Clotilde, and lowered her down over the battlements. When he found that she had reached the ground he made fast the end of the rope and slid down till he stood beside her. They proceeded with the utmost caution until at some distance from the walls; and then shaped their course until, after a long walk, they came down upon the Tiber below the city.

Day had by this time broken, and Malchus bade Clotilde enter a little wood to change her garments and dye her skin. He then proceeded to do the same, and rolling up the clothes he had taken off, hid them under a bush. Clotilde soon joined him again. She wore the dress of a peasant boy, consisting of a tunic of rough cloth reaching to her knees. Her limbs, face, and neck were dyed a sunny brown, and her hair, which was cut quite short, was blackened. Dyes were largely in use by Roman ladies, and Malchus had had no difficulty in procuring those necessary for their disguises.

"I don't think anyone would suspect you, Clotilde," he said; "even I should pass you without notice. What a pity you have had to part with all your sunny hair!"

"It will soon grow again," she said; "and now, Malchus, do not let us waste a moment. I am in terror while those dark walls are in sight."

"We shall soon leave them behind," Malchus said encouragingly. "There are plenty of fishermen's boats moored along the bank here. We shall soon leave Rome behind us."

They stepped into a boat, loosened the moorings, and pushed off, and Malchus, getting out the oars, rowed steadily down the river until they neared its mouth. Then they landed, pushed the boat into the stream again, lest, if it were found fastened up, it might give a clue to any who were in pursuit of them, and then struck off into the country. After travelling some miles they turned into a wood, where they lay down for several hours, and did not resume their course until nightfall.

Malchus had, before starting, entered the kitchen, and had filled a bag with cold meat, oatmeal cakes, and other food, and this, when examined, proved ample for four days' supply, and he

Malchus and Clotilde escape from Rome

had, therefore, no occasion to enter the villages to buy provisions. They kept by the sea-shore until they neared Terracina, and then took to the hills, and skirted these until they had left the state of Latium. They kept along at the foot of the great range which forms the backbone of Italy, and so passing along Samnium, came down upon the Volturnus, having thus avoided the Roman army, which lay between Capua and Rome.

Their journey had been a rough one, for, by the winding road they had followed along the mountains, the distance they traversed was over one hundred miles. The fatigue had been great, and it was well that Clotilde had had a Gaulish training. After their provisions were exhausted they had subsisted upon corn which they gathered in the patches of cultivated ground near the mountain villages, and upon fruits which they picked in the woods.

Twice, too, they had come upon herds of half wild goats in the mountains, and Malchus had succeeded in knocking down a kid with a stone. They had not made very long journeys, resting always for a few hours in the heat of the day, and it was ten days after they had left Rome before, from an eminence, they saw the walls of Capua.

"How can I go in like this?" Clotilde exclaimed in a sudden fit of shyness.

"We will wait until it is dusk," Malchus said; "the dye is fast wearing off, and your arms are strangely white for a peasant girl's. I will take you straight to Hannibal's palace, and you will soon be fitted out gorgeously. There are spoils enough stored up to clothe all the women of Rome."

They sat down in the shade of a clump of trees, and waited till the heat of the day was past; then they rose and walked on until, after darkness had fallen, they entered the town of Capua. They had no difficulty in discovering the palace where Hannibal was lodged. They were stopped at the entrance by the guards, who gave a cry of surprise and pleasure when Malchus revealed himself. At first they could hardly credit that, in the dark-skinned peasant, their own commander stood before them, and as the news spread rapidly the officers of the corps ran down and saluted him with a joyous greeting. While this was going on Clotilde shrank back out of the crowd.

As soon as he could extricate himself from his comrades, Malchus joined her, and led her to Hannibal, who, hearing the unusual stir, was issuing from his apartment to see what had occasioned it. The shouts of "Long live Malchus!" which rose from the soldiers informed him of what had happened, and he at once recognized his kinsman in the figure advancing to meet him.

"My dear Malchus," he exclaimed, "this is a joyous surprise. I have been in vain endeavouring to get you out of the hands of the Romans, but they were obstinate in refusing an exchange; but knowing your adroitness, I have never given up hopes of seeing you appear some day among us. But whom have you here?" he asked as he re-entered his room accompanied by Malchus and his companion.

"This is Clotilde, daughter of Allobrigius, the chief of the Orcan tribe," Malchus replied, "and my affianced wife. Her father has been defeated and killed by Postumius, and she was carried as a slave to Rome. There good fortune and the gods threw us together, and I have managed to bring her with me."

"I remember you, of course," Hannibal said to the girl, "and that I joked my young kinsman about you. This is well, indeed; but we must see at once about providing you with proper garments. There are no females in my palace, but I will send at once for Chalcus, who is now captain of my guard, and who has married here in Capua, and beg him to bring hither his wife; she will I am sure take charge of you, and furnish you with garments."

Clotilde was soon handed over to the care of the Italian lady, and Malchus then proceeded to relate to Hannibal the various incidents which had occurred since he had sailed from Capua for Sardinia. He learned in return that the mission of Mago to Carthage had been unsuccessful. He had brought over a small reinforcement of cavalry and elephants, which had landed in Bruttium and had safely joined the army; but this only repaired a few of the many gaps made by the war, and was useless to enable Hannibal to carry out his great purpose.

"Hanno's influence was too strong," Hannibal said, "and I

foresee that sooner or later the end must come. I may hold out for years here in Southern Italy, but unless Carthage rises from her lethargy, I must finally be overpowered."

"It seems to me," Malchus said, "that the only hope is in rousing the Gauls to invade Italy from the north."

"I know nothing of what is passing there," Hannibal said; "but it is clear from the disaster which has befallen our friends the Orcans that the Romans are more than holding their own north of the Apennines. Still, if a diversion could be made it would be useful. I suppose you are desirous of taking your bride back to her tribe."

"Such is my wish, certainly," Malchus said. "As I have told you, Hannibal, I have made up my mind never to return to Carthage. It is hateful to me. Her tame submission to the intolerable tyranny of Hanno and his faction, her sufferance of the corruption which reigns in every department, her base ingratitude to you and the army which have done and suffered so much, the lethargy which she betrays when dangers are thickening and her fall and destruction are becoming more and more sure, have sickened me of her. I have resolved, as I have told you, to cast her off, and to live and die among the Gauls–a life rough and simple, but at least free."

"But it seems that the Gauls have again been subjected to Rome," Hannibal said.

"On this side of the Alps," Malchus replied, "but beyond are great tribes who have never as yet heard of Rome. It is to them that Clotilde's mother belongs, and we have settled that we will first try and find her mother and persuade her to go with us, and that if she is dead we will journey alone until we join her tribe in Germany. But before I go I will, if it be possible, try and rouse the Gauls to make another effort for freedom by acting in concert, by driving out the Romans and invading Italy. You will, I trust, Hannibal, not oppose my plans."

"Assuredly not, Malchus; I sympathize with you, and were I younger and without ties and responsibilities would fain do the same. It is a sacrifice, no doubt, to give up civilization and to begin life anew, but it is what our colonists are always doing. At anyrate it is freedom—freedom from the corruption, the intrigue, the sloth, and the littleness of a decaying power like that of Carthage. You will be happy at least in having your wife with you, while the gods only know when I shall see the face of my beloved Imilce.

"Yes, Malchus, follow your own devices. Carthage, when she flung you in prison and would have put you to a disgraceful death, forfeited all further claim upon you. You have rendered her great services, you have risked your life over and over again in her cause, you have repaid tenfold the debt which you incurred when she gave you birth. You are free now to carry your sword where you will. I shall deeply regret your loss, but your father has gone and many another true friend of mine, and it is but one more in the list of those I have lost. Follow your own wishes, and live in that freedom which you will never attain in the service of Carthage."

The next day the marriage of Malchus and Clotilde took place. Hannibal himself joined their hands and prayed the gods to bless their union. Three weeks later Hannibal arranged that a body of a hundred Carthaginian horse should accompany Malchus to the north, where he would endeavour to raise the Gaulish tribes. They were to cross into Apulia, to travel up the east coast until past the ranges of the Apennines, and then make their way across the plains to the Alps. A dozen officers accompanied him; these were to aid him in his negotiations with the chiefs, and in organizing the new forces, should his efforts be successful.

To the great joy of Malchus, on the very evening before he started Nessus arrived in the camp. He had, when Malchus was at Rome, been employed with the other Carthaginian soldiers on the fortifications. Malchus had once or twice seen him as, with the others, he was marched from the prison to the walls, and had exchanged a few words with him. He had told him that he intended to escape, but could not say when he should find an opportunity to do so; but that if at any time a month passed without his seeing him, Nessus would know that he had gone.

The extra rigour with which the prisoners were guarded had led Nessus to suspect that a prisoner had escaped, and a month having passed without his seeing Malchus, he determined on making an attempt at flight. So rigourous was the watch that there was no possibility of this being done secretly, and, therefore, one day when they were employed in repairing the foundations of the wall outside the city Nessus seized the opportunity, when the attention of the guards was for a moment directed in another quarter, to start at the top of his speed. He had chosen the hottest hour of the day for the attempt, when few people were about, and the peasants had left the fields for an hour's sleep under the shade of trees.

The Roman guard had started in pursuit, but Nessus had not overrated his powers. Gradually he left them behind him, and, making straight for the Tiber, plunged in and swam the river. He had followed the right bank up to the hills, and on the second evening after starting made his appearance at Capua. When he heard the plans of Malchus he announced, as a matter of course, that he should accompany him. Malchus pointed out that, with the rewards and spoils he had obtained, he had now sufficient money to become a man of importance among his own people. Nessus quietly waved the remark aside as if it were wholly unworthy of consideration.

The cavalry who were to accompany Malchus were light-armed Numidians, whose speed would enable them to distance any bodies of the enemy they might meet on their way. With them were thirty lead horses, some of them carrying a large sum of money, which Hannibal had directed should be paid to Malchus from the treasury, as his share, as an officer of high rank, of the captured booty. The rest of the horses were laden with costly arms, robes of honour, and money as presents for the Gaulish chiefs. These also were furnished from the abundant spoils which had fallen into the hands of the Carthaginians.

Hannibal directed Malchus that, in the event of his failing in his mission, he was not to trouble to send these things back, but was to retain them to win the friendship and good-will of the chiefs of the country to which he proposed to journey. The next morning Malchus took an affectionate farewell of the general and his old comrades, and then, with Clotilde riding by his side—for the women of the Gauls were as well skilled as the men in the management of horses—he started at the head of his party. He followed the route marked out for him without any adventure of importance. He had one or two skirmishes with parties of tribesmen allied with Rome, but his movements were too rapid for any force sufficient to oppose his passage being collected.

After ascending the sea-coast the troop skirted the northern slopes of the Apennines, passing close to the battle-field of Trebia, and crossing the Po by a ford, ascended the banks of the Orcus, and reached Clotilde's native village. A few ruins alone marked where it had stood. Malchus halted there and despatched scouts far up the valley. These succeeded in finding a native, who informed them that Brunilda with the remains of the tribe were living in the forests far up on the slopes. The scouts delivered to them the message with which they were charged: that Clotilde and Malchus, with a Carthaginian force, were at Orca. The following evening Brunilda and her followers came into camp.

Deep was the joy of the mother and daughter. The former had long since given up all hope of ever hearing of Clotilde again, and had devoted her life to vengeance on the Romans. From her fastness in the mountain she had from time to time led her followers down, and carried fire and sword over the fields and plantations of the Roman colonists, retiring rapidly before the garrisons could sally from the towns and fall upon her. She was rejoiced to find that her child had found a husband and protector in the young Carthaginian, still more rejoiced when she found that the latter had determined upon throwing in his lot with the Gauls.

All that night mother and daughter sat talking over the events which had happened since they parted. Brunilda could give Malchus but little encouragement for the mission on which he had come. The legion of Postumius had indeed been defeated and nearly destroyed in a rising which had taken place early in the spring; but fresh troops had arrived, dissensions had as usual, broken out among the chiefs, many of them had again submitted to the Romans, and the rest had been defeated and crushed. Brunilda thought that there was little hope at present of their again taking up arms.

For some weeks Malchus attempted to carry out Hannibal's instructions; he and his lieutenants, accompanied by small parties of horse, rode through the country and visited all the chiefs of

Cisalpine Gaul, but the spirit of the people was broken. The successes they had gained had never been more than partial, the Roman garrison towns had always defied all their efforts, and sooner or later the Roman legions swept down across the Apennines and carried all before them.

In vain Malchus told them of the victories that Hannibal had won, that Southern Italy was in his hands, and the Roman dominion tottering. In reply they pointed to the garrisons and the legion, and said that, were Rome in a sore strait, she would recall her legion for her own defence, and no arguments that Malchus could use could move them to lay aside their own differences and to unite in another effort for freedom. Winter was now at hand. Malchus remained in the mountains with the Orcans until spring came, and then renewed his efforts with no greater success than before. Then he dismissed the Carthaginians, with a letter giving Hannibal an account of all he had done, and bade them find their way back to Capua by the road by which they had come.

Brunilda had joyfully agreed to his proposal that they should cross the Alps and join her kinsmen in Germany, and the remnant of the tribe willingly consented to accompany them. Accordingly in the month of May they set out, and journeying north made their way along the shore of the lake now called the Lago di Guarda, and, crossing by the pass of the Trentino, came down on the northern side of the Alps, and, after journeying for some weeks among the great forests which covered the country, reached the part inhabited by the tribe of the Cherusci, to which Brunilda belonged.

Here they were hospitably received. Brunilda's family were among the noblest of the tribe, and the rich presents which the ample resources of Malchus enabled him to distribute among all the chiefs, at once raised him to a position of high rank and consideration among them. Although accepting the life of barbarism Malchus was not prepared to give up all the usages of civilization. He built a house, which, although it would have been but a small structure in Carthage, was regarded with admiration and wonder by the Gauls. Here he introduced the usages and customs of civilization. The walls, indeed, instead of being hung with silk and tapestry, were covered with the skins of stags, bears, and other animals slain in the chase; but these were warmer and better suited for the rigour of the climate in winter than silks would have been. The wealth, knowledge, and tact of Malchus gained him an immense influence in the tribe, and in time he was elected the chief of that portion of it dwelling near him. He did not succeed in getting his followers to abandon their own modes of life, but he introduced among them many of the customs of civilization, and persuaded them to adopt the military formation in use among the Carthaginians. It was with some reluctance that they submitted to this; but so complete was the victory which they obtained over a rival tribe, upon their first encounter when led by Malchus and his able lieutenant Nessus, that he had no difficulty in future on this score.

The advantages, indeed, of fighting in solid formation, instead of the irregular order in which each man fought for himself, were so overwhelming that the tribe rapidly increased in power and importance, and became one of the leading peoples in that part of Germany. Above all, Malchus inculcated them with a deep hatred of Rome, and warned them that when the time came, as it assuredly would do, that the Romans would cross the Alps and attempt the conquest of the country, it behoved the German tribes to lay aside all their disputes and to join in a common resistance against the enemy.

From time to time rumours, brought by parties of Cisalpine Gauls, who, like the Orcans, fled across the Alps to escape the tyranny of Rome, reached Malchus. For years the news came that no great battle had been fought, that Hannibal was still in the south of Italy defeating all the efforts of the Romans to dislodge him.

It was not until the thirteenth year after Hannibal had crossed the Alps that any considerable reinforcement was sent to aid the Carthaginian general. Then his brother Hasdrubal, having raised an army in Spain and Southern Gaul, crossed the Alps to join him. But he was met, as he marched south, by the consuls Livius and Nero with an army greatly superior to his own; and was crushed by them on the river Metaurus, the Spanish and Ligurian troops being annihilated and Hasdrubal himself killed.

For four years longer Hannibal maintained his position in the south of Italy. No assistance whatever reached him from Carthage, but alone and unaided he carried on the unequal war with Rome until, in 204 B.C., Scipio landed with a Roman force within a few miles of Carthage, captured Utica, defeated two Carthaginian armies with great slaughter, and blockaded Carthage. Then the city recalled the general and the army whom they had so grossly neglected and betrayed.

Hannibal succeeded in safely embarking his army and in sailing to Carthage; but so small was the remnant of the force which remained to him, that when he attempted to give battle to Scipio he was defeated, and Carthage was forced to make peace on terms which left her for the future at the mercy of Rome. She was to give up all her ships of war except ten, and all her elephants, to restore all Roman prisoners, to engage in no war out of Africa, and none in Africa except with the consent of Rome, to restore to Massinissa, a prince of Numidia who had joined Rome, his kingdom, to pay a contribution of two hundred talents a year for fifty years, and to give a hundred hostages between the ages of fourteen and thirty, to be selected by the Roman general.

These terms left Carthage at the mercy of Rome, when the latter, confident in her power, entered upon the third Punic war, the overthrow and the destruction of her rival were a comparatively easy task for her. Hannibal lived nineteen years after his return to Carthage. For eight years he strove to rectify the administration, to reform abuses, and to raise and improve the state; but his exposure of the gross abuses of the public service united against him the faction which had so long profited by them, and, in B. C. 196, the great patriot and general was driven into exile.

He then repaired to the court of Antiochus, King of Syria, who was at that time engaged in a war against Rome; but that monarch would not follow the advice he gave him, and was in consequence defeated at Magnesia, and was forced to sue for peace and to accept the terms the Romans imposed, one of which was that Hannibal should be delivered into their hands.

320

THE LION

Hannibal, being warned in time, left Syria and went to Bithynia. But Rome could not be easy so long as her great enemy lived, and made a demand upon Prusias, King of Bithynia, for his surrender. He was about to comply with the request when Hannibal put an end to his life, dying at the age of sixty-four.

No rumour of this event ever reached Malchus, but he heard, fifteen years after he had passed into Germany, that Hannibal had at last retired from Italy, and had been defeated at Zama, and that Carthage had been obliged to submit to conditions which placed her at the mercy of Rome. Malchus rejoiced more than ever at the choice he had made. His sons were now growing up, and he spared no efforts to instill in them a hatred and distrust of Rome, to teach them the tactics of war, and to fill their minds with noble and lofty thoughts.

Nessus had followed the example of his lord and had married a Gaulish maiden, and he was now a sub-chief in the tribe. Malchus and Clotilde lived to a great age, and the former never once regretted the choice he had made. From afar he heard of the ever-growing power of Rome, and warned his grandsons, as he had warned his sons, against her, and begged them to impress upon their descendants in turn the counsels he had given them. The injunction was observed, and the time came when Arminius, a direct descendant of Malchus, then the leader of the Cherusei, assembled the German tribes and fell upon the legions of Varus, inflicting upon them a defeat as crushing and terrible as the Romans had ever suffered at the hands of Hannibal himself, and checking for once and all the efforts of the Romans to subdue the free people of Germany.

THE END

Preston Speed Publications

Preston Speed Publications RR#4, Box 705, Mill Hall, PA 17751

www.prestonspeed.com (717) 726-7844

Available Henty Titles:

Ancient Civilizations

The Young Carthaginian: A Story of The Times of Hannibal
(Hardcover, 321 pages, 12 illustrations)
For the Temple: A Tale of the Fall of Jerusalem
(hardcover; 333 pages, 10 illustrations, map/plan illustrating the siege of Jersualem)
Beric the Briton: A Story of the Roman Invasion
(hardcover, 398 pages, 12 illustrations)
The Cat of Bubastes: A Tale of Ancient Egypt
(hardcover, pages, 8 illustrations, Special Foreword by Douglas Wilson)

Middle Ages

The Dragon and the Raven: Or the Days of King Alfred
(hardcover, 238 pages, 9 illustrations)
Winning His Spurs: A Tale of the Crusades
(Hardcover, 326 pages, numerous illustrations, Foreword by J. Byron Snapp)
In Freedom's Cause: A Story of Wallace and Bruce
(hardcover, 351 pages, 12 illustrations)

Reformation Times

By Pike and Dyke: A Tale of the Rise of the Dutch Republic
(hardcover, 366 pages, 10 illustrations, 4 maps)
St. Bartholomew's Eve: A Tale of the Huguenot Wars
(hardcover, 376 pages, 12 illustrations, fold out map of France)
Under Drake's Flag: A Tale of the Spanish Main
(hardcover, 298 pages, 12 illustrations, Special Foreword by Rev. Dale Dykema)

American Continents Exploits

By Right of Conquest: or with Cortez in Mexico
(Hardcover, 375 pages, 10 illustrations, 2 maps, Special Foreword by Rev. J. Steven Wilkins)
With Lee in Virginia: A Story of the American Civil War
(hardcover, 337 pages, 12 illustrations, 2 maps (1 of which is a fold out map of Virginia), 4 battle plan maps, includes both British and the extremely rare American 'My Dear Lads' Prefaces, Special Foreword by George M. Calhoun)

Preston/Speed Publications takes great pride in re-printing the complete works of G. A. Henty. New titles are regularly being released. Our editions contain the complete text along with all maps and/or illustrations. In order to ensure the most complete Henty editions, we review all previous releases for the most comprehensive version. Preston/Speed Publications maintains the original vocabulary that Mr. Henty first penned as this will open up to American students the necessary vocabulary skills when conversing with British or other European cultures and/or reading their literature.